Intellectual Property Law in Argentina

Intellectual Property Law in Argentina

Fourth Edition

Guillermo Cabanellas

This book was originally published as a monograph in the International Encyclopaedia of Laws/Intellectual Property Law.

Founding Editor: Roger Blanpain
General Editor: Frank Hendrickx
Volume Editor: Hendrik Vanhees

Wolters Kluwer

Published by:
Kluwer Law International B.V.
PO Box 316
2400 AH Alphen aan den Rijn
The Netherlands
E-mail: international-sales@wolterskluwer.com
Website: lrus.wolterskluwer.com

Sold and distributed in North, Central and South America by:
Wolters Kluwer Legal & Regulatory U.S.
7201 McKinney Circle
Frederick, MD 21704
United States of America
Email: customer.service@wolterskluwer.com

Sold and distributed in all other countries by:
Air Business Subscriptions
Rockwood House
Haywards Heath
West Sussex
RH16 3DH
United Kingdom
Email: international-customerservice@wolterskluwer.com

Printed on acid-free paper

ISBN 978-94-035-0324-0

e-Book: ISBN 978-94-035-0220-5
web-PDF: ISBN 978-94-035-0224-3

Printed in the United Kingdom.

The Author

Prof. Dr Guillermo Cabanellas (born 14 July 1950) obtained degrees in Economics (1971) and Law (1972) from the National University of Buenos Aires. He graduated with Master's in Comparative Law (1975) and as Doctor of the Science of Law (1978) from the University of Illinois. Since 1977, he has taught at the University of Illinois, at the University of Miami and at the Loyola of Los Angeles Law School. He is also Professor at the National University of Buenos Aires, Universidad Austral Argentina and the Universidad de San Andrés (Argentina). He is Honorary Professor at the Catholic University of Arequipa, Perú. Professor Cabanellas was a member of the board of directors of the National Foreign Trade Commission of Argentina. He has also acted as General Director of Economic Legislation of the Ministry of the Economy of Argentina, and as a member of several legislative commissions. In 1981, 1982 and 1987, he was research fellow at the Max Planck Institute for Foreign and International Patent, Copyright and Competition Law, Munich. He is senior partner at the Buenos Aires law firm Cabanellas, Etchebarne and Kelly.

The Author

Table of Contents

List of Abbreviations

CIL	Confidential Information Law
Doct.	Doctrina
IDL	Industrial Designs Law
LS	Law of Seeds
PA	Patent Act
Regs	Regulations
TA	Trademark Act
TM Regs	Trademark Regulations

Preface

This study consists of a description of the Argentine intellectual property law. Because much of this law has been shaped by the influence of international agreements, particularly the Paris Convention and the TRIPS agreement, the basic traits of Argentine intellectual property law will be familiar to foreign lawyers, to whom this work is directed.

The international intellectual property conventions have not been examined in this monograph, although they are part of Argentine law. Rather, this study focuses on Argentine domestic law, as it has evolved on the basis of the statutes that implement Argentina's international commitments in the intellectual property area.

While Argentine intellectual property legal theories are largely based on European precedents and international developments, legal practice has a distinctly local flavour, which is not easy to describe in a study of this type. This should serve as a caveat against easy generalizations about the role and status of intellectual property law in developing countries such as Argentina.

The law is stated as of January 2018.

General Introduction

§1. General Background

I. Geography

1. Argentina is the eighth largest country in the world. It occupies most of South America, south of the Tropic of Capricorn, and east of the Andes. The north of the country is subtropical and includes large areas of natural forests and wetlands. The centre of the country is occupied by the Pampas, a vast flat prairie, where most of the country's population lives. To the south lies the Patagonia, mostly cold and arid, except for its tree-covered mountainous west. Including the Antarctic and the South Atlantic territories, the area of Argentina is 3,761,274 square kilometres, of which approximately 2.8 million square kilometres are part of continental Argentina and Tierra del Fuego, an island province at the southern tip of the continent.

II. Cultural Composition

2. The cultural composition of Argentina has been, to a large extent, determined by the massive immigration that took place after 1860. At the time of independence, in 1810, the population was around 500,000. In the 1860s, it was around 1 million. The population has grown rapidly thanks to a net immigration of approximately 9 million people, about 7 million from Europe, and the rest predominantly from neighbouring countries. The European immigrants came mostly from the Mediterranean basin, especially from Italy and Spain. Hence, the prevailing cultural influence has come from these countries. Spanish is the national language, and most of the population is Catholic.

The different ethnic groups that originated the Argentine population have mixed to a large extent, so that ethnic divisions or identities within Argentina are presently weak.

There are very few pure American Indians in Argentina. Some communities in the north of the country still speak Indian languages, as well as Spanish. A significant percentage of the population has partial Indian ancestry.

The illiteracy rate is about 3%; it is higher in the Northern provinces. The proportion of the population pursuing university careers is similar to that in industrialized countries. However, the comparative weakness of science, technology and research has influenced the development of the country's intellectual property regime.

III. Political System

3. Argentina has always been a republic. The present constitution – dating from 1853, one of the oldest in the world still in effect – is the result of multiple amendments, the most recent of which was approved in 1994. The national constitution is based on the American constitution and retains several main characteristics of the latter, including a federal system; a division of powers into the judiciary, legislative and executive branches; and a legislature divided into a House of Representatives (*diputados*) and a Senate. These parallels are not the result of mere imitation but rather the consequence of certain characteristics of the Argentine political organization that made the use of the American model advantageous: the pre-existence of autonomous provinces; the size of the country, which made centralization impossible; the prestige of the executive power in comparison with the legislature; and the ideological rejection of the European monarchic traditions.

The executive power, which in the Argentine system holds vast legal and practical prerogatives, is exercised by the president. A vice president is elected together with the chief executive, to replace the president in case of death, absence or disability. The president is elected by popular vote every four years. He may be re-elected once; thereafter re-election is only possible after a period of four years has elapsed since the candidate's last term in office. To be elected, a candidate must obtain at least 45% of the popular vote; if a candidate garnishes more than 40% of the vote, the difference with the second-most-voted candidate must be at least 10%. If no candidate meets these conditions, a second round is necessary; the two most-voted candidates participate in this round.

The constitution also provides for the appointment of a cabinet chief. Although this position holds certain similarities with European prime ministers, its inclusion in the Argentine constitution in 1994 has been the result of political compromise, and the powers of the cabinet chief are significantly more limited than those of the president. The cabinet chief is appointed by the president and may be removed by the vote of the majority of the Senate and of the majority of the House of Representatives (*diputados*). The cabinet chief acts mainly as a coordinator of the ministers' work; ministers are appointed and removed by the president.

The legislative branch of government consists of two bodies: the Senate and the Chamber or House of Representatives (*Cámara de Diputados*). The Senate has seventy-two members, three per province, as well as three from the Federal District of the City of Buenos Aires. They are directly elected by voters for six-year terms and may be re-elected. Under the electoral system for senators, two represent the most-voted party and one the second-most-voted party. One-third of the Senate comes up for election every two years. The representatives (*diputados*) are elected by popular vote. The number of representatives is determined per province in rough proportion to the population of the provinces. A proportional representation system, applied within each province, is used for the election of representatives. They are elected for four-year terms and may be re-elected. One half of the representatives are subject to a new election every two years.

The enactment of laws requires a majority vote of both the Senate and the House of Representatives. The president has veto power and exercises such power frequently.

Congress may override a presidential veto with a two-thirds majority vote in each house. Veto overrides are unusual.

The judiciary consists of a federal Supreme Court and lower provincial and federal courts. The federal judiciary system includes courts of appeals in the city of Buenos Aires as well as federal courts of appeals with jurisdiction in federal matters sitting in different parts of the country. Federal courts of the first instance are subordinated to these courts of appeals. In addition, each province organizes its own judicial system, which has jurisdiction on matters not declared federal by the National Constitution and the laws enacted thereunder. Provincial systems normally have three tiers of courts. Under certain circumstances, it is possible to appeal before the federal Supreme Court and other federal courts the decisions of provincial courts.

4. Argentina is a federal country. This political and constitutional structure is not the consequence of theoretical preferences or academic analysis but rather the result of a violent and protracted struggle that predated the enactment of the Constitution of 1853. After independence, which was formally declared in 1816, several efforts were made to impose 'unitarian' constitutions, to be applied in the territory of what was roughly the previous Viceroyalty of the River Plate, an administrative division within the Spanish kingdom. These constitutions were strongly rejected by most of the provinces, which had, in fact, resulted from the breakdown of Spanish authority. Several parts of what had previously been the Viceroyalty of the River Plate broke away, either spontaneously or as a consequence of international disputes; present-day Bolivia, Paraguay and Uruguay are the result of this process. The rest of the provinces refused to submit to any central authority, and between 1826 and 1853 no such authority was to be found in what is now Argentina. There was no federal or central government, and no federal or national constitutions; the only formally centralizing element was the fact that the province of Buenos Aires conducted the foreign affairs of the country in the name of a loosely organized 'federation'. The Constitution of 1853, drafted after a short civil war, reflects the pre-existence of the provinces. These enact their own constitutions and laws and elect their own authorities. However, the power of the provinces in the Argentine constitutional system is somewhat more limited than the power of the states under US law. Federal legislation is constitutionally allowed to extend into areas that in the US are reserved to the states, such as commercial law. Also, provinces may be subject to a process called *intervención*, whereby the federal government, in certain specific circumstances, may remove and replace temporarily the provincial authorities. In addition, historically the power of the provinces has been further eroded by the centralization of economic resources by the federal government.

5. A noteworthy characteristic of the Argentine constitutional system, after the 1994 amendments, particularly from the point of view of intellectual property protection, is the position international law treaties occupy in the Argentine legal structure. Several international treaties on human rights are declared to be part of the Constitution, and Argentina's participation in such treaties may only be terminated by the executive branch with the approval of two-thirds of the members of each of the houses of Congress. In addition, all the treaties approved by Congress and enacted into law are declared to have a legal status superior to ordinary laws.[1]

---

1. *See* National Constitution, Art. 75(22).

Recent court decisions have strengthened the status of international treaties within the Argentine legal system. In *Ekmekdjian, M.A. v. Sofovich, G. and others*,[2] the federal Supreme Court stated that the rules derived from an international treaty duly approved by the Argentine authorities are immediately applicable and enforceable in Argentina, provided such rules are sufficiently specific to become operative without further legislation or regulations.

6. The Argentine political system is characterized by the electoral domination by two parties: the Justicialista or Peronist Party and the Radical Party. Under normal circumstances, these two parties obtain approximately 80% of the popular vote. Most provincial governors also are elected through these parties. However, after 2001, the power and electoral vote of the Radical Party has diminished significantly, and opposition to the Peronist Party became highly fragmented. This picture changed dramatically in 2015. The Radical Party joined a broad coalition – called 'Cambiemos' (Let us change) – headed by the PRO party, which until then had a significant presence only in the city of Buenos Aires. The presidential candidate of 'Cambiemos', Mauricio Macri, won the 2015 election, and that party also won governorships in several provinces, including the larger one, the province of Buenos Aires. In 2017, the 'Cambiemos' coalition was again successful, this time in federal legislative elections held that year.

The Justicialista or Peronist Party originated in the political activity of Juan Domingo Perón, who was elected president of Argentina in 1946, 1952 and 1973. In the beginning, the ideology of the Peronist Party was strongly nationalist and favourable to state intervention in economic matters. The backbone of its support was in the trade unions. A military coup removed Perón from the presidency in 1955, but he returned to power in 1973, only to die shortly afterward. During the 1990s, under the presidency of Carlos Menem, then leader of the Peronist Party, the international and the economic policies of the government were radically different from the original Peronist policies. In foreign affairs, the government pursued a policy of strong integration in international organizations, of openness to world trade, and of cooperation with the US, a traditional foe of the first Peronist governments. In economic matters, the Menem administration, elected in 1989 and re-elected in 1995, followed a policy of liberalization, deregulation and privatization. After 2001, the Peronist Party returned to power. Nestor Kirchner was elected president in 2003, and his wife Cristina Fernández de Kirchner followed in 2007, being re-elected in 2011. From several perspectives, the Kirchners' administration moved significantly to the left of traditional Peronist policies. It partially reversed the privatization process of the 1990s and followed a relatively confrontational policy with regard to the US. The electoral support of the Peronist Party still lies in the traditional groups in which it originated: blue-collar workers, trade unions and the small and poor provinces of the North. The Peronist Party is nowadays fragmented to a significant degree, some of its members having supported the Kirchners' government and other groups having acted in opposition to the Kirchner government with regard to certain matters, although without forming a separate party.

The Radical Party is much older, dating back to the last decades of the nineteenth century. Its original driving force was electoral fairness. The progress it achieved towards this end is reflected in electoral reforms enacted in 1912. Soon after, in 1916, the Radical Party leader, Hipolito Yrigoyen, was elected to the presidency, which

2. Federal Supreme Court, 7 Jul. 1992, *La Ley*, vol. 1992-C, (1992), 543.

Radical Party candidates then occupied until 1930. In 1963 and 1983, the Radical Party also won the presidential elections. In recent years, the electoral strength of the Radical Party has diminished significantly, particularly after the economic misfortunes of hyperinflation and financial crisis that characterized the final years of the Radical administrations headed by Raúl Alfonsín and Fernando de la Rúa. Contrary to what its name might suggest – and the claims of some of its leaders – the Radical Party is basically conservative in outlook. Its supporters are found mainly among the middle class. For several decades, it has had the support of the majority of university students in elections to choose university authorities. The Radical Party is now part of the coalition which supports the present president, Mauricio Macri.

Other minor parties are the Socialist, ARI and PRO parties. On the left, the Socialist Party has a long but not very successful history in Argentina; its strength is based in certain provinces. With a vague and moderate agenda, the ARI (Afirmación para una República Igualitaria) Party is based on the figure of Elisa Carrió and has enjoyed significant support in elections held throughout this decade; it is now part of the governing 'Cambiemos' coalition. On the right, the PRO (Propuesta Republicana) Party is led by Mauricio Macri, the former mayor of the city of Buenos Aires and now president of the Republic. Another group of right-wing or conservative parties consists of independent provincial parties. In general, they are formed around a specific individual or family. They consistently win the elections in some provinces, such as Neuquén and Corrientes.

In the general elections held in 2015, a coalition named 'Cambiemos' led by the PRO Party and including the Radical Party and former members of ARI prevailed, winning the federal presidency and the governorship of the province of Buenos Aires, as well as several other provincial governments. Thus Mauricio Macri became president for the period 2015–2019. The previously ruling coalition, called 'Frente para la Victoria' (Front for victory), including the main part of the Peronist Party, lost the elections in all the main provinces.

Political activity is significant, and voter participation in elections is high. The proportion of voters formally affiliated to parties is also relatively high. Electoral swings are strong. A compulsory system of primary elections is applied, and in the main parties such elections are strongly contested by the leading candidates.

IV. Population Statistics

7. The population of Argentina is approximately 44 million inhabitants. Of these, about 15 million live in the city of Buenos Aires and its suburbs. Two-thirds of the population lives in the central provinces of Buenos Aires, Cordoba and Santa Fe, and in the city of Buenos Aires.

Argentina is a sparsely populated country. With an area comparable to that of western and central Europe, its population is smaller than that of several member countries of the European Union. This low population is more striking in view of the fact that most of continental Argentina's area consists of arable land and has the benefit of a temperate climate. Two immediate results of this low population density have been the continuous flow of immigration – presently, mostly from neighbouring countries and from the Far East – and the production of huge agricultural surpluses.

At 1.4% per annum, the domestic population growth is higher than in Europe, but lower than in most developing countries.

§2. Historical Background

8. The historical development of Argentina has been determined, to a significant extent, by the situation of the indigenous population at the time of the Spanish conquest, in the sixteenth century. Apart from the northwest of the country, the population was extremely low, estimated at about 500,000 individuals. Again with the exception of the northwest, most of the indigenous tribes were at the hunting-and-gathering stage of economic development, which helps explain the low population density. These circumstances, together with the absence of precious metals, meant that during the period of Spanish domination, what is now Argentina became one of the least developed areas of Spanish America. The social and economic patterns characteristic of the most developed parts of Spanish America – large relatively integrated Indian population, agriculture and exports of precious metals – were, to a large extent, nonexistent in what is now the Argentine territory. In fact, more than half of this territory was fully in possession of Indian tribes at the time of independence, in the early nineteenth century.

At the end of the eighteenth century, a reorganization of the Spanish administration led to the creation of the Viceroyalty of the River Plate. The limits of this Viceroyalty were to serve as a basis for the determination of Argentina's territorial boundaries.

In the context of the political and military disturbances created by the Napoleonic wars, Argentina became self-governing in 1810. It formally declared independence in 1816. The first years after independence were marked by multiple foreign and civil wars: first against Spain, then against Brazil and repeatedly between the different provinces of what had previously been the Viceroyalty of the River Plate. Paraguay and Bolivia, originally parts of that Viceroyalty, became independent and so did Uruguay, in this case as a consequence of a protracted war with Brazil.

Until 1853, it was not possible to achieve any type of stable national organization. The efforts to enact a national constitution failed because of the opposition by the majority of the provinces. After 1826, the provinces existed as semi-independent entities, under the influence of the province of Buenos Aires, ruled until 1851 by a conservative dictator, Juan Manuel de Rosas.

Rosas was defeated in the battle of Caseros in 1851. In 1853, a federal constitution was approved. The promotion of immigration became one of the central elements of this constitution. This legal background, together with the gradual disappearance of wars between the provinces, political stability and the expansion of the territory effectively controlled by the Argentine state – at the expense of the indigenous tribes – resulted in a massive increase in immigration.

The rapid increase in population became viable thanks to the inflow of foreign capital, mainly British, and the rapid growth of agricultural production and exports. Legislation was generally adapted to be 'hospitable' to foreign individuals and capital.

According to the available statistical evidence, between 1900 and 1950 Argentina was among the ten richest countries of the world in terms of per capita income.

Between 1860 and 1930, there were no successful military coups in Argentina. Governmental succession complied with the constitutional terms. In 1912, effective universal manhood suffrage was achieved.

This institutional stability was broken in 1930 by a military coup headed by General Uriburu. This coup was followed by several right-wing governments, elected by fraud or brought into power by new coups. The economy suffered severely from the world recession of the 1930s and never again recovered its previous relative position in the world.

In 1946, Juan Domingo Perón, heading a populist movement, was elected to the presidency. He promptly nationalized large sectors of the economy and followed a protectionist economic policy. He was re-elected in 1952. After this re-election, his government became increasingly repressive. He was removed by a military coup in 1955. Neither this coup nor several others that took place in 1963, 1966 and 1976 managed to solve the division of the country into Peronist and anti-Peronist camps. The military governments, opposed to the return of Perón or the Peronist party to office, either prohibited the participation of Peronist candidates in elections or removed them from office after their election. A permanent struggle between the Peronist-led trade unions and the army was characteristic of this period. Inflation and institutional instability hampered economic growth.

In 1983, the Radical Party's candidate, Raúl Alfonsín, was elected in open and clean elections. Thereafter, restrictions against the Peronist Party or its candidates were dropped.

The Peronist Party's candidate in the 1989 presidential election, Carlos Menem, obtained a clear majority and was re-elected in 1995, after the amendment of the federal constitution. Mr Menem's government followed a policy generally different from that associated with former Peronist governments. A broad privatization plan was implemented, barriers to foreign trade were dropped, deregulation was pursued and the country's foreign policy became generally aligned with that of the United States. In addition, Argentina participated together with Brazil, Paraguay and Uruguay in an economic integration scheme known as Mercosur, which – after a successful start – is in the process of being extended to Venezuela and Bolivia.

In 1999, Fernando de la Rúa of the Radical Party was elected president. He was not able to maintain the financial structure established by the Menem administration, based on the convertibility of the Argentine Peso (ARS) at a one-to-one rate to the US Dollar (USD). At the end of 2001, the financial system became generally insolvent, and Mr de la Rúa was forced to resign. Soon after, Argentina finished the convertibility system – the exchange rate is now floating – and declared a moratorium on its public debt.

After several short-lived presidencies, Nestor Kirchner, then representing one sector of the Peronist Party, was elected president in 2003. He restructured the public debt and followed a policy of greater governmental intervention in the economy. His wife, Cristina Fernández de Kirchner, was in turn elected president in 2007. She has generally followed the policies of her predecessor and was re-elected in 2011 for a new four-year term.

Mrs Kirchner's political vehicle, the 'Frente para la Victoria', including a large part of the Peronist Party, was defeated by a broad, more pro-business, coalition named 'Cambiemos', led by Mauricio Macri, in the 2015 general elections.

Part I. Intellectual Property Law

Chapter 1. Copyright and Neighbouring Rights

§1. Sources: Legislation

9. The sources of Argentine copyright law are the common ones in civil law countries: legislation, custom, court decisions and legal doctrine. However, the sources of Argentine copyright law have certain noteworthy characteristics. First, legislation has a prominent position. Case law, which in other areas of Argentine legal practice is extremely important, is relatively underdeveloped in the copyright area. Second, treaties have played a significant role in the development of Argentine copyright law. These treaties are approved by federal laws and have a legal status superior to that of ordinary laws.[3]

The main statutory source of copyright law is Law 11,723. This law, dating back to 1933, has been amended several times. It includes the basic rules on copyright, as well as provisions on related matters, such as publishing contracts.

Other laws applicable to copyright are the following:

(a) Law 17,648, of 1968, on the Argentine Association of Authors and Composers of Music (SADAIC). It grants special powers to this association with regard to the collective enforcement of copyright on musical works.
(b) Law 17,741, of 1968, as amended, on promotion and regulation of cinematography.
(c) Law 20,115, on the General Association of Argentine Authors (ARGENTORES). It grants special powers to this association with regard to the collective enforcement of copyright.
(d) Law 22,399, of 1981. It regulates the use of the International Standard Book Number (ISBN) in Argentina.
(e) Law 22,963, of 1983. It governs the publication of maps.

10. Argentina has ratified several international treaties applicable to copyright and neighbouring rights. These treaties are directly applicable as part of the Argentine legal system. Their effects within Argentina may be affected or influenced by other laws and regulations applicable to the same subject matter.

The following ratified treaties may be mentioned:

3. *See* para. 5, *supra* .

(a) The Treaty of Montevideo of 1889, on Literary and Artistic Property, ratified by Law 3,192, of 1894. Under this agreement, several South American countries agreed on certain minimum rules on copyright protection.
(b) The Convention of Buenos Aires, of 1910, on Literary and Artistic Property, ratified by Law 13,585, of 1949. It provides certain minimum standards for the protection of literary and artistic property. It was signed by several countries of North, Central and South America.
(c) The Inter-American Convention on Copyright, signed in Washington, DC, in 1946. It was ratified by Law 14,186, of 1953. For the parties ratifying this Convention, it replaces the Buenos Aires Convention of 1910.
(d) The Universal Copyright Convention, created in Geneva in 1952. It was ratified by Argentina through Decree 12,088 of 1957.
(e) The Berne Convention on the Protection of Literary and Artistic Works. By means of Law 17,251, of 1967, Argentina has ratified this Convention, including its revisions up to the Brussels revision of 1948. By means of Law 22,195, Argentina has also ratified the amendments agreed on in Paris in 1971, with the exception of Articles 1–21 and the Annex provided by Article 28, section 1(b).
(f) The Stockholm Agreement of 1967, creating the World Intellectual Property Organization (WIPO). It was ratified by Argentina by means of Law 22,195, of 1980.
(g) The Convention for the Protection of Phonograms approved in Geneva in 1971. It was ratified by Argentina in 1972, by means of Law 19,963.
(h) The Rome Convention of 1961, on the Protection of Artists, Players and Phonogram Producers. Argentina ratified this Convention in 1991, through Law 23,921.
(i) The Treaty on the International Registration of Audio-visual Works, signed in Geneva in 1989. This Treaty was ratified by Law 24,039, of 1992.
(j) The Latin American Agreement on Cinematographic Coproduction, signed in Caracas in 1989. It was approved by Argentina in 1993, by Law 24,202.
(k) The Agreement creating the Latin American Common Market for Cinematography, signed in Caracas in 1989 and approved by Argentina in 1993, by Law 24,203.
(l) The TRIPS *(Trade-Related Aspects of Intellectual Property Rights)* agreement approved in Marrakech in 1994. It was ratified by Argentina in 1995, by means of Law 24,425.
(m) The WIPO Copyright Treaty. It was ratified by Argentina in 1999, by means of Law 25,140.
(n) The WIPO Performances and Phonograms Treaty. It was ratified by Argentina in 1999, by means of Law 25,140.

11. Multiple regulations have been issued and are in effect with regard to copyright and related fields. The main regulations applicable in this area are the following:

(a) Decree 41,233, of 1934, regulating the application of the Copyright Law 11,723.
(b) Decree 31,964, of 1939, on the deposit of unpublished works for copyright purposes.

(c) Decree 71,180, of 1940, on the return of unpublished works deposited for copyright purposes.
(d) Decree-law 6,422, of 1957, on the indication of editors and publishers of journalistic publications.
(e) Decree 1,155, of 1958, on the licenses for the translation of foreign works.
(f) Decree-law 1,224, of 1958, creating the National Arts Fund and regulating the use of works in the public domain.
(g) Decree 6,255, of 1958, regulating the activities of the National Arts Fund.
(h) Decree 16,697 of 1959, providing the filing of sworn affidavits with regard to published works.
(i) Decree 7,616, of 1963, on the renewal of the deposit of unpublished works.
(j) Decree 8,478, of 1965, on the public use of musical works.
(k) Decree 5,146, of 1969, regulating the powers of the SADAIC of Music.
(l) Decree 746, of 1973, on the rights of performers.
(m) Decree 1,670, of 1974, on rights related to phonographic reproduction.
(n) Decree 1,671, of 1974, on the management of performer's rights.
(o) Regulation 15,850, of 1977, of the National Arts Fund, on payments due for the use of works in the public domain.
(p) Decree 165, of 1994, on the protection of software and databases.

§2. Subject Matter of Protection

I. Different Categories of Protected Works

12. Article 1 of Law 11,723, as amended, sets out the basic rules on the subject matter of copyright protection. It provides as follows:

> For purposes of this law, scientific, literary and artistic works include writings of every nature and extension, including source and object computer programs; compilations of data and of other materials; dramatic, musical and musical-dramatic works; cinematographic, choreographic and pantomimical works; drawings, paintings, sculptures and architectural works; models and works of art or science applied to commerce and industry; printings, blueprints and maps; plastics, photographies, engravings and phonograms, and finally: every scientific, literary, artistic or didactic production, whatever its reproduction procedure.
>
> Copyright protection covers the expression of ideas, procedures, operation methods and mathematical concepts, but not such ideas, procedures, methods or concepts in themselves.

It is generally admitted that the essential element of these provisions is the last part of the first paragraph. In other words, all types of scientific, literary, artistic or didactic works are granted copyright protection, regardless of whether they fall under any of the specific categories listed in Article 1 of Law 11,723.[4]

It is also common under Argentine law to distinguish between original and derivative works.[5] The first include literary, musical, theatrical, dramatic, artistic, scientific, audio-visual and software works. Derivative works include adaptations, translations, compilations, annotations, commentaries, summaries, extracts, musical arrangements and other transformations. Both groups of works are legally protected, although the type of protection varies for each category.

13. Particular characteristics of certain types of subject matter of copyright under Argentine law may be mentioned as follows:

(a) *Literary works*. These include written and oral works. Protection covers both traditional literary production as well as other types of work implying a significant intellectual effort, such as slogans, nomenclatures, catalogues, forms, brochures, compilations, etc. The protection of oral works is supported by Article 2(1) of the Berne Convention.

(b) *Musical works*. Melody is considered to be the key element protected by copyright in this area. The determination of whether the limits of the protected element have been breached normally requires the help of expert witnesses.[6]

(c) *Theatrical works*. These are considered to include – *inter alia* – choreographic works, even if these have not been described in writing or by means of pictures.[7]

(d) *Artistic works*. These include – *inter alia* – paintings, drawings, engravings, sculpture, photography and architecture. A clear distinction is made in these cases between the protection of the artistic creation – regarding which copyright is granted – and the protection of the physical object – a painting, a sculpture, etc. – that embodies the artistic creation, which is governed by the rules on real property. Property of a physical object embodying an artistic creation grants no right to the reproduction or exhibition of that object or of the artistic creation embodied therein, which in principle belongs to the copyright owner.[8]

In general, the artist is entitled to prevent any changes or modifications to his or her work, in the process of reproduction. However, in the case of architecture the owner of the building is considered to be allowed to introduce changes required for practical or technical reasons.[9] With regard to photographies, they are clearly covered by copyright protection if they have an artistic value. The prevailing

4. *See* M. Goldstein, *Derecho de autor* (Buenos Aires: La Rocca, 1995), 51 et seq.
5. *Ibid.*, 59 et seq.; D. Lipszyc, *Derecho de autor y derechos conexos* (Buenos Aires: UNESCO, Cerlalc, Zavalía, 1993), 69.
6. *See* D. Lipszyc, *Derecho de autor y derechos conexos* (Buenos Aires: UNESCO, Cerlalc, Zavalía, 1993), 69.
7. *Ibid.*, 76.
8. *Ibid.*, 77, 78.
9. *See Iramain, J.C. v. Province of Tucumán*, Supreme Court of Tucumán, 11 Dec. 1947, *La Ley*, vol. 49 (1948), 888.

tendency is to admit copyright protection even in connection with photographs of a purely mechanical nature.[10]

Artistic works with a practical or ornamental value may also be protected under other intellectual property rules, particularly those on industrial designs.[11]

(e) *Scientific works*. They are protected to the extent that they result in the expression of a given theory, observation or scientific result. Scientific inventions, discoveries or projects are not protected by copyright, but their description is subject to copyright protection.[12] Maps are protected, provided they imply an original expression by their author.[13]

(f) *Audio-visual works*. Films and other audio-visual works are expressly covered by copyright protection. Special rules are included in the Argentine copyright law in connection with these works,[14] particularly with regard to films.[15]

(g) Law 25,036 has added to the list of works expressly covered by copyright protection software and data compilations. The extent of this protection is determined by the general copyright rules; that is, protection refers to the expression of ideas and other concepts, and a certain degree of creativity is required. Law 25,036 has thus incorporated into the text of Law 11,723 rules that were previously included in Decree 165 of 1994.[16]

14. Case law has repeatedly established that the listing of works included in Article 1 of Law 11,723 is not exclusive of other intellectual works not expressly mentioned in that article.[17] Thus, copyright protection has been extended to culinary publications,[18] catalogues,[19] software,[20] etc. Therefore, to determine whether certain subject matter may be protected by copyright under Argentine law, it is essential to evaluate such subject matter under the substantive requirements that case law has developed with regard to all types of intellectual property.[21]

---

10. *See Curutchet, J. v. Editorial Atlántida*, National Criminal and Correctional Court of Appeals III, 24 Aug. 1976, *La Ley*, vol. 1976-D, 333.
11. *See* Lipszyc, *Derecho de autor y derechos conexos*, 86 and 87.
12. *Ibid.*, 87 et seq.
13. *See Estate of Ribero Duffy, V. v. Beluzzi, S.*, Civil Court of Appeals of the City of Buenos Aires 1, 17 Jul. 1940, *La Ley*, vol. 24 (1941), 865.
14. *See* Law 11,723, Arts 17 et seq.
15. *Ibid.*
16. Software and compilation protection is discussed in s. III, *infra.*
17. *See Guía Práctica del Exportador e Importador S.R.L. v. Empresa I.A.R.A.*, National Civil Court of Appeals IV, 30 Apr. 1974, *El Derecho*, vol. 56, 344.
18. *See Figueredo, F. v. Gonzaga, A.*, Civil Court of Appeals of the City of Buenos Aires, 1, 23 Dec. 1935, *La Ley*, vol. 1(1936), 271.
19. *See Enrique Debat y Cía. SRL. v. Lippi, A.F.*, National Civil Court of Appeals B, 3 Oct. 1951, *La Ley*, vol. 64(1952), 500.
20. *See* Decree 165, of 1994. Software protection is now expressly provided by Law 11,723.
21. To be discussed in s. III, *infra* .

II. Works Excluded from Protection

15. Article 1 of Law 11,723 sets out positively the possible scope of copyright protection. Pursuant to that basic provision, works may be excluded from protection owing to any of the following reasons:

- they do not meet the substantive requirements set out by Argentine law for copyright protection;
- their subject matter is outside the limits of Law 11,723 and other statutes granting copyright protection; or
- a provision or legal principle excludes certain subject matter from protection.

With regard to the works identified under (i), courts have decided that copyright protection does not extend to mere ideas; the expression of ideas is protected, but the subject matter of protection is the expression of the idea and not the idea itself.[22] Also, while courts will not evaluate the artistic or scientific merit of works to determine whether they merit copyright protection, a minimum level of creativity is always required, depending on the nature of the work claiming protection.[23]

With regard to works identified under (ii), courts have distinguished between the creator of intellectual works and the manufacturers of the goods embodying such works; the latter are excluded from claiming copyright protection.[24] Also, gambling procedures or game instructions have been considered to be outside the scope of copyright protection.[25]

Under (iii), it is possible to mention different regulations that limit or prohibit the private use or appropriation of expressions indicating or suggesting an official nature, such as 'national',[26] 'official',[27] 'police',[28] and words related to the armed forces.[29] These prohibitions are particularly relevant in connection with the protection of titles.

---

22. *See* P. Chaloupka, 'La propiedad de las ideas', *Derechos Intelectuales* 3 (1988): 50 et seq.
23. *See* Lipszyc, *Derecho de autor y derechos conexos*, 67.
24. *See* *Mangiante, G. v. Aadi Capif A.C.R.*, National Civil Court of Appeals I, 4 Jun. 1991, *La Ley*, vol. 1991-E, 229.
25. *See* *Pantano, J.C. v. Jockey Club de Buenos Aires*, National Civil Court of Appeals C, 18 Apr. 1974, *La Ley*, vol. 155, 82.
26. *See* Decree 42,366, of 1934.
27. *See* Decree 23,813, of 1944.
28. *See* Decree 24,381, of 1944.
29. *See* Decree 7,926, of 1944.

III. Special Categories of Works

A. Computer Software

16. As in other countries, the protection of software in Argentina has been subject to extensive discussions.[30] From a practical point of view, however, the matter has been largely settled. Decree 165, of 1994, provides the protection and registration of software under copyright law, while the Patent Act (PA) is basically exclusive of software as subject matter of patent protection.[31] Law 25,036 has strengthened the position taken by Decree 165, expressly including software within the subject matter protected by copyright.

Nevertheless, the discussions regarding the possibility of protecting software under copyright law still retain certain practical meaning. As in other countries, the limits of the protection derived from copyright law, with regard to software, are extremely vague, and these limits have not been defined by case law. Although the copyright protection of software is provided by the TRIPS agreement included in the Marrakech Act, which is part of Argentine law,[32] neither these rules nor the amendments introduced by Law 25,036 set out the limits of the rights resulting in favour of software from copyright protection.

Several reasons have mitigated the impact that the vague limits of the copyright protection of software under Argentine law have on the effective rights of software producers or purchasers. First, as in other intellectual property areas, litigation regarding software in Argentina tends to be limited. Many of the cases involve blatant acts of piracy that do not require any fine analysis as to the limits of the legal protection of software. Complex cases, involving relevant legal issues, tend to be settled, as both parties try to maintain long-term relationships and prestige and to avoid the uncertainties, costs and time consumption resulting from litigation. Second, much of the software used in Argentina is already in the public domain and has little commercial value. Third, much of the software with commercial value used in Argentina is protected by confidentiality mechanisms, which are independent from copyright protection.

17. Decree 165, of 1994, sets out certain basic rules on the copyright protection of software. Article l, section (a), provides that software is included among the works listed in Article 1 of Law 11,723; these are the works that receive copyright protection under general intellectual law rules and principles.

---

30. *See* C. Correa et al., *Derecho Informático* (Buenos Aires: Depalma, 1987), 55 et seq.; G. Cabanellas, *Propiedad intelectual sobre los programas de computación* (Buenos Aires: Heliasta, 2011); Lipszyc, *Derecho de autor y derechos conexos*, 104 et seq.; G. Cabanellas, 'The Legal Protection of Computer Technology under Argentine Law', *Copyright World* II (1990): 34 et seq.
31. Law 24,481, as amended, consolidated text established by Decree 260, of 1996, hereinafter cited as 'Patent Act'. *See* Art. 6(c).
32. *See* Law 24,425.

Software is defined by Article 1, section (a), of Decree 165, as including the following 'expressions':[33]

- Designs, both general and detailed, of the logical flow of data in a computer system.
- Computer programs, both in their 'source' version, principally directed to a human reader, and in their 'object' version, principally directed to be executed by a computer.
- Technical documentations with purposes such as explanation, support or training for the development, use or maintenance of software.

Article 1, section (c), of Decree 165 provides that writings or diagrams directly or indirectly perceptible by human senses, as well as records made by means of any technique, directly or indirectly subject to processing by information-processing equipment shall be considered to be adequate procedures for the reproduction of software.[34]

Article 1, sections (d) and (e), of Decree 165 distinguish between published and unpublished software.[35] Published software is that which has been made available to the public in general, either by its reproduction in multiple commercially distributed copies or by a general offer of its transmission with exploitation purposes. Unpublished software is that which has been kept in reserve or has been transferred by means of negotiations with specific parties.[36]

Registration of software in the copyright registry takes place by means of the deposit of the different expressions of the work as the owner considers sufficient for purposes of identifying the software to be protected.[37]

Decree 165 has been criticized for being based on the assumption that software was included in the original subject matter of the copyright law.[38] This has been a debatable question both under Argentine law and other comparable copyright systems. However, this criticism has been overcome by the express inclusion of software in the subject matter of the copyright law, by means of Law 25,036.

33. By using the term 'expressions', Decree 165 tries to make its provisions compatible with traditional copyright law; it is not the idea underlying a given software that is protected but rather specific expressions of that idea.
34. As with other provisions of Decree 165, Art. 1(c) intends to provide the limits of the copyright protection of software and of the violations of such limits. *See* M.F. Bohmer, 'La protección jurídica del mercado informático y un decreto que se anula a sí mismo', *La Ley* (1994-D): 1019.
35. This distinction intends to connect software with the basic copyright rules applicable to published and unpublished works.
36. The definitions of published and unpublished works do not cover the whole logical spectrum of software. For example, they do not foresee the case of software which has been transferred non-commercially to specific parties, without adequate confidentiality precautions. Cases such as this have to be tackled on the basis of the general copyright rules distinguishing between published and unpublished works.
37. *See* Decree 165, of 1994, Art. 3.
38. *See* M.F. Bohmer, 'La protección jurídica del mercado informático y un decreto que se anula a sí mismo', *La Ley* (1994-D).

Decree 165 rules that software is protected by copyright but does not set out the limits of such protection, regarding which traditional copyright law is vague or insufficient. As in other countries, it is likely that the development of the economic value of software will require more specific legislation, setting out clearly what constitutes a violation of the rights granted as to software.[39]

18. Decree 165, together with the TRIPS agreement approved by Law 24,425, clearly put software within the possible subject matter of copyright protection. However, this protection, to the extent that it applies to software, is subject to several limitations:

(a) The Argentine copyright rules have been drafted having in mind the protection of scientific, literary and artistic works.[40] These rules do not protect ideas but rather the expression of ideas.[41] Such 'expression', in the framework of traditional copyright law, refers to signs and elements directed to human beings, in the sense that it will be through human perception that the esthetical, logical or conceptual value of signs and elements will be understood. Software, on the contrary, consists basically of instructions directed to a machine. Even though such instructions may be understood by a human being, they only acquire their proper sense and purpose in the context of the computer processes in which software is made to work. Decree 165 has tried to overcome this hurdle by means of a *sui generis* definition of 'expression'. This definition, however, is not coherent with basic copyright concepts, as they have been developed under Law 11,723, which is the basic copyright statute in Argentina and has a legal hierarchy superior to Decree 165.

(b) Although Article 1 of Law 11,723 includes a broad definition of the works that may receive copyright protection[42] and that definition expressly extends to include software,[43] it is also true that the body of copyright law effective in Argentina has been drafted with the purpose of dealing with issues and matters that vary to a significant extent from those related to software. This leads to three types of difficulties, common to all copyright systems that have not been specially adapted to the issues created by software:[44] uncertainty as to the applicability of specific copyright rules and as to their effects on software; enforcement of rules that are not adapted to the factual circumstances of software; and lack of protection of elements related to software that cannot fall within the bounds of copyright law even under an extensive interpretation of such law.[45]

(c) The effort leading to protected artistic, literary or scientific works is generally focused on the expression of a given idea, and not on the idea itself. Thus, the literary and economic value of a Sherlock Holmes story lies in the words chosen

39. *See* Lipszyc, *Derecho de autor y derechos conexos*, 111.
40. *See* Law 11,723, Art. 1.
41. *See* P. Chaloupka, 'La propiedad de las ideas', *Derechos Intelectuales* 3 (1988).
42. *See* *supra* nn. 12 et seq.
43. *See* Lipszyc, *Derecho de autor y derechos conexos*, 104 et seq.
44. *See* E. Galán Corona, 'En torno de la protección jurídica del soporte lógico', *Revista del Derecho Comercial y de las Obligaciones* 16 (1983): 335.
45. *See* P. Samuelson et al., 'A Manifesto Concerning the Legal Protection of Computer Programs', *Columbia Law Review* 94 (1994): 2308 et seq.

to develop a given plot and certain characters, and not in the plot or character itself. A misogynist London detective may be chosen as a character by any other writer; this will be legal and will not bear on the economic value of the rights on stories involving Sherlock Holmes. The situation of software is different. It has been defined as an organized or structured expression of a set of instructions used to ensure that a computer works in a given way.[46] If the expression of that set of instructions is altered, but its function and results are maintained, it may be possible to avoid the effects of the copyright protection of software, while preserving the economic content of that software and, furthermore, profiting from the creative effort of whoever has developed the conceptual aspects or the logical content of the software.

(d) Under the category of software it is common to include several stages or aspects. The following have been mentioned under Argentine law:[47]

- the idea for the solution of a given problem;
- an algorithm or method to be followed, generally expressed by means of mathematical formulae;
- a solution or treatment plan based on the algorithm;
- a text in programming language following the elements set out in the treatment plan (source program);
- a text in an intermediate language;
- a text that is directly legible by the hardware to be used, expressed in binary language (object program).

In all these cases, we find either ideas, which as such are not covered by copyright, or elements that are not directed to the expression of an idea in a way that is perceptible by human beings. The elements that are directly perceptible by human beings may be practically or economically irrelevant or may be avoided by a user wishing to avoid the effects of copyright protection. The end of the sequence is always, by definition, the operation of computer equipment. Argentine court law has tried to avoid these difficulties, declaring software to be protected by copyright even if it is meant to be 'read' by a machine.[48] But even following this line of interpretation of copyright law, as it relates to software, does not establish whether copyright protection extends to conduct that does not imply the expression, nor the reproduction or the marketing of software, but rather only the unauthorized use of software by means of computers.[49] This use has an economic importance normally lacking in the case of use of the information or ideas included in other works protected by copyright. Thus, listening to music or reading a book does not infringe the copyright on the music or book, but it does not affect the commercial

46. *See* C. Correa et al., *Derecho Informático* (Buenos Aires: Depalma, 1987), 57.
47. *Ibid.*
48. *See* G. García Zivano et al., 'National Court for Preliminary Criminal Proceedings', *Jurisprudencia Argentina* (1989-III), no. 11 (31 Jul. 1989): 709.
49. *See* Correa et al., *Derecho Informático*, 83.

value of the music or book. This is frequently not the case when software is put into use.[50]

(e) All intellectual property rights imply the definition of a conceptual area within which the owner of the intellectual property right has an exclusionary power against non-authorized third parties. Different criteria are used for purposes of defining this exclusive area, such as the concept of confusion in trademark law and concepts such as the reproduction of essential means under patent law. Similar criteria have been developed in the case of copyright, with regard to literary, artistic, musical and other types of work. These criteria clearly determine an area of protection that goes beyond an identical replication of the original work. Thus, if someone published García Márquez's *One Hundred Years of Solitude*, changing the name of one of the characters from Buendía to Buenasnoches, this would be held to be a violation of the exclusive rights on that book. When the differences become more extensive, it is necessary to examine in more detail the criteria developed by case law with regard to each type of work, to decide whether infringement exists.

These criteria are still lacking under Argentine copyright law with respect to software. The criteria that have been developed for literary, scientific, artistic or musical works – basically related with the impression on humans – may not be directed without further analysis to software, whose purpose is to perform a mechanical task in connection with machinery. In addition, for the legal protection of software to be economically effective, it must protect the creative effort required by the development of software. However, this creative effort is to a large extent focused not on the typical subject matter of copyright – the expression of an idea – but rather in the idea itself. This becomes apparent once the different stages in the development of software are examined.[51] Copyright in its traditional meaning and scope should not be applied to the idea for the solution of a problem, nor to the algorithm that applies such idea, since that algorithm may be expressed differently without violating the copyright on a prior expression. Nor should copyright be applied to the solution or plan based on the algorithm, which, again, is a type of idea and not a precise expression. Therefore, only after the source program stage is it possible to obtain copyright protection for the different stages of software development.

Certainly, either court decision or legislation may expand the traditional limits of copyright protection as they apply to software; this has been the case in other countries.[52] That expansion, however, has taken place in Argentina only imperfectly.[53] Decree 165, of 1994, does not have the legal status to extend the limits of copyright protection provided by Law 11,723 and by the copyright treaties approved by

---

50. Decree 165, of 1994, has tried to deal with this problem by means of a broad definition of 'expression'. As indicated in (a), *supra* , this solution is probably invalid. *See* M.F. Bohmer, 'La protección jurídica del mercado informático y un decreto que se anula a sí mismo', *La Ley* (1994-D).
51. *See* the text following n. 8, *supra* .
52. *See* UNESCO-OMPI, 'Protección jurídica de los programas de ordenador. Inventario y análisis de la legislación y jurisprudencia nacionales', *Revista del Derecho Industrial* 7 (1985): 630.
53. *See* Correa et al., *Derecho Informático*, 85 and 86.

Argentina.[54] Therefore, it has been necessary to enact Law 25,036, amending Article 1 of Law 11,723, so as to expressly include copyright within the subject matter covered by copyright protection. Law 25,036, however, does not solve the limits and uncertainties, described above, as to the proper or actual limits of copyright protection for software.

These shortcomings of Argentine software law are frequently hidden – in theory and in practice – by the statement that software receives copyright protection in Argentina.[55] This statement is true but leaves unanswered the basic questions related to that protection, namely the extent and limits of copyright protection as it applies to software.[56] A formal right that does not protect the economic value of its subject matter is of no practical interest.

The conclusion may be fairly reached that only with the help of special legislation, or after the development of a substantial body of case law, will it be possible to set out clearly and effectively the limits of the copyright protection of software under Argentine law.

B. *Databases*

19. The copyright protection of databases under Argentine law presents problems similar to those described above, in section A, with regard to software. The basic copyright statute, Law 11,723, included no express provision on databases. That law was drafted decades before databases acquired their present significance, which is closely related to the use of computers. The prevailing view was that databases could be protected by copyright,[57] but the limits of that protection were uncertain.[58] Decree 165, of 1994, included provisions intended to strengthen the copyright protection of databases, but such provisions were of limited value, specially since, under Argentine law, a decree may interpret or regulate the enforcement of copyright but not extend or limit the scope of such right, which must be fully defined by formal laws or treaties.

The status of databases under copyright law has been clarified, to some extent, by Law 25,036, which amended Article 1 of Law 11,723 to include compilations of data or of other materials within the subject matter protected by copyright. However, this amendment does not settle one of the central issues of database protection, namely the conditions that a database must satisfy to be considered a work subject to copyright protection.

Article 1, section (b), of Decree 165, of 1994, defines databases as 'the productions formed by an organized set of interrelated data, compiled with the view of storing, processing and recovering such data by means of informatic techniques and systems'. It includes databases under the category of literary works.

---

54. *See* I.B. Langenauer, 'El software en la ley 11.723', *El Derecho* 132 (1989): 628.
55. *See* M.F. Bohmer, 'La protección jurídica del mercado informático y un decreto que se anula a sí mismo', *La Ley* (1994-D).
56. *See* E. Galan Corona, 'En torno de la protección jurídica del soporte lógico', *Revista del Derecho Comercial y de las Obligaciones* 16 (1983): 335.
57. *See* Lipszyc, *Derecho de autor y derechos conexos*, 114 et seq.
58. *See* Correa et al., *Derecho Informático*, 299 et seq.

The definitions of reproduction of software[59] and of published and unpublished software[60] have been extended by Decree 165 to databases.

Registration of published database works whose exploitation is conducted by means of distance transmission takes place by means of the filing of broad extracts of the database's contents and of a written description of the database's structure, organization and principal characteristics to allow a sufficient determination of the work and of its contents.[61] Registration of unpublished database works takes place by means of the filing in the copyright registry of the different expressions of the work the owner considers sufficient for purposes of identifying the database to be protected.[62]

Several issues, common in comparative law, are left unanswered by the Argentine database regime, as follows:

(a) The right of the authors of material stored in a database to allow the inclusion of such materials.[63] The prevailing view is favourable to the existence of such right to allow or prohibit the inclusion of protected works in databases.[64]

(b) The right of database producers on the system, organization and processing of data.[65] The prevailing view is also favourable to the existence of this right.[66] The legal basis for such right is unclear. Some authors mention the traditional copyright protection of collections and anthologies,[67] while others base their position in the need to protect database producers from the parasitic exploitation of their efforts and investment,[68] a justification that appears to be closer to unfair competition law than to traditional copyright protection.

(c) The right of database producers on the databases that have been formed by means of computers.[69] Some authors question this right, since the work would have been the result of non-human activity.[70] The objection does not appear to be strong, since computers only play an instrumental role in these cases, common to many other musical and scientific works.

(d) The right of a given person to obtain information included in databases referred to that same person. Article 43 of the National Constitution, amended in 1994, includes this right, as well as the right to obtain the suppression, rectification, confidentiality or updating of information that is 'false or discriminatory'. The relation of this right – *habeas data* – with the copyright on databases has not yet been regulated or determined by the courts. Law 25,326 determines in more detail the protection of personal data, including information entered in public or private

59. *See* para. 17, n. 2, *supra* and accompanying text.
60. *Ibid.*, nn. 3, 4 and accompanying text.
61. *See* Decree 165, of 1994, Art. 2.
62. *Ibid.*, Art. 3.
63. *See* Correa et al., *Derecho Informático*, 300.
64. *See* Lipszyc, *Derecho de autor y derechos conexos*, 115.
65. *See* Correa et al., *Derecho Informático*, 300.
66. *See* Lipszyc, *Derecho de autor y derechos conexos*, 116.
67. *See* Correa et al., *Derecho Informático*, 302.
68. *See* Lipszyc, *Derecho de autor y derechos conexos*, 116.
69. *See* Correa et al., *Derecho Informático*, 300.
70. *Ibid.*

databases, thus implementing the basic rules provided by Article 43 of the National Constitution.

C. *Others*

20. Different types of intellectual works have created specific legal problems within the framework of copyright law, either because of their novelty or because of changes in the economic value of such works. The following may be mentioned:

(a) *Folklore.* It is governed by the general copyright rules included in Law 11,723 and in the international treaties approved by Argentina.[71] The contemporary tendency, however, is towards enhanced protection of local folklore, although this tendency has not yet materialized ineffective legislation.
(b) *Adaptations.* To the extent that an adaption is based on material protected by copyright, it is necessary to obtain the authorization of the owner of such copyright. The possible extent of the adaptation depends on the term of the authorization given by the copyright owner.[72] Once adaptation has been authorized, the author of the adaptation has the rights of a co-author with regard to such adaptation.[73] The author of an adaptation of a work that has fallen into the public domain has an exclusive right on such adaptation but may not prevent other adaptations.[74]
(c) *Translations.* Translators have an exclusive right on their translations, subject to the terms agreed with the author of the translated work.[75] The agreement between the translator and the author must be registered with the National Intellectual Property Registry to become enforceable.[76] The translator of a work that has fallen into the public domain has an exclusive right on the translation but may not prevent other translations.[77]
(d) *Anthologies.* A right as to the anthology, distinguishable from the rights related to the works included in such anthology, is recognized under Argentine law.[78] When not more than a thousand words of a given work are included in an anthology, it is not necessary to obtain the authorization of the copyright owner of such work; however, an equitable compensation must be paid to such copyright owner.[79]
(e) *Arrangements and orchestrations.* It is necessary to obtain the authorization of the copyright owner of the work subject to the arrangements or orchestrations. A distinction is introduced between 'technical' and 'creative' arrangements and

---

71. *See* Lipszyc, *Derecho de autor y derechos conexos*, 93 et seq. If the work has fallen in the public domain, a fee for its exploitation is payable to the National Articles Fund. *See* M. Goldstein, *Derecho de autor* (Buenos Aires: La Rocca, 1995), 79.
72. *See* Lipszyc, *Derecho de autor y derechos conexos*, 113.
73. *See* Law 11,723, Art. 25.
74. *Ibid.*, Art. 26.
75. *Ibid.*, Art. 23.
76. *Ibid.*
77. *Ibid.*, Art. 24.
78. *See* The Berne Convention on the Protection of Literary and Artistic Works, Art. 2(5); Lipszyc, *Derecho de autor y derechos conexos*, 116, 117.
79. *See* Law 11,723, Art. 10.

orchestration; only the latter category gives rise to a separate right on the arrangement or orchestration.[80]

(f) *Journalistic publications*. Unsigned articles, reports, interviews, drawing, engravings and general information included in a journal, magazine or periodical publication are considered to be the property of the publisher of such journal, magazine or periodical, unless they have been acquired from a third party, provided they are original.[81] General interest information may be used, transmitted or retransmitted, but if it is published in its original version, it is necessary to indicate its source.[82] The authors of signed articles, reports, interviews and other journalistic material are the owners of the intellectual property rights on such material.[83]

§3. Conditions of Protection

I. Formal Requirements

21. The basic principle under Argentine law is that copyright arises by virtue of the creation of an original work and that registration is not necessary for an exclusive right on intellectual property to result.[84] However, registration is a condition for the exercise of certain rights. In particular, in the case of published works, the exclusive rights of the editor resulting from copyright may only be exercised if the work has been registered in the National Intellectual Property Registry.[85] If registration has not taken place within three months from publication of the work, the editor loses his or her rights with regard to unauthorized publications until registration takes place.[86] After such registration the editor's rights only extend to publications taking place after registration.[87]

Registration takes place by means of the deposit of three complete copies of the published work in the National Intellectual Property Registry.[88] Registration must take place within three months of publication.[89] In the case of paintings, architectural works, sculptures and similar works, it is enough to deposit a drawing or photograph of the original, with the indications necessary to identify such original.[90] Cinematographic works are registered by means of a summary of their elements.[91]

80. *See* Lipszyc, *Derecho de autor y derechos conexos*, 117, 118.
81. *See* Law 11,723, Art. 28.
82. *Ibid.*
83. *Ibid.*, Art. 29.
84. *See* Lipszyc, *Derecho de autor y derechos conexos*, 68; Goldstein, *Derecho de autor*, 199.
85. *See* Law 11,723, Arts 57, 61 and 63.
86. *Ibid.*, Art. 63.
87. *See* Lipszyc, *Derecho de autor y derechos conexos*, 538.
88. *See* Law 11,723, Art. 57.
89. *Ibid.*
90. *Ibid.*
91. *Ibid.*

Unpublished works may be registered by means of the deposit of only one copy of the work.[92]

Argentine courts have decided that foreign works covered by the Universal Copyright Convention are fully protected under Argentine law, even if they have not complied with the deposit or registration requirements provided by local statutes, if they comply with the formal requirements included in that convention.[93] These rules extend even in the field of criminal law protection of copyright.[94] On the basis of this case law, it has been proposed that compliance with the formal requirements of the Universal Copyright Convention should be sufficient for full copyright protection also for Argentine works or authors.[95] This position, however, has not yet found support in case law.[96]

The registration of a given work, as provided by Argentine copyright law, creates a rebuttable presumption of validity of the copyright claimed through that registration.[97] However, the different aspects of such presumption may be overruled if sufficient evidence is produced showing that a substantive element of the copyright protection being claimed through registration is lacking. Thus, the presumption created through registration may be destroyed if the subject matter claimed through registration is not a work that may be protected by copyright[98] or if the actual author of the work is not the person who claimed authorship through registration.[99]

In addition, registration creates evidence that may be used in future litigation connected with the subject matter of such registration.[100]

Registration pursuant to Argentine copyright law is also possible or is required with regard to several aspects or transactions related to intellectual works:

(a) Acts or transactions through which the exploitation of works is authorized.[101]
(b) Acts or transactions assigning or modifying copyright.[102]
(c) Articles of incorporation and bylaws of entities in charge of the collective management of copyright.[103]

92. *Ibid.*, Art. 62.
93. *See* N Ferrari de Gnisi, et al., 'National Criminal and Correctional Court of Appeals in Banc', *Jurisprudencia Argentina* 1982-II (30 Nov. 1982): 562.
94. *Ibid.*
95. *See* Lipszyc, *Derecho de autor y derechos conexos*, 540.
96. *See* n. 10, *supra* . But *see SADAIC v. Puig Major Discotheque*, National Civil Court of Appeals F, 8 Aug. 1991, *El Derecho*, vol. 145, 135. This was a case that dealt with a foreign work but in which no distinction was made between local and foreign works for the purposes of applying only the formal requirements of the Berne Convention, and not those originally required by Argentine law.
97. *See* Lipszyc, *Derecho de autor y derechos conexos*, 542.
98. *See Martínez, A.D. v. ATC Canal 7 TV LS 82*, National Civil Court of Appeals B, 28 Oct. 1988, *Jurisprudencia Argentina*, vol. 1989-II (1989), 492.
99. *See* Goldstein, *Derecho de autor*, 197.
100. *See* Lipszyc, *Derecho de autor y derechos conexos*, 543.
101. *See* Law 11,723, Art. 66.
102. *Ibid.*
103. *See* Lipszyc, *Derecho de autor y derechos conexos*, 547.

(d) Agency agreements between entities in charge of the collective management of copyright, acting in Argentina and abroad.[104]
(e) Preliminary injunctions, liens and other precautionary measures related to copyright.[105]
(f) Transfer of copyright due to inheritance.[106]

The registration of transactions related to copyright is not necessary for the validity of such transactions;[107] however, a third party – for example, a creditor of the assignor – may disregard the transaction until it is registered.[108]

Any of the parties to a copyright transaction may request the registration of such transaction.[109]

In the case of registration of new works, the registration claim is published in the Official Gazette after the claim has been filed.[110] A thirty-day period as from the last publication is provided for interested third parties to file their possible opposition to the registration claim.[111] If no opposition is filed, registration must take place immediately.[112] If an opposition is filed, the National Intellectual Property Registry decides whether the opposition is justified.[113] This decision only affects the registration procedure and is not decisive with regard to the underlying copyright ownership.[114]

The National Copyright Office (*Dirección Nacional del Derecho de Autor*) is presently in charge of the National Intellectual Property Registry.[115]

II. Substantive Requirements

22. It has been repeatedly stated under Argentine copyright law that the subject matter of copyright protection is the expression of an idea, and not the idea itself.[116] As in other jurisdictions, the exact meaning and practical consequences of this rule is vague and debatable. Procedures to obtain practical results are clearly beyond the

104. *Ibid., see also* Decree 41,233, of 1934, Art. 31.
105. *See* Law 11,723, Art. 65.
106. *Ibid.*
107. *See* Lipszyc, *Derecho de autor y derechos conexos*, 547, 548; A. G. Spota, *Instituciones de Derecho Civil. Contratos*, vol. 6 (Buenos Aires: Depalma, 1981), 340, 341.
108. *Ibid.*
109. *See* A. G. Spota, *Instituciones de Derecho Civil. Contratos*, vol. 6 (Buenos Aires: Depalma, 1981), 341.
110. *See* Decree 41,233, of 1934, Art. 18.
111. *Ibid.*, Art. 19.
112. *Ibid.*
113. *Ibid.*, Art. 20.
114. *See* Goldstein, *Derecho de autor*, 197 et seq.
115. *See* Decree 800, of 1971.
116. *See* Lipszyc, *Derecho de autor y derechos conexos*, 61 et seq.; D. Chaloupka, 'La propiedad de las ideas', *Derechos Intelectuales* 3 (1988): 56 et seq.; C.A. Villalba, 'La apuesta triple. Un fallo que pone en juego los elementos básicos que regulan la actividad intelectual', *La Ley* 156 (1974): 1222. *See also* Law 11,723, Art. 1, as amended by Law 25,036.

scope of copyright protection;[117] if such procedures are not protected by industrial property rights, such as patents, the procedures may be used even if they have been described in a work that receives copyright protection.[118]

In addition, copyright only applies to original works.[119] As with similar intellectual property concepts, the originality test encompasses two distinct aspects. First, for a work to be original it must be new; that is, it must differ from pre-existing works. Second, the differences between the purportedly original work and other pre-existing works must be such that the new work implies a process of artistic, scientific, literary or intellectual creation.[120]

The originality requirements, although applicable to all types of subject matter protected by copyright, have different implications for each type of creation. Thus, for example, in the case of musical works, special emphasis has been placed on the melody;[121] in the case of musical arrangements, a distinction has been introduced between 'mechanical' and 'creative' arrangements.[122] In some areas, particularly software, little progress has been made in legal literature or in court decisions with regard to the specific meaning and limits of originality.

Argentine copyright law excludes several possible substantive requirements of protection. First, the artistic, scientific, cultural or intellectual value or merit of a work is irrelevant in defining copyright protection, provided such work is original and implies a process of intellectual creation.[123] If the originality requirements are satisfied, it is not for the courts or for the administrative authorities to weigh the value of the work;[124] such assessment is left to the public.

Second, the purpose of the work is also irrelevant in defining copyright protection.[125] A work with a purely practical application receives copyright protection. However, it is the expression of the intellectual work that is protected, and not the use to which the ideas included in such work may be put.[126]

Third, the means or medium used for the expression or transmission of an intellectual work are irrelevant for purposes of defining copyright protection. If the nature of the work permits it, a given work may be expressed in different ways – orally,

117. *See* Lipszyc, *Derecho de autor y derechos conexos*, 64.
118. *Ibid*., *See also Gibellini, E.J. v. Plan Ovalo S.A.* National Civil Court of Appeals A, 9 Apr. 1986, *Jurisprudencia Argentina*, vol. 1987-I, 436.
119. *See* Lipszyc, *Derecho de autor y derechos conexos*, 65; *Neer, E. v. Lotería de Beneficencia Nacional y Casinos*, National Criminal and Correctional Court of Appeals II, 23 Mar. 1988, *Jurisprudencia Argentina*, vol. 1989-II, 403.
120. *Ibid.*
121. *See* Lipszyc, *Derecho de autor y derechos conexos*, 74.
122. *Ibid*., 118.
123. *Ibid*., 67; R.E. Witthaus, 'Propiedad intelectual de la traducción', *Jurisprudencia Argentina* (1972-Doctrina): 243.
124. *See Cesani, P.E. v. Mortero y Cía*., National Commercial Court of Appeals A, 19 Oct. 1989, *Jurisprudencia Argentina*, vol. 1991-I, 134.
125. *See* Lipszyc, *Derecho de autor y derechos conexos*, 67.
126. This distinction is particularly important in the area of software.

in writing, in electronic media and so forth – and all these expressions will receive copyright protection.[127]

Finally, there is no *numerum clausum* as to the types of intellectual work that may be protected. Thus, if technology permits the development of new types of work, as has been the case with software, these new types will be protected provided they meet the general requirements applicable to all types of intellectual creations subject to copyright protection.[128]

Certain possible substantive requirements for copyright protection have not yet been sufficiently discussed by the Argentine courts. In particular, it is not clear whether 'creations' made by machines, and not by humans, may be considered to be 'works' for copyright purposes.[129] Also, if a given expression is necessary to achieve certain practical results, as may be the case with certain software, it is debatable whether copyright protection is still admissible.[130]

§4. Ownership

I. The Author

23. The author of a work is the original owner of the copyright on such work. This basic principle is stated in Article 4 of Law 11,723. This provision distinguishes between the author of the work – the original owner of the intellectual property rights – and the heirs and other successors and beneficiaries of such rights. In addition, Article 4 mentions the category of persons who, with the permission of the author of the work, proceed to its translation, consolidation, adaptation, modification or inclusion in a new work. In this case, the authors of these changes are considered original owners with respect to the intellectual creation implicit in such changes.

Because authorship implies an intellectual creation and this, in turn, requires a human activity, it has been stated that only individuals may be the original owners of copyright.[131] The fact that the duration of copyright under Argentine law is generally calculated on the basis of the death of the author[132] would confirm that the law is built on the idea of individuals as authors and original owners of works covered by copyright. There are certain exceptions to the rule that corporations may not be the original owners of copyright. Anonymous collective works are considered to belong immediately to

127. *See* Villalba, 'La apuesta triple', 1222; E. O'Farrell, 'La apropiación de las ideas en la ley 11,723', *La Ley* (1989-C): 250.
128. *See* A. Mille, 'El software y los bancos de datos a la luz de la jurisprudencia', *V Congreso Internacional sobre la Protección de los Derechos Intelectuales* (1990): 151.
129. *See* Correa et al., *Derecho Informático*, 300. Some court decisions have required that the subject matter of copyright protection be perceptible by human beings; *see Cesani, P.E. v. Mortero y Cía., supra* n. 124.
130. The prevailing view appears to be favourable to copyright protection in these cases; *see* Goldstein, *Derecho de autor*, 53.
131. *See* Lipszyc, *Derecho de autor y derechos conexos*, 123 et seq.
132. *See* Law 11,723, Art. 5.

the institutions, corporations or other legal entities that organized such collective works.[133] Also, works resulting from an employment relationship are considered to be immediately transferred to the employer.[134] Strictly speaking, the original owner of the copyright is still the individual who created the underlying work,[135] but the economic content of such copyright is immediately transferred to the employer.[136]

24. Several special rules on authorship have been developed under Argentine law with regard to specific types of works:

(a) In case of musical works including wording, the music and the words are two different works that may have two separate individual original authors.[137]
(b) Translators have a separate individual right on their translation, even if it refers to a translated work that has fallen into the public domain.[138]
(c) In the case of anonymous works, copyright belongs to the editor, but the anonymous author may at any time claim the copyright by showing his or her identity and authorship.[139]
(d) In the case of cinematographic works, the director of the film, the producer and the author of the script have similar rights with regard to the resulting work.[140] In the case of 'musical cinematographic works', the composer of the music has the same rights as the director of the film, the producer and the author of the script.[141] In both cases, it is possible to alter contractually these rules.[142]
(e) The author of an adaptation, modification or parody or of the inclusion of a pre-existing work in a different work is the owner of the adaptation, modification, parody or inclusion.[143] The new derived work can only be published or otherwise exploited with the authorization of the owner of the copyright on the original work.[144]
(f) Special rules have also been developed with regard to anthologies,[145] arrangements and orchestrations[146] and journalistic publications.[147]
(g) In the case of computer programs produced by persons hired for that purpose, in the course of their employment, the employer owns the copyright over such programs, except if the parties have agreed otherwise.[148]

---

133. *Ibid.*, Art. 16.
134. *See* Lipszyc, *Derecho de autor y derechos conexos*, 146.
135. *Ibid.*
136. *Ibid.*, *See also* the Employment Contract Law (Law 20,744, as amended), Art. 82.
137. *See* Law 11,723, Art. 17.
138. *Ibid.*, Arts 23, 24.
139. *Ibid.*, Art. 3. *See also* Decree 41,233, of 1934, Art. 26.
140. *See* Law 11,723, Art. 20, as amended by Law 25,847.
141. *Ibid.*
142. *Ibid.*
143. *Ibid.*, Arts 25, 26.
144. *Ibid.*, Art. 25.
145. *See supra* para. 20(d).
146. *See supra* para. 20(e).
147. *See supra* para. 20(f).
148. *See* Law 11,723, Art. 4(d), as included by Law 25,036.

II. Joint Works: Works Created by Several Persons

25. A basic distinction is applied under Argentine law between works done through cooperation, collective works and composite works.

Works done through cooperation (*obras en colaboración*) imply a creative collaboration between different authors. Such authors do not merely add the results of their creative efforts but rather direct and organize their work with a view towards a common result. Cooperation is defined as 'perfect' if the resulting work is indivisible and 'imperfect' if it is possible to distinguish the results attributable to each co-author.[149]

Collective works are those created through the initiative or direction of one or more individuals, who coordinate or direct the efforts of several other individuals to achieve a joint result. These include dictionaries, encyclopaedias, compilations, etc.[150] Composite works are the result of adding different separate works, each one with a possible separate author and owner, into one final result. This result may take place after a considerable time has elapsed after the creation of each or some of the original separate works. Composite works include translations, adaptations, music with words, etc.[151]

Works done through cooperation and collective works are considered as categories within the concept of co-authorship. Composite works may result in a situation termed 'plurality of authors', under which each element of the composite work has a separate set of authors with specific rights as to such element.[152]

It is not clear what authorization requirements must be met for the exploitation of works done through cooperation. Some authorities consider it necessary to obtain the consent of all the co-authors for such authorization to be valid.[153] Other sources understand that the authorization of only one co-author is sufficient, on the basis of the rule to that effect included in Article 19 of Law 11,723, with regard to lyrical or dramatic works.[154] If this second mechanism is accepted, the proceeds of the exploitation must be divided among the different co-authors, in proportion to their participation in the joint property of the copyright.

In cases of 'imperfect' cooperation, each co-author may exploit separately the elements he or she has contributed to the joint work and authorize a similar exploitation by third parties, in both cases provided no damage is caused to the joint work or to the rights related thereto.[155]

Comparable doubts exist in connection with collective works. It may be argued, on the basis of the provisions of Article 16 of Law 11,723, that the anonymous authors participating in a collective work relinquish their original copyright in favour of the

149. *See* Lipszyc, *Derecho de autor y derechos conexos*, 131.
150. *Ibid.*, 132 et seq.
151. *Ibid.*, 130.
152. Law 11,723, Art. 17, provides that the mere plurality of authors shall not be considered cooperation and that this shall only exist if the property may not be divided without altering the nature of the work. It adds that in the case of musical works with words, the music and the words shall be considered to be two different works.
153. *See* Lipszyc, *Derecho de autor y derechos conexos*, 132.
154. *See* Goldstein, *Derecho de autor*, 70.
155. *See* Lipszyc, *Derecho de autor y derechos conexos*, 132.

publisher, unless a different solution has been agreed between the parties.[156] If the authors of the collective work are not anonymous, they would hold the same rights as authors in a joint work created through cooperation,[157] unless a different agreement is reached between the parties.

In the case of composite works, the general rule is that each author has the right to authorize or prohibit the exploitation of the part of the work attributable to such author. Law 11,723 provides special statutory rules to that effect,[158] although certain exceptional different solutions are also provided in that law with regard to specific types of composite works.[159]

III. Works Made for Hire

26. There were no specific provisions under Argentine statutory law with regard to copyright relative to works made for hire.

If works have been developed or created in the course of employment, the rules of the Employment Contract Law (Law 20,744 as amended) would be applicable. These rules do not make specific reference to copyright, but they do provide a specific regime for inventions and discoveries obtained in the course of employment, which would also be extendable to works covered by copyright. On the basis of these rules, if the employee has been hired to develop or create certain works, the property rights on such works would belong to the employer,[160] and the employee would retain the moral rights.[161] The employer would also have the right to modify or adapt the works it has thus obtained.[162]

If works have been developed on the basis of intellectual property previously belonging to the employer, he or she would also be entitled to copyright on such works, with the limits described in the preceding paragraph.

All the other works developed or created by employees would be the property of such employees and would only be transferred to employers through specific transactions accepted by the employees.

If works are made for hire in circumstances that do not involve employment relationships, the property rights on such works will depend on the contractual terms agreed by the parties. The original right on these works will still belong to their authors, except in the case of anonymous works.[163] Moral rights will always belong to the

156. *Ibid.*, 133, 134.
157. *See* Goldstein, *Derecho de autor*, 70.
158. *See* Art. 18 (music with words); Art. 20 (musical cinematographic works); Art. 23 (translations); and Art. 25 (adaptations, modifications, parodies, etc.).
159. For example, under Art. 21 of Law 11,723, the producer of a cinematographic film has the right to exhibit such film, even without the authorization of the author of the script or of the music. The authors of the script and of the music have a similar right with regard to the script and the music, respectively, but not with regard to the cinematographic work that includes their script or music.
160. *See* C.A. Villalba, 'Derecho de autor y trabajo subordinado', *La Ley* (1990-E): 320.
161. *See* Lipszyc, *Derecho de autor y derechos conexos*, 147.
162. *Ibid.*, 149.
163. *See* Law 11,723, Art. 16; Lipszyc, *Derecho de autor y derechos conexos*, 145.

author.[164] Exploitation rights will also belong to the author, unless express or implied covenants between the parties provide otherwise.[165]

Argentine authorities have generally been reluctant to infer the transfer of copyright from agreements under which certain works will be supplied by their author with specific purposes,[166] such as architectural works.[167] In the absence of express provisions, it will normally be inferred that the acquirer has the right to put the work into his or her own use, but not to reproduce or otherwise exploit it in connection with third parties.[168] In a similar vein, if a given work has been developed for a specific project of the hirer, the author's consent is necessary if the work is to be put into a different use by the hirer.[169]

Law 25,036 has amended Article 4 of Law 11,723, which now includes a section (d) providing that in the case of computer programs produced by persons hired with that purpose, in the course of their employment, the employer owns the copyright over such programs, except if the parties have agreed otherwise. The result does not differ from what follows from the general rules included in the Employment Contract Law, described previously in this section.

§5. Transfer

I. Assignment of Copyright

27. It has been debated whether it is possible under Argentine law to agree to a full assignment of copyright. Certain authorities suggest that such assignment is not legally possible, and the original copyright owner may only grant licenses or other types of authorization to exploit works for a limited period or with a limited scope.[170] This position does not find support in Argentine statutory law[171] nor in court decisions.[172] The general principle, under Argentine civil law, is that all rights may be assigned by their owner, except in the cases in which a rule prohibits or limits such assignment.[173] Copyright falls under this general rule. Article 51 of Law 11,723 sets out the basic rule to that effect in the copyright area, providing that the author or his or her successors or assignees may sell or assign totally or partially the work.

There are, however, several exceptions to the general possibility of copyright assignment. The following may be mentioned:

164. *See* D. Lipszyc, *ibid.*
165. *Ibid.*
166. *See* Law 11,723, Arts 54 and 55.
167. *See* D.E. Butlow & P.M. Bustos, 'Derechos intelectuales en las obras de arquitectura', *La Ley* (1988-E): 835.
168. *See* Lipszyc, *Derecho de autor y derechos conexos*, 145.
169. *See* Butlow & Bustos, 'Derechos' 837.
170. *See* Lipszyc, *Derecho de autor y derechos conexos*, 272.
171. *See* Law 11,723, Art. 51.
172. *See* Goldstein, *Derecho de autor*, 132 et seq.
173. *See* Civil and Commercial Code, Arts 398 and 1616.

(a) The assignment is valid only for the term provided by law.[174] Strictly speaking, this is not a restriction on assignments of copyright, since the term in question is that provided by the copyright statutes for the duration of copyright; it is a general principle of Argentine law that an assignor may not, by means of the assignment, extend the scope or duration of the rights previously held by such assignor.[175]
(b) The assignment only extends to the economic or exploitation aspects of copyright,[176] and not to the author's moral rights.[177] In particular, the author retains the right to have his or her work properly reproduced and to have his or her name mentioned in connection with the assigned work.[178]
(c) The assignee is not allowed to change the title, form or contents of the assigned work.[179]

In addition, several restrictions apply to the contractual obligations that may be included in copyright assignment agreements. Thus, clauses where under an author agrees to assign all future intellectual production are considered void.[180] This restriction would not apply to specific future works. Clauses of this type are considered to be contrary to the constitutional right to work and to the property of intellectual creations.[181] Also, clauses providing that the assignor may not obtain copyright in the future with respect to new works or that prohibit the assignor from creating new intellectual works would also be void,[182] for similar reasons.

For a copyright assignment to be fully legally effective, it must be in writing and registered in the National Intellectual Property Registry.[183] However, if the agreement is not thus registered, it will not be void, but rather invalid with relation to bona fide third parties, such as the assignor's creditors.[184]

Certain special provisions apply to specific types of assignment. Thus, under Article 54 of Law 11,723, the assignment of rights related to paintings, sculptures, photographs and other similar tangible works does not imply the right to reproduce such work, unless an express contractual provision assigns the copyright together with the right to individual tangible works.[185] In a similar vein, the sale of charts, blueprints and other similar works implies the right of the purchaser to undertake the work or

174. *See* Law 11,723, Art. 51.
175. *See* Civil and Commercial Code, Art. 399.
176. *See* Law 11,723, Art. 51.
177. *Ibid.*, Art. 52. *See also* Lipszyc, *Derecho de autor y derechos conexos*, 281, 282; *Szabo, L. v. Remington Rand Sudamericana*, National Civil Court of Appeals B, 22 Jul. 1963, *La Ley*, vol. 112, 211.
178. *See* Law 11,723, Art. 52.
179. *Ibid.*, Art. 51.
180. *See* Lipszyc, *Derecho de autor y derechos conexos*, 278.
181. *See* National Constitution, Arts 14, 14*bis* and 17.
182. *See* Lipszyc, *Derecho de autor y derechos conexos*, 278.
183. *See* Law 11,723, Art. 53.
184. *See* Lipszyc, *Derecho de autor y derechos conexos*, 275; *Bollo, J.N. v. Gonzalez, H.*, Civil Court of Appeals of the City of Buenos Aires 2, 6 Aug. 1940, *Jurisprudencia Argentina*, vol. 71, 700.
185. *See Piranian, A.A. v. Gona, R.*, National Civil Court of Appeals C, 15 Mar. 1991, *La Ley*, vol. 1991-C, 401.

project described in such elements but does not allow such purchaser to reproduce the charts and other similar elements, nor to use them for other projects, nor to sell them to third parties, unless the copyright owner has expressly allowed such further uses.[186]

It has been proposed that assignments of copyright should be interpreted restrictively so that the transfer of an element of copyright would be the exception, and the retention of such right by the original copyright owner would be the rule.[187] Thus, for example, the transfer of copyright would not extend to the use of new reproduction media if they were not expressly mentioned in the assignment documentation.[188] This type of interpretation, however, appears to be more a reflection of comparative legal tendencies than a description of the actual Argentine practice. The latter continues to be based on the contract interpretation rules generally derived from the Civil and Commercial Code.[189]

II. Licenses

28. Argentine law does not include a set of general provisions applicable to copyright licenses. This field is thus governed by two very different types of rules: specific copyright provisions applicable to particular types of licenses and general contract law rules applicable to all types of contracts and, therefore, also to copyright licenses.

Law 11,723 includes relatively detailed provisions on publishing agreements. Such agreements are defined as those in which a party owning property rights over an intellectual work undertakes the obligation to deliver it to the publisher, and this second party agrees to reproduce it, divulge it and sell it.[190] If these conditions are met, a publishing agreement exists regardless of the media used for such publishing.[191]

A publishing agreement generally implies that the copyright owner retains such ownership, unless a contractual provision to the contrary is agreed.[192] The rights to translate or modify the work are retained by the copyright owner.[193] Also, the copyright owner retains the right to file legal actions against infringers of such copyright.[194]

The publisher acquires the right to reproduce, divulge and sell the work.[195] The extent and limits of these rights may be contractually arranged between the parties.[196]

186. *See* Law 11,723, Art. 55.
187. *See* Lipszyc, *Derecho de autor y derechos conexos*, 275 et seq.; M.A. Emery, 'La interpretación restrictiva en la cesión de derechos intelectuales', *La Ley* (1991-C): 401.
188. *See* Lipszyc, *Derecho de autor y derechos conexos*, 279.
189. *See* Law 11,723, Art. 12.
190. *Ibid.*, Art. 37.
191. *Ibid.*
192. *Ibid.*, Art. 38.
193. *Ibid.*
194. *Ibid.*
195. *Ibid.*, Art. 39.
196. *See* Lipszyc, *Derecho de autor y derechos conexos*, 294; *see also* R. Bottaro, 'Contrato de edición', *La Ley* (1981-D): 1112; C.A. Villalba, 'El denominado contrato de edición musical. Los contratos en la ley sobre propiedad intelectual', *La Ley* (1990-A): 551.

The contract must state the number of authorized editions and their size.[197] If no provisions are included in that respect, the issue is decided on the basis of the customs prevailing in the place where the publishing contract is completed.[198]

The publishing contract must also state the consideration to be paid by the publisher.[199] There is a general presumption to the effect that a price is owed to the copyright owner.[200] Again, in the absence of contractual determination, the price is fixed on the basis of the prevailing customs.[201] In the case of musical works, a monthly royalty statement must be submitted by the publisher, including the indication of the number of copies sold.[202]

If a work is delivered to the publisher and is lost by such publisher before publication, the publisher must pay the author an indemnity equivalent to the royalties or other consideration that would have been payable if publishing had taken place.[203]

The author has the obligation to deliver the work stated in the publishing agreement. If no date is set for such delivery, the date is equitably fixed by a court.[204] If the work is lost before the delivery, the author or his assignees must return any price they may have previously received for future delivery of the work and indemnify any damages suffered by the publisher.[205]

The agreement expires due to termination of the agreed term, or pursuant to other termination provisions included in the publishing contract. If a specified number of editions or copies is provided in the agreement, publication rights expire together with the total sale of such editions or copies.[206]

Several special customs and practices have developed in connection with the publishing of musical or artistic works. Thus, in the case of musical works, it is common for the publisher to have the right to sublicense publishing rights[207] and to obtain a participation from any type of exploitation of the published work, even if such exploitation is not directly undertaken by the publisher.[208] In the case of artistic works, it is common to agree upon a flat fee which will be payable to the artist, regardless of the exploitation of the work by the publisher, particularly if the works have been specially commissioned by the publisher.[209]

197. *See* Law 11,723, Art. 40.
198. *Ibid.*
199. *Ibid.*
200. *Ibid.*
201. *Ibid.*
202. *See* Decree 4,233, of 1934, Art. 39.
203. *See* Law 11,723, Art. 41.
204. *Ibid.*, Art. 42.
205. *Ibid.*, Art. 41.
206. *Ibid.*, Art. 44. If the agreement expires due to termination of the agreed term and the publisher, at the termination date, still holds unsold copies, the author may purchase them at a price equivalent to cost plus a 10% bonus. If the author does not exercise this option, the publisher may continue selling such copies under the terms provided in the publishing agreement. *See* Law 11,723, Art. 43.
207. *See* Lipszyc, *Derecho de autor y derechos conexos*, 304.
208. *Ibid.*
209. *Ibid.*, 307.

These special characteristics of the publishing of musical or artistic works have not yet resulted in a special statutory regulation of these agreements.[210]

29. Law 11,723 includes specific provisions applicable to performance agreements. These are defined by this law[211] as those in which an author or its assignors or successors deliver to an entrepreneur a theatrical work for public performance and such work is accepted by the entrepreneur.[212]

In the case of new works, whose first performance is provided by the performance agreement, the entrepreneur, upon receiving the work, must state within a thirty-day term whether he or she elects to perform the work.[213]

Any work accepted for performance must be performed within one year from the moment in which it was presented to the entrepreneur.[214] If this obligation is not fulfilled, damages equivalent to the royalties that would accrue from twenty performances of a similar work must be paid to the author.[215]

Acceptance of a work for performance does not allow the entrepreneur to publish such work or to have it performed by a different entrepreneur.[216] Performance must take place as agreed with the author.[217] If any copies of the work to be performed are made for purposes of organizing the performance, such copies may not be sold or leased without the author's consent.[218]

If the entrepreneur loses the original copy of the work, and this results in the loss of the work, for lack of additional copies, the entrepreneur is liable for the damages thus caused to the author.[219] Also, if the work is performed by unauthorized third parties who have had access to copies of the work due to the entrepreneur's fault, the entrepreneur shall be liable for damages.[220]

If an unpublished work is delivered pursuant to a performance agreement and accepted for performance as a consequence of such agreement, the author is not allowed to authorize other parties to perform the same work, until it has been performed under the first performance agreement, unless the parties to such agreement have jointly decided otherwise.[221]

For purposes of the application of these rules on performance agreements, performance shall include not only theatrical stagings, but also radio transmissions, cinema or television exhibitions, and any other procedure for the reproduction and exhibition of a work.[222]

---

210. *Ibid.*, 304.
211. Article 45.
212. In practice, the concept and rules of performance agreements extend to all types of work that may be performed in public, such as literary, dramatic, musical, pantomimic or choreographic works; *see* Lipszyc, *Derecho de autor y derechos conexos*, 312.
213. *See* Law 11,723, Art. 46.
214. *Ibid.*
215. *Ibid.*
216. *Ibid.*, Art. 47.
217. *Ibid.*
218. *Ibid.*
219. *Ibid.*, Art. 48.
220. *Ibid.*
221. *Ibid.*, Art. 49.
222. *Ibid.*, Art. 50.

30. There are other types of copyright licenses, not regulated by Argentine statutory law, but which are nevertheless valid pursuant to general contractual law and copyright principles. The following may be mentioned:

(a) *Mechanical reproduction agreements*. These agreements may be defined as those in which the owner of the copyright on a musical work authorizes its reproduction by means of discs, tapes or other similar mechanical means.[223] These contracts are generally governed by the same rules applicable to publishing contracts.[224] There are, however, certain differences as to customary provisions to include in mechanical reproduction agreements, as compared with the usual provisions in agreements for the publishing of printed works. These differences, in turn, may result in divergent results in case of litigation related to the interpretation of specific agreements. In particular, mechanical reproduction agreements are heavily influenced by the contractual practice of authors' associations,[225] which have a much smaller role in the case of printed works.

(b) *Radio and television performance agreements*. These agreements are a variation within the category of performance agreements;[226] this broader category is expressly governed by Argentine statutory law.[227] As in the case of mechanical reproduction agreements, radio and television performance agreements have been drafted primarily under the influence of authors' associations.[228]

(c) *Audio-visual works production agreements*. These have been defined as those in which the author of a literary, dramatic or artistic work authorizes its inclusion by a producer in an audio-visual work, particularly cinematography or television works that will be distributed and exhibited by the producer.[229] In general, these works are governed by the rules on publishing contracts.[230] However, certain specific rules apply to these agreements: There is a presumption that the author of the script retains the same rights as the producer, unless the production agreement provides otherwise;[231] the author of the script retains the right to publish it as a separate literary work,[232] etc.

223. *See* Lipszyc, *Derecho de autor y derechos conexos*, 324.
224. *Ibid.*, 325.
225. *Ibid.*, 326 et seq.
226. *Ibid.*, 332 et seq.
227. *See* para. 29, *supra* .
228. *See* Lipszyc, *Derecho de autor y derechos conexos*, 332 et seq.
229. *Ibid.*, 342.
230. *Ibid.*, 343.
231. *See* Law 11,723, Art. 20.
232. *Ibid.*, Art. 21.

§6. Scope of Exclusive Rights

I. Moral Rights

31. Moral rights are considered to be an essential constituent element of copyright under Argentine law.[233] Moral rights related to a given work result together with the creation of such work[234] and are part of the original copyright granted to the author.[235]

Moral rights consist of several different elements:

(a) The right to preserve the text, title and other contents of the work, even if property rights on such work have been assigned.[236] This right extends to any publication, printing or reproduction of the work.[237]
(b) The right to have the author named and identified as such together with the work, regardless of who holds property rights in connection with such work.[238]
(c) The right to decide whether the work will be published.[239] This right would only apply for as long as the author has not taken the decision to publish the work. If such decision has been taken, and contracts have been entered into by the author as a consequence of such decision, the author would be bound by such decision.[240] As a result, the author's creditors would not be allowed to act against an unpublished work, requiring its publication, but if such work is published, the creditors may garnish or otherwise act against the proceeds from publication.[241]
(d) The right to modify the work, even after it has been published.[242]

Argentine law, however, does not recognize the right to withdraw the contractual consent given by the author with respect to the publication of a work, even if proper indemnification is offered.[243]

Moral rights, as described above, are considered to be non-assignable.[244] They may not be waived or surrendered in a general way,[245] although they may be waived

233. *See Casiraghi, F. et al. v. Province of La Rioja*, Federal Supreme Court, 23 Nov. 1989, *El Derecho*, vol. 138, 330.
234. *Ibid.*
235. *Ibid.*
236. *See* Law 11,723, Art. 52.
237. *Ibid.*
238. *Ibid.*
239. *Ibid.*, Art. 2. *See also* Lipszyc, *Derecho de autor y derechos conexos*, 159 et seq.
240. *See* Law 11,723, Art. 38.
241. *See* Lipszyc, *Derecho de autor y derechos conexos*, 163.
242. *See* Law 11,723, Art. 38.
243. *Ibid., see also* Lipszyc, *Derecho de autor y derechos conexos*, 172 et seq.
244. *See* R. Arlt Cristophersen et al., 'National Civil Court of Appeals B', *La Ley* 128 (7 Sept. 1967): 906.
245. *Ibid.*

in connection with specific conducts or situations.[246] They are not part of the marital property.[247]

Some aspects of moral rights have been specially regulated in connection with specific types of works. Thus, in the case of cinematographic works, the exhibited copies must show not only the name of the producer but also the names of the authors of the script, the book on which such script may have been based, the music composer, the artistic director, the adapter and the main actors.[248] In the case of printed works, the correction of the proofs is part of the author's rights and may only be undertaken by the publisher if the author does not do it.[249]

II. Exploitation Rights

A. Reproduction Right

32. The copyright owner's reproduction right applies to all types of works and to any form of reproduction of such works.[250] The copyright owner has an exclusive right to reproduce the relevant work by means such as printing, drawings, engravings, photographs, photocopies, microfilms, films, tapes, discs, etc.

Reproduction rights extend to the tri-dimensional expression of works originally made in the bi-dimensional form, and vice versa, to bi-dimensional expressions of tri-dimensional works.[251]

The storage of a work in a computer system would be an act of reproduction, subject to the limitations the copyright owner may impose on such acts.[252] It is debatable, however, whether such rule applies even in cases in which the storage will never be accessible to individuals but rather is done for operational purposes that will not lead to a visible expression of the protected work.[253]

The basic content of the reproduction right inherent in copyright ownership is a *ius prohibendi*. No reproduction of the work is legally valid without the copyright owner's consent. Such consent takes place by means of one of the possible licensing transactions previously described.[254] The consent for reproduction may be extended with respect to limited copies or instances of reproduction, or in an unlimited way.[255]

246. For example, an author may accept changes to his work, proposed by a publisher.
247. *See* Arlt Cristophersen et al., 'National Civil Court of Appeals B', 906.
248. *See* Law 11,723, Art. 22.
249. *Ibid.*, Art. 39.
250. *See* Law 11,723, Art. 2.
251. *See* Lipszyc, *Derecho de autor y derechos conexos*, 179.
252. *See* Decree 165, of 1994, Art. 1(c). Licensees of computer software are allowed to make a safety copy of such software; *see* Law 11,723, Art. 9, as amended by Law 25,036.
253. This situation differs from that of compact discs or other elements that by themselves do render a work accessible to human individuals, but that will make such work thus accessible by means of the proper equipment.
254. *See* paras 28, 29 and 30, *supra* .
255. *See* Law 11,723, Art. 40.

It may refer to specific parts of a given work, extend only to certain expression means, or be limited to a given geographical area.[256]

The copyright owner may impose the conditions under which the work shall be reproduced or exploited, including its price,[257] provided no violation of competition law takes place.[258]

The reproduction right extends also to complex works in which the work on which copyright is held is only an element, or in which this work has been modified, while maintaining the creative elements of the original.[259]

It is irrelevant, for purposes of determining the extent of reproduction rights, whether reproduction will take place with a commercial or a non-commercial or non-lucrative purpose.[260]

B. *Performing Right*

33. Copyright includes, under Argentine law, the property on performing rights.[261] All works covered by copyright may be the subject matter of such right, within the limits set by the physical or intellectual nature of the work involved. Also, all types and means of performance are included within the performing right, which is a constitutive part of copyright.[262]

Performing rights may be assigned or licensed. Such assignments or licenses may be total or may refer to specific types of performance, or to performances directed to a specific public. If performance is authorized within a certain area or for certain public, a new consent by the copyright owner is necessary for the transfer of more extensive performing rights.[263]

Performing rights have been considered to include the following types of performance, without prejudice to other possible types of performance which may be developed on the basis of new techniques and which would also be encompassed by copyright:[264]

(a) Exhibitions of artistic works, either by means of the original or through films, television or other means.

256. *See* Lipszyc, *Derecho de autor y derechos conexos*, 182.
257. *See* Goldstein, *Derecho de autor*, 109.
258. The Argentine Competition Law (Law 25,156, as amended) does not expressly prohibit price-fixing in licensing transactions, and no court decisions have implemented such a prohibition. However, Law 25,156 is based on Arts 85 and 86 of the Treaty of Rome, and its broad drafting could be used to attack at least certain types of pricing clauses in copyright licensing transactions.
259. *See Creserri, A. v. SADAIC*, National Civil Court of Appeals B, 16 May 1977, *La Ley*, vol. 1977-D, 337.
260. *Brinkmann de Roldán, A. et al. v. Peinados Pozzi S.R.L.*, National Civil Court of Appeals D, 28 Feb. 1957, *La Ley*, vol. 86, 648.
261. *See* Law 11,723, Arts 2 and 36.
262. *Ibid.*, Arts 36 and 50.
263. *See* D. Lipszyc, *Derecho de autor y derechos conexos* (Buenos Aires: UNESCO, Cerlalc, Zavalía, 1993), 184.
264. *Ibid.*, 185 et seq.

(b) Scenic performances of dramatic, musical, choreographic or theatrical works.[265]
(c) Readings and recitals of literary works.
(d) Conferences, lectures or sermons.[266]
(e) Public performances by means of mechanical instruments, particularly in the case of musical works.
(f) Radio and television transmissions.
(g) Satellite broadcasting.[267]
(h) Cable transmissions.
(i) Public access to databases or other elements stored by electronic means.[268]

The copyright owner has exclusive control over public performances,[269] thereby implicitly excluding private performances from the effects of copyright.[270] Article 50 of Law 11,723 provides that radio or television transmission, cinematographic exhibitions or any procedure for the mechanical reproduction of literary or artistic works shall constitute public performances. This provision does not exclude other possible types of public performance mentioned in other provisions of the same Law, particularly its Article 36. Article 33 of Decree 41,233, of 1934, further defines public performance as that which takes place outside 'family homes', as well as that which, while taking place in 'family homes', is propagated or projected outside such homes.

Article 36 of Law 11,723 provides certain exceptions to the performance right element of copyright. These include performances for educational purposes and performances of musical works, without payment by the public, by governmental entities.

C. *Adaptation Right*

34. This right is expressly included within copyright by Article 2 of Law 11,723.

The copyright owner may decide to make adaptations by himself or herself or authorize third parties to make such adaptations. In case of such an authorization, the adaptation must comply with the limits set by the author of the original work.[271]

Also in case of an adaptation authorization by the author of a work, the author of the original work and of the adaptation will share rights as co-authors of the adapted work.[272] It is possible for these rights to be contractually regulated by the parties, provided the moral rights of the author of the original work and of the author of the adaptation are respected.[273]

265. *See* Law 11,723, Art. 36.
266. *See* Lipszyc, *Derecho de autor y derechos conexos*, 185.
267. *Ibid.*, 189 et seq. *See also Bauleo, R.V. et al. v. Arte Radiotelevisivo Argentino S.A,* National Civil Court of Appeals H, 27 Mar. 2014.
268. *See* Decree 165, of 1994, Art. 1(d).
269. *See* Law 11,723, Art. 36.
270. *See* Decree 41,233, of 1934, Art. 33.
271. *See* Lipszyc, *Derecho de autor y derechos conexos*, 168 et seq.
272. *See* Law 11,723, Art. 25.
273. *See* para. 31, *supra* .

If the owner of an original work authorizes its adaptation, he or she may still authorize new and different adaptations, and different sets of rights will apply to each separate adaptation.[274] In the case of publishing and other copyright licensing agreements, the author retains the right to authorize the adaptation or modification of the work, even if the exploitation rights have been transferred to the publisher or licensee.[275]

D. Translation Right

35. Article 2 of Law 11,723 includes the right to translate a work within the property rights derived from copyright.

Translation rights include the right of the author to translate works by himself or herself or to have them translated by a third party, with the copyright owner's authorization. The author of the translation acquires a property right over such translation, subject to the conditions agreed with the copyright owner of the translated work.[276] These conditions should not conflict with both parties' moral rights. The agreement governing the translation rights must be registered in the National Intellectual Property Registry[277] and becomes effective against third parties only once such registration has taken place. However, the translation authorized under a non-registered agreement is valid and may not be attacked by the copyright owner of the translated work.[278]

The possibility of authorizing additional independent translations is governed by the agreement between the copyright owner of the translated work and the translator. If different translations of the same work exist, each translation is covered by a separate copyright.[279]

E. Other Rights

1. Droit De Suite

36. Although some authorities state that the *droit de suite* is applicable under Argentine law,[280] no effective provisions have been enacted or applied to make such right, as it is understood in comparative law, a constituent element of copyright under Argentine law. The only effective rights of the author with regard to successive transmissions of right to his or her work are those derived from moral rights,[281] which do not imply the participation in the proceeds of such successive transmissions, characteristic of the *droit de suite*.

---

274. *See* Law 11,723, Art. 25.
275. *Ibid.*, Art. 38.
276. *Ibid.*, Art. 23.
277. *Ibid.*
278. *Ibid.*
279. *See* Lipszyc, *Derecho de autor y derechos conexos*, 113.
280. *Ibid.*, 213.
281. *See* para. 31, *supra* .

2. Public Lending Right

37. Argentine law does not include a specific public lending right as part of copyright. Although a general right of the copyright owner with regard to public communications of protected works is recognized by the pertinent authorities,[282] this right has not been construed or applied in a way that extends to public lending activities.

3. Others

38. Although Argentine law does not include a restrictive listing of the exploitation rights or of the property rights derived from copyright,[283] it is not possible to infer additional rights inherent in copyright without a rule or provision authorizing such extension. Thus, the right to withdraw a work from circulation or to unilaterally terminate a copyright license would not exist under Argentine law, given the fact that no provision, rule or legal principle provides the existence of such right.[284] However, certain rights may be inferred from the listing of rights inherent in copyright, included in Article 2 of Law 11,723. Thus, the copyright owner has a general right to transform a work,[285] going beyond its mere adaptation, provided the moral rights related to such work are respected in cases in which the author's moral rights have been separated from the exploitation rights inherent in copyright.

§7. Limitations or Exemptions to the Scope of Copyright Protection

39. Argentine law has developed a number of limitations and exemptions to the general scope of copyright protection described in preceding section. Some of these limitations and exemptions are included in express statutory provisions, while others are the consequence of the provisions describing the scope and effects of copyright. The following limitations and exemptions may be mentioned:

(a) *Private copies:* Private copies for personal use are considered not to be in violation of the copyright that may exist with regard to the copied work.[286] This exemption is not the result of express statutory provisions, but rather the result of a customary interpretation of the limits of copyright, followed by the courts.[287]

282. *See* Lipszyc, *Derecho de autor y derechos conexos*, 183.
283. *Ibid.*, 175.
284. In addition, the statutory provisions on publishing agreements are incompatible with the hypothetical existence of a right to unilaterally terminate copyright licenses.
285. *See* Lipszyc, *Derecho de autor y derechos conexos*, 111, 112.
286. *See* Goldstein, *Derecho de autor*, 114, 115; C.A. Villalba & D. Lipszyc, 'La copia privada de obras musicales y audiovisuales. Necesidad de regular este nuevo ámbito de explotación', *La Ley* (1988-E): 971.
287. *See* L.A. Dragani et al., 'National Criminal and Correctional Court of Appeals V', *La Ley* 1992-A (5 Jul. 1991): 436.

The exemption for private copies has been the basis for multiple intended abuses in Argentine legal practice. If such abuses have not resulted in widespread prosecutions, this has been more the result of lack of enforcement means than the consequence of judicial interpretation. Under the latter, it is clear that the exemption for private copies does not extend to multiple copies of the same work done with a commercial purpose,[288] or to the practice under which several persons associate themselves with the purpose of making multiple copies to be used by such persons.[289]

It is not equally certain, however, whether copies made by an enterprise for internal use are exempt from the effects of the copyright owner's reproduction rights.[290] The limits set by Argentine statutory law with regard to other exemptions[291] would suggest that such copies would not qualify as private and would not be exempt. No system to compensate authors for the use of their works by means of private copies has been developed in Argentina.

(b) *Educational purposes:* There is no general exemption under Argentine law for the use of works protected by copyright for educational purposes. However, certain educational uses have benefited from limited statutory exemptions. Thus, it is possible to include up to one thousand words of a literary or scientific work, or up to eight bars of musical works, in educational works, without any prior authorization, provided the inclusion is necessary for the alleged educational purposes.[292] In addition, it is possible to perform or recite literary or artistic published works, at the occasion of public ceremonies organized by educational institutions, without authorization from the copyright owner or payment to such owner, provided the performance or recital is linked to educational purposes, the performance or recital is not transmitted beyond the place where it occurs, and no payments are made to the performers.

(c) *Quotation rights:* A right to quote up to one thousand words of literary or scientific works, or up to eight bars of musical works, without prior authorization, is granted by Article 10 of Law 11,723. Apart from the cases in which the quotation rights are exercised for educational purposes, described in (b) above, quotation rights, within the quantitative limits described above, exist when a reference must be made for scientific or critical purposes, or in commentaries and notes referred to the quoted works.[293] Only the parts of the work whose quotation is necessary for the scientific or critical purposes, or for the purpose of the commentary or note, are included within this exemption. The exemption also extends to quotations

288. *Ibid.*
289. However, the lack of a commercial purpose may result in an exemption from criminal liabilities, even when the remaining effects of copyright – e.g., injunctions – remain possible.
290. *See* Lipszyc, *Derecho de autor y derechos conexos*, 224, 225. An express statutory exemption exists in favour of safety copies of software programs, made by a licensee; *see* Law 11,723, Art. 9, as amended by Law 25.036.
291. *See* Decree 41,233, of 1934, Art. 33.
292. *See* Law 11,723, Art. 10.
293. *Ibid.*

– within the quantitative limits described above – included in collections, anthologies and other similar works.[294]

When these exemptions apply, no payment is due to the copyright owner, unless quotations constitute the principal element of a new work. In such case, the copyright owners whose works are quoted are entitled to compensation, to be fixed and allotted on an equitable basis by means of a summary judicial proceeding.[295]

(d) *News of general interest:* Articles including such news, as part of a newspaper or periodical publication, may be used, transmitted or retransmitted.[296] They may be published in their original version provided the source is mentioned.[297]

(e) *Speeches:* Parliamentary speeches may be published without the author's authorization, provided the publication has no profit motive.[298] This exception has been extended by case law to other speeches delivered in the course of governmental functions.[299] Speeches not included within these exemptions, even those of a political nature,[300] are covered by copyright but may be commented on or quoted by the news media.[301]

(f) *Public performances of musical works:* Article 36 of Law 11,723 authorizes these performances, free from any payment to the author or to the copyright owner, provided the performance takes place in concerts, auditions or shows by orchestras, bands and other musical organizations belonging to governmental institutions, if admission for the general public is free of charge.[302]

(g) *Portraits:* The publication of portraits is free if it is related with scientific, educational or cultural purposes or with public interest events or with events that have been open to the general public.[303]

(h) *Translation of works written in a foreign language:* Any person may obtain a non-exclusive license to translate and publish in Argentina works written in a foreign language and protected by the Geneva Universal Copyright Convention, if such works have not been published in Spanish with the authorization of the copyright owner within a term of seven years from the original foreign language publication.[304] The license is granted by the Ministry of Justice.[305] The potential licensee must show that he or she has taken the steps necessary to locate the

294. *Ibid.*
295. *Ibid.*, The exemption relative to quotation rights is generally construed narrowly. Exceeding the maximum quotation limits results in a copyright infringement, and not just in a royalty right in favour of the copyright owner. *See* J. Paganelli et al., 'National Criminal and Correctional Court of Appeals V', *Jurisprudencia Argentina* 1989-III (28 Oct. 1988): 261.
296. *See* Law 11,723, Art. 28.
297. *Ibid.*
298. *Ibid.*, Art. 27.
299. *See Brinkmann de Roldán, A. et al. v. Virgilio Fossati e Hijos S.R.L.*, National Civil Court of Appeals C, 10 May 1956, *La Ley*, vol. 83 (1956), 215.
300. *See Brinkmann de Roldán, A. et al. v. Peinados Pozzi S. R. L.*, National Civil Court of Appeals D, 28 Feb. 1957, *La Ley*, vol. 86 (1957), 648.
301. *See* Law 11,723, Art. 27.
302. *See also* Decree 41,233, of 1934, Art. 33.
303. *See* Law 11,723, Art. 31.
304. *See* Decree 1,155, of 1958, Art. 1.
305. *Ibid.*

copyright owner and to obtain a voluntary license from such owner.[306] If the copyright owner has not been located, the prospective licensee must also produce evidence to the effect that the original publisher of the work and the diplomatic and consular authorities of the country whose nationality is held by the copyright owner were given copies of the request of a voluntary license.[307]
The translation must be undertaken by a person approved by an ad hoc commission.[308] A 10% royalty on the retail sales of the licensed publication is payable to the copyright owner.[309] One-third of this amount, calculated on the initial licensed edition, must be immediately deposited in a special account.[310] A bond for the remaining two-thirds must also be supplied immediately by the licensee, and the payment of such remaining two-thirds of the royalties on the initial licensed edition must be fully paid within two years from the granting of the license.[311]
Similar licensing rights exist when the publication of the Spanish translation of a foreign language work has been out of print for at least seven years.[312]
These licensing rights are inapplicable if the author has withdrawn from circulation the foreign language original version of the work.[313]

(i) *Works of deceased authors:* If these works are not published for a term of ten years from the death of the author, any person is authorized to republish them, regardless of the heirs', legatees' or assignees' authorization or refusal thereof.[314] This exemption would not be applicable to works that were not published before the author's death.[315] Similar rights exist to have the work translated.[316] In both cases, if no agreement is reached between the new publisher or the author of the translation, on one side, and the heirs, legatees or assignees, on the other side, as to the consideration payable to the latter, such consideration is determined by means of arbitration.[317]
In cases of publications governed by this special regime for works of deceased authors, the publisher has the obligation to deposit copies of the new publication in the National Intellectual Property Registry, as would be the case with regular editions.[318] Translations under this special regime enjoy copyright protection and are also subject to registration as described above.[319]

(j) *Performer's rights:* The performer of a literary or musical work does not have the power to prevent the transmission or reproduction of the performance, unless

306. *Ibid.*, Art. 2(b).
307. *Ibid.*, Art. 2(c).
308. *Ibid.*, Art. 2(d).
309. *Ibid.*, Art. 2(f), (g).
310. *Ibid.*, Art. 2(f).
311. *Ibid.*, Art. 2(g).
312. *Ibid.*, Art. 3.
313. *Ibid.*, Art. 9.
314. *See* Law 11,723, Art. 6.
315. The text of the statutory exemption refers to 'reediting', implying the existence of a prior edition. But *see* Goldstein, *Derecho de autor*, 119.
316. *See* Law 11,723, Art. 6.
317. *Ibid.*
318. *See* Law 11,723, Arts 57 and 61. *See also* Decree 16,697, of 1959.
319. *See* Decree 41,233, of 1934, Art. 28.

such reproduction or transmission may result in damage to the performer's artistic interest.[320]

If no agreement is reached between a performer and a person interested in the transmission or reproduction of the performance as to the payments to be made to the performer in consideration for such transmission or reproduction, the performer has the right to have such payments determined by means of a summary judicial proceeding.[321]

(k) *Visually handicapped persons:* Law 26,285 introduced a new Article 36*bis* to Law 11,723, creating exceptions regarding the reproduction and distribution of scientific and literary works to be used in special systems for the use of blind or visually handicapped persons.

§8. Duration of Protection

40. The basic provision on the duration of copyright protection is Article 5 of Law 11,723, as amended. Pursuant to this provision, copyright protection lasts for a term of seventy years, counted as of 1 January of the first year after the death of the author, as well as through the life of the author.

In the case of works done through cooperation,[322] the seventy-year term is computed from the death of the last person who participated in the joint authorship of the work involved.[323]

In the case of posthumous works, the seventy-year term is computed from the death of the author.[324]

If an author dies without heir or legatees, the duration of the protection term remains unaltered, but the beneficiary of the deceased author's copyright is the State.[325]

The duration of protection of anonymous works whose copyright belongs to institutions, corporations or legal entities is fifty years from the date of publication of the work.[326]

When the duration of copyright protection depends on the date of publication, and the work consists of several volumes or parts, the term of protection is calculated with respect to each such volume or part.[327] If the work consists of several periodical publications, only the last publication shall be taken into account to determine the duration of protection.[328]

320. *See* Law 11,723, Art. 56.
321. *Ibid.*
322. *See* para. 25, *supra* .
323. *See* Law 11,723, Art. 5.
324. *Ibid.*
325. *Ibid.*
326. *Ibid.*, Art. 8.
327. *Ibid.*, Art. 11.
328. *Ibid.*

41. Law 11,723 provides certain special periods of protection for certain types of work. In the case of photographic works, the period of protection is twenty years counted from the first publication of the work.[329]

Cinematographic works are protected for fifty years counted from the date of the death of the last of their co-authors.[330] This limit does not apply to the literary or musical works used in a film or on which the film is based;[331] such literary or musical works are governed by the general rules on copyright duration, described above.[332]

The consent for the publication of portraits, by a deceased person's family, is no longer required after the expiration of a twenty-year term from the death of such person.[333]

In a similar vein, in the case of letters, no consent by a deceased person's family is required for the publication of the letters written by such deceased person, after the expiration of a twenty-year term from the death of the author.[334] This rule applies even if the letters qualify as a work for copyright purposes.[335]

42. Moral rights exist during the whole term of copyright protection, including the applicable term after the author's death.[336]

Once the statutory term of copyright protection has expired it is still possible to protect several of the elements that constitute moral rights by means of a special procedure provided by Article 83 of Law 11,723. Pursuant to this provision, any person may request the formation of a special jury to determine whether any of the possible situations has taken place with regard to a work: additions, transposition, translation mistakes, conceptual errors or mistaken use of the language. The composition of the jury, which is determined by Article 83, varies depending on the type of work involved. If the jury decides that the situation that was denounced existed, it may order that the necessary corrections be made in the way the work involved is used, published or communicated and that any mistaken use, publication or communication be prevented or stopped.

43. Once the copyright protection has expired, as provided in the rules described above, works enter into the public domain. They thereby become subject to a system of fees, payable to the National Arts Fund (*Fondo Nacional de las Artes*). These fees are set in accordance with a schedule, which provides different types and amounts of payment depending on the type of use made of the works that have entered into the public domain: performance, inclusion within other works, exhibition, reproduction, publishing, etc.[337]

44. Several exceptions apply to the obligation to pay fees on works that have entered the public domain, namely the following:

329. *Ibid.*, Art. 34.
330. *Ibid.*, as amended by Law 25,006.
331. *Ibid.*
332. *See* para. 40, *supra* .
333. *See* Law 11,723, Art. 35. Strictly speaking, this is not a question of copyright protection, but rather of privacy protection.
334. *Ibid.*
335. *Ibid.*
336. *See* Lipszyc, *Derecho de autor y derechos conexos*, 260 et seq.
337. *See* Decree-Law 1,224, of 1958; Regulation 15,850, of 1977, of the National Articles Fund.

(a) Use of works for exclusively cultural or educational purposes, provided the public has free access to the use or performance of the work and no paid advertisement is included together with such use or performance.[338]
(b) Publishing of books, textbooks and other publications, approved by governmental authorities for use in primary and secondary education.[339]
(c) Publication of works that qualify as 'children's literature', provided the price per unit does not exceed a maximum amount set by the National Arts Fund.[340]

§9. Neighbouring Rights

45. Although the category of neighbouring rights, in connection with copyright, is not expressly acknowledged by Argentine statutory law, it has been repeatedly recognized and examined in Argentine legal literature.[341]

46. The following are the principal types of neighbouring rights that have been protected under Argentine copyright law:

(a) According to Article 56 of Law 11,723, the performer of a literary or musical work has the right to obtain a consideration in exchange for any performance transmitted or retransmitted by means of radio or television or recorded on discs, film, tapes, wires or any other substance or body suitable for the reproduction of sounds or images. If no agreement is reached between a performer and a person interested in the transmission or reproduction of his performance, as to the payments to be made to the performer in consideration for such transmission or reproduction, the performer has the right to have such payments determined by means of a summary judicial proceeding. In addition to this economic right, performers have a moral right[342] under which they may oppose the transmission or reproduction of their performance if it is done in a way that may result in a major and unfair damage to the performer's artistic interest.[343] In the case of performance by a chorus or orchestra, this so-called opposition right belongs to the director of the chorus or orchestra.[344] However, a work performed in a theatre or in a public hall may be transmitted or retransmitted by means of radio or television, provided the entrepreneur who organized the performance authorizes such transmission or retransmission, and provided also that the owner of the copyright on the work performed consents to such performance.[345]

338. *See* Regulation 15,850, of 1977, Art. 6.
339. *Ibid.*, Art. 31.
340. *Ibid.*, Art. 30.
341. *See* Lipszyc, *Derecho de autor y derechos conexos* 347 et seq.; Goldstein, Derecho de autor, 173 et seq.; C.A. Villalba & D. Lipszyc, Derechos de los artistas, intérpretes o ejecutantes, productores de fonogramas y organismos de radiodifusión. Relaciones con el derecho de autor (Buenos Aires: Zavalía, 1976).
342. *See Asociación Argentina de Intérpretes v. LS5 Radio Rivadavia*, National Civil Court of Appeals C, 13 Jul. 1965, *La Ley*, vol. 120 (1966), 331.
343. *See* Law 11,723, Art. 56.
344. *Ibid.*
345. *Ibid.*

The meaning of 'performers', for purposes of determining the extent of the protection granted by Article 56 of Law 11,723 has been intensely debated.[346] Some court decisions distinguished between 'performers' (*ejecutantes*) and 'interpreters' (*intérpretes*) and provided that only the latter enjoyed the opposition and economic rights provided by Article 56.[347] In this perspective, 'interpreters' are considered to be a species within the more general category of 'performers', and would be distinguished from the latter due to the level of creativity involved in their performance.[348] Thus, it was held that a musician who played for a tango orchestra was excluded from the protection granted by Article 56 of Law 11,723 to 'performers'.[349] In the context of statutory interpretation, this position was weakened by the fact that Article 56 does not deny the existence of the rights described therein in favour of orchestra players but rather places on the orchestra's director the exercise of such rights, presumably in favour of all the members of the orchestra. This was the interpretation made in other court decisions that have tended to abolish any practical legal distinction between 'performers' and 'interpreters'.[350]

The issue was the subject matter of specific regulation by Decree 746, of 1973. It provides that for the purposes of Article 56 of Law 11,723, '*intérpretes*' – that is, the category granted moral and economic rights under Article 56 – shall be considered to include orchestra directors, singers and performing musicians, individually; the director and actors of cinematographic works and of recordings with images and sound in magnetic tape, for television; and singers, dancers and any other person who plays a part, sings, recites, performs or plays in any way a literary, cinematographic or musical work. In spite of Decree 746, of 1973, the discussion persists with regard to the level of creativity required for performers to qualify for the rights granted by copyright law, and in particular by Article 56 of Law 11,723.[351]

Several other regulatory provisions have tended to determine more clearly the rights of performers. Article 2 of Decree 746, of 1973, provides that the following shall be considered to be appropriate means for the transmission of performers' works: discs, the different types of recording in magnetic tapes and recordings with images and sound in magnetic tapes for television, films and any other technical element that may be used for radio or television transmission, cinematographic theatres, dance clubs or halls, and any other public place where direct or indirect commercial exploitation takes place. In addition, Article 3 of

346. *See* M. Mouchet, 'Los derechos de los artistas intérpretes en las ejecuciones colectivas', *La Ley* 120 (1965): 330.
347. *See* Judge Padilla's vote in *Asociación Argentina de Intérpretes v. LS5 Radio Rivadavia*, National Civil Court of Appeals C, 13 Jul. 1965, *La Ley*, vol. 120, 331. *See also* M.A. Lancelotti, 'Una disidencia importante', *Jurisprudencia Argentina* (1965-V): 267.
348. *See* M.A. Lancelotti, *ibid.*, 267 et seq.
349. *See* Judge Padilla's vote in *Asociación Argentina de Intérpretes v. LS5 Radio Rivadavia*, National Civil Court of Appeals C, 13 Jul. 1965, *La Ley*, vol. 120 (1966), 331.
350. *See* Asociación *Argentina de Intérpretes v. Villa Malcom Club Social y Deportivo*, National Civil Court of Appeals B, 24 Oct. 1969, La Ley, vol. 133 (1970), 168.
351. *See* Goldstein, *Derecho de autor*, 173 et seq.

Decree 1,670, of 1974, provides that the incorporation of the performance of a musical work to a tangible element requires the prior consent of the 'principal performers'[352] who participated in such performance. Article 4 of Decree 1,670, of 1974, provides that the 'principal performer' of a musical or literary work has the right to demand that his or her name or pseudonym be mentioned in case of transmission or communication of the performance and to demand that his or her name or pseudonym be included in the label, envelope or other packaging of the tangible element including the performance. Decree 1,671, of 1974, has regulated the collective exercise of performer's rights, by means of the Argentine Association of Performers (*Asociación Argentina de Intérpretes*).

Argentine statutory law does not set a time frame for the performer's rights. It has been reasonably suggested that the general provisions on copyright duration[353] should also be applicable to performer's rights.[354] This would agree with the identity of the performer's creative work and its relation with the works traditionally protected by copyright.

(b) Article 35 of Decree 41,233, of 1934, as amended, provides that without prejudice to the rights of the authors of lyrics and the composers of music and of the principal and secondary performers, the producers of phonograms or their heirs, legatees and assignees have the right to receive a consideration from any person who occasionally or permanently obtains a direct or indirect benefit from the public use of the reproduction of the phonogram, such as: radio, television and other similar organizations; bars; cinematographic theatres; theatres; social clubs; recreational centres; restaurants; cabarets and in general, whoever communicates to the public the reproduction of the phonogram by any direct or indirect means. No consideration is payable for occasional uses for educational purposes or in national celebrations, by officially or publicly authorized educational institutions. Decree 1,671, of 1974, provides the collective exercise of the phonogram producers' rights by means of the Argentine Chamber of Phonogram Producers and Manufacturers (*Cámara Argentina de Productores e Industriales de Fonogramas*). It is highly debatable whether the rights of phonogram producers are a type of copyright and are, therefore, subject to the general statutory provisions on copyright, as to the duration of protection, for example. The inclusion of the provisions of Article 35 of Decree 41,233, of 1934, would imply that the drafters of that provision tended to have a view of the rights of phonogram producers as a type of copyright, since Decree 41,233 includes the regulations applicable to Law 11,723, on copyright. However, from the point of view of the nature and province of copyright protection, phonograms would not qualify as works and would not have the

352. This provision does not appear to be in accordance with the general Argentine legal system for the protection of performers' rights, which does not distinguish, for legal purposes, between 'principal' and 'secondary' performers. Where distinctions are introduced, as in the case of chorus or orchestra directors (Law 11,723, Art. 56), this does not imply that the director is the holder of performers' rights, but rather that the director acts in representation of the rest of the performers. *See Asociación Argentina de Intérpretes v. Villa Malcom Club Social y Deportivo*, National Civil Court of Appeals B, 24 Oct. 1969, *La Ley*, vol. 133 (1970), 168.

353. *Supra* n. 40.

354. *See* Lipszyc, *Derecho de autor y derechos conexos*, 389.

element of intellectual creativity generally deemed necessary for copyright protection.[355] Therefore, the rights of phonogram producers are neighbouring rights with respect to copyright, but not copyright proper.[356] Therefore, the general copyright provisions are only applicable to the rights of phonogram producers by way of analogy, in particular in cases in which the scope of the rights of phonogram producers may not be determined on the basis of the very limited statutory provisions expressly applicable to such rights. The violation of phonogram producers' rights is subject to special punitive provisions.[357] This special penal regime has been to a large extent necessary due to the impossibility of extending by means of analogy the penal rules applicable to copyright to a subject matter – phonogram producers' rights – which, strictly speaking, is not copyright.

(c) Some authorities have mentioned, as a right neighbouring to copyright, the right of sportsmen to authorize and profit from the exhibition of their sport activities.[358] The prevailing view, however, is that in these cases there is no work in the sense of copyright law, and that whatsoever protection may be due must be obtained under the rules applicable to the protection of the personal image.[359]

(d) Other authorities have mentioned the rights of television and radio producers as a type of neighbouring rights in relation with copyright.[360] This view has little support in Argentine law. If the works of television and radio producers do not fit within the limits of traditional copyright protection, there is no statutory provision or legal principle granting neighbouring rights to such producers. Protection for the programs and transmissions made by such producers – if exceeding the scope of copyright law – must be obtained on the basis of the administrative law regulations governing radio and television, or on the broader basis of unfair competition law.[361]

§10. Infringement and Remedies

47. The limits of copyright, described in the preceding sections of this chapter, are also the limits of the conducts that qualify as infringements from the point of view of copyright law. If a right exists under copyright law, the violation of such right is an infringement that may result in different types of remedies. These remedies, in turn, may be of a civil, punitive or administrative nature.

48. Although civil remedies constitute the backbone of copyright protection, there are few specific provisions on such remedies. The basic reason for this is that

355. *Ibid.*, 392.
356. *Ibid.*, 390 et seq.
357. *See* Law 11,723, Art. *72bis*.
358. *See* Goldstein, *Derecho de autor*, 187.
359. *Ibid.*
360. *See* Lipszyc, *Derecho de autor y derechos conexos*, 398 et seq.
361. Although it can be argued that protection may be claimed under the Rome Convention and the TRIPS agreement's provisions on broadcasting organizations, the extent of this protection under Argentine law has not yet been tested. *See* Villalba & Lipszyc, *Derechos de los artistas*, 243 et seq.

infringements and the remedies thereof are determined on the basis of general provisions included in or derived from the Civil and Commercial Code.[362] Thus, if a certain conduct infringes any of the elements of copyright and causes a damage, due to the negligence or intent of the person to whom such conduct is attributed, an obligation will arise in favour of the holder of the infringed right to compensate any damages caused by the infringement;[363] this rule is derived from the general Civil and Commercial Code rules on torts.[364] In addition, if a certain conduct infringes any of the elements of copyright, it will be possible to obtain an injunction from civil courts, ordering the termination of such conduct.[365]

49. A special civil procedure applies under Argentine law for cases involving infringements of copyright.[366] This procedure also applies to civil litigation related to contracts or transactions on copyright matters.[367] This special procedure is summary.[368] The parties may request that all evidence be produced within thirty court days from the moment in which the period for the production of evidence is opened.[369] The court may require additional evidence *sua sponte*.[370] The parties may request that evidence be produced in a public hearing.[371] A special jury of experts may be appointed by the court;[372] Law 11,723 provides the institutions that will supply or appoint members of such jury.[373] The special jury decides whether there has been a violation of statutory or contractual rights,[374] but the final judgment is issued by the court hearing the case.[375]

50. During the course of civil procedures, the party whose copyright has allegedly been infringed may obtain different precautionary measures, to be ordered by the court. Some of these measures are provided by copyright law, and some are derived from the general rules on civil procedure.

The basic copyright statute – Law 11,723, Article 79 – provides that courts may, once the interested party has supplied a satisfactory bond, order as a precautionary measure the suspension of a theatrical, cinematographic, philharmonic or other analogous exhibitions; the attachment of the works that have been indicated as in violation of copyright; the attachment of the proceeds derived from infringing exhibitions or works, and any other precautionary measure deemed necessary for the protection of the rights involved.

362. *See* Law 11,723, Art. 12.
363. *See* Lipszyc, *Derecho de autor y derechos conexos*, 577.
364. *See* Civil and Commercial Code, Arts 1716 and 1721.
365. *See* Lipszyc, *Derecho de autor y derechos conexos*, 572, 573.
366. *See* Law 11,723, Arts 80 and 81.
367. *Ibid.*, Art. 80.
368. *Ibid.*, Art. 81.
369. *Ibid.*, Art. 81(a).
370. *Ibid.*
371. *Ibid.*, Art. 81(b).
372. *Ibid.*, Art. 81(c).
373. *Ibid.*
374. *Ibid.*
375. *Ibid.*, Although the jury's decision is not binding for the court, in practice it tends to be decisive as to the issues submitted to the jury; *see Terragno, J.D. et al. v. Edami S.R.L.*, National Civil Court (B. Montero, Judge), 1 Feb. 1968, *La Ley*, vol. 133, 154 (decision not appealed).

The general rules on civil procedure provide different types of precautionary measures[376] that may be used in copyright cases: attachments, garnishments, deposit in court of property subject to litigation, designation of court-appointed officers to receive the proceeds from exhibitions or other activities or to obtain information regarding such activities, filing of lis pendens, temporary restraining orders preventing a party from encumbering or selling property, injunctions, etc. Courts are allowed to issue other types of precautionary measures, to be structured by such courts, if they are necessary to prevent an imminent or irreparable damage to a legal right.[377]

Some court decisions have stated that the precautionary measures provided by Article 79 of Law 11,723 are only applicable in connection with registered works.[378] It is debatable whether these decisions are practically correct, taking into account that the precautionary measures derived from the general rules on civil procedure are at least as broad as those allowed by Law 11,723, and are applicable to all types of rights. Also debatable is whether intellectual property rights exist prior to registration of works, even if such registration may broaden the effects of such rights.

As a general rule, courts have been relatively liberal as to the types of bond required for the granting of precautionary measures; for example, the plaintiff's personal bond has been deemed sufficient to order the precautionary measures provided by Law 11,723.[379]

51. Law 11,723 includes the punitive provisions applicable to copyright infringements.[380] Article 71 applies to any 'fraud' against intellectual property rights derived from Law 11,723. The penalties included in Article 172 of the Criminal Code for all cases of fraud, namely imprisonment for a period ranging from one month to six years, are to be fixed by the court on the basis of the gravity of the offence. Article 71 has to be construed in conjunction with the remaining provisions of Law 11,723 and other pertinent copyright statutes, to determine the scope of the rights that allegedly have been infringed and which have therefore become the subject matter of a 'fraud'.[381] In principle, any type of wilful infringement of copyright is subject to the penalties provided by Article 71 of Law 11,723.[382]

Article 72 provides certain special types of 'fraud' against intellectual property rights. These cases are also governed by and penalized in accordance with Article 71 of Law 11,723, and they may result, in addition, in the sequestration of any infringing publications. The infringements listed by Article 72 are the following:

---

376. *See* National Code of Civil and Commercial Procedure, Arts 195 et seq.

377. *Ibid.*, Art. 232.

378. *See Agi S.A. v. Kaiser, A.J.*, National Civil Court of Appeals D, 23 Dec. 1987, *El Derecho*, vol. 132, 629. For a criticism of this decision, *see* I.B. Langenauer, 'El software en la ley 11,723', *El Derecho*, 628 ff. *See also* D. Lipszyc, 'Las medidas precautorias', in *Los ilícitos civiles y penales en derecho de autor* (Buenos Aires: IIDA, 1981), 68 et seq.

379. *See Guastavino, E. v. S.A. Pampa Films S.A.*, Civil Court of Appeals of the City of Buenos Aires 1, 10 Jul. 1944, *La Ley*, vol. 35 (1945), 217.

380. *See* generally J.C. Ledesma, *Derecho penal intelectual* (Buenos Aires: Universidad, 1992).

381. *See Franceschini, R.*, 'National Criminal and Correctional Court of Appeals II', *La Ley* 1990-C (5 Apr. 1990): 310.

382. *See* Ledesma, *Derecho penal intelectual*, 249 et seq.

(a) Publishing, selling or reproducing by any means or instrument an unpublished or a published work without the authorization of the author or his heir, legatees or assignees.
(b) Falsifying intellectual works, this being understood as the publication of a previously published work, falsely bearing the name of the properly authorized publisher.
(c) Suppressing or changing the name of the author or title of a work, or wilfully altering the text of a work upon its publication, sale or reproduction.
(d) Publishing or reproducing a higher number of copies than authorized.

52. In addition, Articles 72*bis* and 73 of Law 11,723 provide special penalties for specific types of intellectual property infringements. Article 72*bis* applies to violations related to phonograms. These include: reproducing with a profit motive a phonogram, without the written authorization of the producer or of the producer's licensee; facilitating with a profit motive the illegal reproduction of phonograms by means of renting phonographic discs or other tangible elements; reproducing unauthorized copies of a phonogram, requested by third parties in exchange for a price; storing or exhibiting illegal copies of phonograms, if the person thus acting is unable to show – by means of an invoice derived from a legitimate producer – the origin of such goods; importing illegal copies with the purpose of distributing them to the public. In any of these cases it is possible to obtain a court order for the sequestration of the illegal copies and of the elements used for the illegal reproduction of phonograms. The court may order this sequestration *sua sponte*. If the sequestration is requested by a petitioner, the court may require an adequate bond, unless the petitioner produces evidence showing that he or she has assets to pay for the possible damages resulting from the sequestration. No bond is required in the case of a petition by legally recognized authors' or producers' associations. Once sequestration has taken place, the criminal action must be filed in the following fifteen days; otherwise, the sequestration order may lapse.

Article 73 of Law 11,723 provides penalties consisting of one month to one year of imprisonment or a fine of between ARS 1,000 and ARS 30,000 against whoever performs or organizes the public performance of theatrical, literary or musical works, without the authorization of their authors or of their heirs, legatees or assignees.

The criminal procedure with regard to copyright violations is governed by the procedural rules enacted by each province or by the federal rules in the case of violations subject to federal jurisdiction.[383]

The criminal procedure may be started *sua sponte* by a court that has knowledge of an apparent criminal violation of copyright, as well as by means of an accusation made to the competent authorities, or by means of criminal complaints or charges brought by the allegedly injured parties.[384]

In case both a civil and a criminal procedure take place with regard to the same violations, the results of both procedures are independent of each other.[385] This is understandable, since the violations and the consequences of such violations examined

383. *See* Law 11,723, Art. 76.
384. *Ibid.*, Art. 75.
385. *Ibid.*, Art. 77.

in both types of procedure are different. However, the evidence obtained in one procedure may be used in the other.[386]

If the right to obtain preliminary injunctions, in civil or criminal actions, is abused, and an otherwise valid public performance is thus unfairly prevented, the party who caused the injunction by falsely claiming the character of author, assignee or agent may be subject to imprisonment or fine penalties.[387]

53. Administrative remedies exist with regard to works that entered into the public domain. These remedies were previously discussed.[388]

§11. Overlapping and Relation to Other Intellectual Property Laws

54. Several subject matters protected by copyright under Argentine law are also protected by other intellectual property rights. In addition, there are instances in which the demarcation between the subject matter of copyright and of other intellectual property rights is vague, creating the possibility of protection claims under different intellectual property laws for the same subject matter.

Several basic concepts have been used under Argentine law to determine the limits of copyright protection, with relation to other intellectual property rights. One is that copyright protects the expression of ideas and not the ideas themselves.[389] The second is that the expression of practical ideas is protected by copyright, but this protection does not encompass the practical application of such ideas; for example, the culinary recipes included in a book may be freely used, although the book itself may not be published without the copyright owner's authorization.[390]

It is possible, on the basis of these rules, to solve most of the possible conflicts of intellectual property rights potentially covering the same subject matter. These potential conflicts will be examined below.

55. There have been in practice few conflicts between copyright and patent protection. In several cases, authors have claimed that copyright extended to the actual use of the processes or subject matter described in their works.[391] These claims have been generally rejected.[392] The practical application of ideas is protected by patents, which are subject to patentability conditions that differ significantly from the requisites applied for copyright protection.

56. Overlapping between copyright and trademark protection has been more frequent. One common area of such overlapping has been the protection of advertisement

386. *Ibid.*
387. *Ibid.*, Art. 74.
388. *See* para. 42, *supra* .
389. *See* para. 15, *supra* .
390. *See* P. Chaloupka, 'La propiedad de las ideas', *Derechos Intelectuales* 3 (1988), 65.
391. *See Pantano, J.C. v. Jockey Club de Buenos Aires*, National Civil Court of Appeals C, 18 Apr. 1974, *La Ley*, vol. 155, 82.
392. *See Gibellini, E.J. v. Plan Ovalo S.A.*, National Civil Court of Appeals A, 9 Apr. 1986, *Jurisprudencia Argentina*, vol. 1987-I, 436.

slogans and phrases.[393] Trademark law grants trademark protection to advertisement slogans and phrases,[394] provided they have originality[395] and have not been part of general usage before registration.[396] This trademark protection does not pre-empt or contradict copyright protection of slogans and phrases used for advertisement, even if they are potentially subject to protection as trademarks.[397] In fact, if a slogan or phrase meets the conditions of both trademark and copyright protection, it would be possible to obtain both types of protection, each one within the limits set out by the relevant intellectual property regime. It is, therefore, possible to distinguish between the following types of advertisement slogans and phrases:[398]

(a) Advertisement slogans and phrases that lack originality. They are not protected either by copyright or by trademark law.
(b) Advertisement slogans and phrases that are original but lack the necessary elements for copyright protection. They may be protected under trademark law.
(c) Advertisement slogans and phrases that are original and have the necessary elements for copyright protection. They may be protected under both copyright and trademark law.

Other trademarks, and particularly those involving drawings, pictures or other images may also be protected by copyright if they meet the necessary conditions of creativity required by copyright law.[399]

57. Sculptures and other works with an ornamental value are protected by the rules on industrial models and designs.[400] It is thus possible for the same subject matter to be protected both under the rules on industrial models and designs and under copyright law.[401] However, in cases of violation of the rights protecting such sculptures or ornamental works, the party whose rights have been infringed has to elect in each specific case under which set of rights to act against the infringer.[402] Such an election, in a specific case, would not preclude a different election in the future.[403]

---

393. *See* P. Chaloupka, 'La propiedad intelectual y la publicidad', *Derechos Intelectuales* 7 (1996): 41 et seq.
394. *See* Law 22,362, Art. 1.
395. *Ibid.*, Art. 3(j).
396. *Ibid.*, Art. 2(b).
397. *See* Chaloupka, 'La propiedad' 52.
398. *Ibid.*, 51, 52.
399. *See* L.E. Bertone & G. Cabanellas, *Derecho de Marcas*, vol. 1 (Buenos Aires: Heliasta, 1989), 231 et seq.
400. *See* Decree-law 6,673, of 1963, Art. 3.
401. *See* D. Lipszyc, 'Las medidas precautorias', in *Los ilícitos civiles y penales en derecho de autor* (Buenos Aires: IIDA, 1981), 86, 87.
402. *See* Decree-law 6,673, of 1963, Art. 28.
403. Registration under copyright law may coexist with registration under the rules on industrial models and designs protection. *See* Decree-law 6,673, of 1963, Art. 28. The owner of the relevant rights chooses in each specific case which set of rights to enforce. Extinction of one set of rights would not affect the continued existence of the other set.

Chapter 2. Patents

§1. Sources: Legislation

58. The statutory framework of Argentine patent law has changed drastically in recent years. For more than a century, Argentine patent law was based on Law 111, which was enacted in 1869. Law 111 had been the object of constant attacks by a significant sector of the legal profession[404] based on contentions that it was outmoded and unsuitable for the present-day technological environment. A second ground was that the protection derived from Law 111 was too weak to create adequate incentives for potential inventors; in particular, the fact that patents lapsed after two years without proper exploitation of the patented invention[405] meant that most patents became practically ineffective in view of the rather stringent standards set by the courts with regard to the exploitation requirement set out by Law 111.[406] Third, Law 111 did not meet the conditions required by the Paris Convention on the protection of industrial property, which Argentina had ratified in 1966.[407] Finally, Law 111 did not grant patent protection to pharmaceutical compositions;[408] multinational pharmaceutical laboratories and the US government led the charge for change on this front.

The pressure to grant patent protection to pharmaceuticals was countered for many years by the opposition of the Argentine pharmaceutical industry, which argued that the campaign to change Law 111 would benefit foreign multinationals to the detriment of local companies, which obtained much of their technology from foreign sources.

Pressure for a change in the patent area became irresistible with the Uruguay round of multilateral trade negotiations. Law 111 was clearly incompatible with the TRIPS agreement included in the Marrakech Act, which concluded the Uruguay round. When the Marrakech Act was ratified by Argentina, the enactment of a new patent law became inevitable.

59. The conflicting views held by different business groups over patent laws resulted in one of the most convoluted approval processes in recent Argentine legal history.

The procedure was set in motion by the enactment of Law 24,425, in 1994. Law 24,425 ratified the Marrakech Act resulting from the Uruguay round of multilateral negotiations and, in the process, the TRIPS agreement included in that act. Several bills were presented in Congress with the purpose of adjusting Argentine patent law to the provisions of the TRIPS agreement. In early 1995, Congress approved one of these bills. However, it was vetoed by the Executive Power, by means of Decree 549,

404. *See* , e.g., R. Frank, 'Ideas para la reforma de la ley argentina sobre patentes de invención', *Derechos Intelectuales* 4 (1989): 190 et seq.
405. *See* Law 111, Art. 47.
406. *See* P. Chaloupka, '¿In dubio contra patentem?', *Derechos Intelectuales* 2 (1987): 34 et seq.
407. *Ibid.*, 35.
408. *See* Law 111, Art. 4.

of 18 April 1995. Shortly thereafter, the Executive Power passed Decree 621, which provided a new general patent regime. This regime was based on Law 111, which had not yet been repealed; Law 17,011, which had ratified the Paris Convention; and Law 24,425, which had ratified the TRIPS agreement. Decree 621, of 1995, purportedly 'consolidated' the pre-existing legal rules on patents; in fact, it was a new patent law, which infringed the constitutional powers of Congress in patent matters.[409]

On 23 May 1995, Congress voted a veto override on the bill that had been vetoed by Decree 549. According to the Federal Constitution, this meant that a veto by the Executive Power was no longer possible and that the bill, as amended together with the veto override, was enacted.[410] The Executive Power, however, prevented the effective enactment of the amended bill by means of the irregular procedure of not allowing the publication of the new Law in the Official Gazette. This procedure, which lacked any form of justification under Argentine constitutional law, was justified by the Executive Power on two grounds: first, that the veto override was partial, whereas Congress, in the Executive Power's view, had to accept or override the Executive Power's veto as a whole; and second, that the bill approved by Congress was unconstitutional, since it violated several provisions of the TRIPS agreement, which, according to Article 75, section 22, of the Federal Constitution, had a legal hierarchy superior to ordinary laws.

Whatsoever the constitutional validity of these arguments, the Executive Power's position was untenable in the long run, since constitutional disputes must be resolved by the judiciary. The Executive Power is not allowed to take justice into its own hands by means of publishing or not publishing enactments it deems unconstitutional. The Executive Power, therefore, entered into negotiations with Congress, and the Congressional veto override was finally accepted. The resulting PA was published as Law 24,481, on 20 September 1995. Article 102 of Law 24,481 repealed Law 111.

The new law did not end the conflict between Congress and the Executive Power with regard to the enactment of new patent rules. Law 24,481 was amended by Law 24,572. This amendment was duly enacted and published by the Executive Power. However, on 18 October 1995, the Executive Power issued Decree 590, which approved a consolidated text of Laws 111, 17,011, 24,425, 24,481 and 24,572. Although the Executive Power is authorized to publish consolidated texts of the legislation in force, these consolidated texts imply merely reproducing previously enacted rules and not interpreting them to create a new set of rules. The purpose of the consolidated text of the patent laws was, in fact, to assure that the Paris Convention and the TRIPS agreement prevailed over other provisions of Argentine patent law.[411] This prevalence may have been constitutionally correct – under Article 75, section 22, of the Federal Constitution – but again, the conflict was for the judiciary and not the Executive Power to resolve. Thus, Argentine patent law entered again into a situation of unacceptable uncertainty. This uncertainty was exacerbated by Law 24,603, passed by Congress on 7 December 1995 and vetoed by the Executive Power by means of Decree 3, of 3 January 1996. Decree 3 declared that the valid text of the PA was that resulting from Laws 24,481 and 24,572, and that Laws 24,481 and 24,572 did not violate the Paris Convention nor

409. *See* National Constitution, Art. 17.
410. *Ibid.*, Art. 83.
411. *See* the preliminary recitals of Decree 590.

the TRIPS agreement; the purpose of Law 24,603 was to prevent the consolidated text of the patent laws, approved by Decree 590, from entering into effect.

After a new set of negotiations between Congress and the Executive Power, Decree 590 was repealed and replaced by Decree 260, of 20 March 1996. Decree 260 includes a new consolidated text of the patent laws (hereinafter referred to as the PA), based on Laws 24,481 and 24,572. Decree 260 also includes the regulations applicable to the implementation of the patent laws (hereinafter referred to as Regs).

The PA was amended to a significant extent in 2004, by means of Law 25,859. This law reflects the agreement reached by Argentina and the US on legislative solutions to overcome alleged violation of the TRIPS agreement by Argentine patent law.[412] It has also been amended recently by Decree 27 of 2018, which has not yet been ratified by Congress; the main purpose of these amendments is to simplify and speed the relevant procedures.

The National Industrial Property Institute has issued a set of Directives on Patenting (hereinafter referred to as Directives) which have periodically been subject to amendments. These Directives include rules both on procedure and on the substantive standards for patenting.

60. As should be obvious from its recent history, Argentine patent law has been shaped to a significant extent by the Paris Convention and by the TRIPS agreement. These international agreements have been ratified by Argentina and therefore incorporated into Argentine law. Their effects differ from those of purely domestic statutes from two perspectives. First, pursuant to Article 75, section 22, of the Federal Constitution, in case of conflict between international treaties ratified by Argentina and domestic laws, the former prevail. Second, although the provisions of international treaties ratified by Argentina become immediately part of Argentine law, and are enforceable as such,[413] some of these provisions may be practically inoperative in the absence of the necessary regulations, and this may actually impede the effectiveness of treaty provisions in specific cases.[414]

In addition to these international conventions, Argentina is part of several industrial property conventions with effects in the patent area, with a limited geographical scope.[415] The following may be mentioned:

(a) Montevideo Treaty on patents of invention, of 1889. It was ratified by several South American countries, including Argentina.
(b) The Treaty of Asunción, of 1991. It created the *Mercado Común del Sur*, or Mercosur, a common market comprising Argentina, Brazil, Paraguay, Uruguay. Although it includes few provisions expressly applicable to patents, its rules on

412. *See* C.M. Correa et al., *Medidas cautelares en el régimen de patentes* (Buenos Aires: Abeledo-Perrot, 2006).
413. *See* *E.I. Dupont de Nemours & Co. v. Estado Nacional*, National Court of Appeals for Federal Civil and Commercial Matters I, 9 Nov. 1995, *La Ley*, 5 Feb. 1996, 5.
414. *See* C.M. Correa, 'Los acuerdos de la Rueda Uruguay y las patentes', *La Ley* (10 Oct. 1995): 1; J. Otamendi, 'Respecto de un comentario sobre el acuerdo TRIPS y las patentes de invención', *La Ley* (28 Nov. 1995): 1.
415. *See* E. Aracama Zorraquin, 'El derecho convencional americano de la propiedad industrial', *Revista del Derecho Comercial y de las Obligaciones* 22 (1989): 641.

the circulation of goods are likely to have significant consequences on the effects of patents, which presently are purely national in scope.[416]

61. There is a general absence of valid judicial precedents under contemporary Argentine patent law. Court decisions under Law 111 were relatively few and were based on a legal regime that was fundamentally different from that enacted in the PA. Also, many of those decisions were incompatible with the Paris Convention and the TRIPS agreement, which contemporary legislation intends to respect.[417] The relatively short span of time since the sanction of the PA implies that very few court decisions have been pronounced on the basis of the new patent regime; most of these decisions refer to specific matters, such as the scope of provisional measures.

§2. Patentable Subject Matter

62. The elimination of several of the exclusions of patentable subject matter provided by Law 111 has been one of the guiding motives of the new Argentine patent legislation. The PA has been drafted, in this respect, on the basis of the limitation of exclusions from patentability provided by the TRIPS agreement, particularly its Article 27.

Article 1 of the PA provides generally that the inventions related to all the types and branches of production shall 'confer to their authors the rights and obligations specified in this Act'. This provision, drafted in terms that conflict with basic patent law principles – reference is made to 'authors' instead of 'inventors'; obligations are 'conferred' to such authors, etc., – has little operative effect and is mainly intended to express the elimination of pre-existing exclusions from the scope of patentable subject matter.

Article 6 of the PA excludes from the concept of invention several types of subject matter, namely the following:

(a) Discoveries, scientific theories and mathematical methods.
(b) Literary or artistic works or any other aesthetic creation, as well as scientific works.
(c) Plans, rules and methods for the exercise of intellectual activities, for games, economic-commercial activities or software.
(d) The form of presentation of information.
(e) Methods for surgical, therapeutical or diagnostic treatment applicable to the human body or related to animals.
(f) The juxtaposition of known inventions or the mixture of known products, and the variations in their form, dimensions and materials, except when they are combined or merged in such a way that they may not function separately or that the qualities or functions characteristic of these elements become modified so as

416. *See* R.M. Beraldi, *El derecho de la propiedad industrial y el Mercosur* (Buenos Aires: Abeledo-Perrot, 1992).
417. *See* Chaloupka, '¿In dubio contra patentem?', 34 et seq.

to obtain an industrial result that is not obvious to a technician with knowledge on the same subject matter.

(g) Every class of living matter and of substances pre-existing in nature.

Several of these exclusions may only be properly understood in the general context of the PA. Thus, the concept of discovery is related to that of industrial application. Industrial application is necessary for the patentability of inventions, pursuant to Article 4 of the PA. Every invention implies the 'discovery' of a causal relationship derived from the laws of matter; however, if this 'discovery' permits a practical industrial application, it becomes no longer qualified as 'discovery' for purposes of exclusion from the patentable subject matter. In a similar vein, inventions imply the express or implied use of scientific theories and mathematical methods; it is only when such scientific theories or mathematical methods are not applied in a concrete way so as to permit an industrial application that the exclusion from patentable subject matter becomes valid.

With regard to literary, artistic or scientific works and to aesthetic creations, the fact that an invention may have aesthetic value or that it may be part of a literary, artistic or scientific work does not imply that it may not be patented. Rather, the meaning of this exclusion is that the scientific work itself is protected by copyright, which does not prevent the exploitation of the inventions described in a scientific work but rather the unauthorized reproduction of the work itself. Meanwhile, the invention, and in particular its industrial application, may only be protected from unauthorized exploitation by meeting the substantive and formal requirements provided by patent law.[418] In other words, a given text describing an invention may be viewed as a scientific work and as such protected by copyright law; this will not prevent the patenting of the invention described by such text, provided compliance with the requirements of patent law. In a similar vein, the fact that an invention has aesthetic qualities will not prevent its patenting, if the PA standards are met. The invention must have – to this effect – an industrial application, and its aesthetic qualities will not qualify as such.

The exclusion of plans, rules and methods for the exercise of intellectual activities once again coincides with the requirement of industrial application. In the case of other plans, methods and rules, the exclusion is more problematic. Process patents imply a description of 'plans, rules, and methods' to achieve a certain end, and the industrial application requirement in turn implies that patented inventions must be applicable in 'economic-commercial activities'. The probable intent of the drafters of the PA is hidden – as is often the case – under its rather careless drafting. With regard to games, the effective meaning of the exclusion being examined refers to the rules of the game and to the tactics and techniques that may be used to obtain better results in the context of such rules. The exclusion would not be applicable to processes used to improve or permit the mechanical results of machines and other instruments used in connection with games. Thus, a process for a more efficient – for example, energy-saving – use of slot machines should not be excluded from patentability. With regard to 'economic-commercial activities', the probable intent of the drafters of the PA was to exclude management, business or financial techniques. The exclusion of software from the

418. *See* para. 55, *supra* .

patentable subject matter, although theoretically debatable,[419] is coherent with the protection granted by Argentine law to software under copyright[420] and with the position taken by the TRIPS agreement.[421] The use of software as part of a more complex process or machine should not hamper the possibility of patenting such process or machine as a whole.

The form of presentation of information is not an industrial process – in the sense patent law gives to that concept. Nor does it imply an industrial application. Therefore, the exclusion from patentability is self-explanatory with regard to that category. However, inventions implying new mechanical, electronic or industrial techniques for the presentation of information – for example, a new machine for the display of transparencies – would not be excluded from patent protection.

Surgical, therapeutic and diagnostic methods have no industrial application, in the sense applied to these terms by patent law.[422] Machines and tools used for surgical, therapeutic or diagnostic treatment would not be subject to the patentability exclusion, since they are not 'methods' and imply an industrial result applicable in the rendering of services.

With regard to the exclusion described in (f), above, it is an ill-conceived effort to deal with certain problems created by the application of the basic conditions of patentability. If a new 'quality' or 'function' is obvious to a technician with knowledge on the same subject matter, it will not be patentable, not because of the exclusion provided by Article 6(f) of the PA, but simply because of lack of novelty.[423] The exception from the patentability exclusion for combinations of elements that may not function separately is also void of content; if such combination exists, it is no longer possible to speak of a mere juxtaposition, mixture or variation. The application of the basic conditions of patentability would have been enough to deal with the exclusion provided by Article 6(f).

The exclusion for living matter, described in g) above, is complemented by Article 6 of the Regs. It provides that plants, animals and the 'essentially biological procedures for their reproduction' shall be considered to be non-patentable. This regulation creates some confusion as to the meaning of Article 6(g) of the PA that only living matter pre-existing in nature would be excluded from patentability; such understanding would be coherent with Article 27(3)(b) of the TRIPS agreement, which requires the patentability of microorganisms. However, Article 6 of the Regs also excludes from patentability plants or animals even if they are not pre-existing in nature. This exclusion would be acceptable from the point of view of the TRIPS agreement, but since it was not included in the PA, it would be unconstitutional.

The exclusion listed in Article 6 of the PA refers to cases in which no invention is deemed to exist. Article 7 lists cases in which an invention may exist but would not be patentable.

419. *See* G. Cabanellas, 'The Legal Protection of Computer Technology under Argentine Law', *Copyright World* 11 (1990): 34 et seq.
420. *See* paras 16–18, *supra* .
421. *See* TRIPS agreement, Art. 10.
422. *See* PA, Art. 4(e).
423. *Ibid.*, Art. 4(b), (c).

The first of these cases refers to inventions whose exploitation in the territory of Argentina must be prevented to protect public order or morality, to protect the health or life of persons or animals, to preserve plants or to prevent grave damages to the environment. This exclusion will normally apply to inventions that necessarily have the negative effects described by Article 7; in other words, the fact that an invention may be put to an improper or harmful use should not be sufficient ground for its non-patentability.

The second exclusion listed in Article 7 refers to the biological and genetic material existing in nature, or its replicate, and to the biological processes inherent to animal, vegetable and human reproduction, including the genetic processes related to material that may replicate itself under normal conditions occurring in nature. This exclusion is broader than that described in Article 6(g) of the PA; it is not clear, however, why the PA considers biological and genetic material existing in nature as unpatentable inventions, instead as a situation in which no invention exists, which is the position taken by Article 6(g) in connection with 'living matter'.

The Directives, as amended by Joint Resolutions 118/2012 of the Ministry of Industry and 546/2012 of the Ministry of Health, include several exceptions and exclusions regarding patentability in the fields of health and pharmaceuticals. Although these exceptions and exclusions are meant to be the implementation of the general rules on patentability in the areas covered by such Joint Resolutions, they have a very general scope and reach, which raises doubts about their coherence with the PA. The Directives includes rules applicable in the following fields:

- Polymorphs. Claims on polymorphs are considered not to be separately patentable, since they would lack inventive activity. Similarly, the standard procedures to obtain polymorphs are considered to be obvious.
- Hydrates and solvates are classified as 'pseudopolymorphs' and are considered not to be subject to separate patentability.
- Optic isomers. They are considered not be possible subject matter of patents once the basic molecular structure from which they can be derived has lost its novelty.
- Metabolites. They are considered not be separately patentable. They result from the action of the body on active pharmaceutical substances; these substances may be patented according to the usual rules.
- Drugs which generate active substances in the body are considered to be patentable, but they require special information about the way the active substances are generated and about how they operate.

§3. Conditions of Patentability

63. Article 4 of the PA provides the patentability of product or process inventions, provided they meet three basic conditions: that they are new, they imply an inventive activity, and they have industrial applicability.

These basic conditions, which have been drafted along the lines set by Article 27(1) of the TRIPS agreement, become somewhat muddled by Article 4(a) of the PA. It provides that for the purposes of that Act, an invention shall be every human creation that allows the transformation of matter or energy for use by mankind. This incursion into the rarefied air of philosophy, although unjustified, is unlikely to do much harm. Many human creations allow the transformation of energy but lack inventive activity and would, therefore, not qualify as inventions either legally or in common use. The fact that the PA still defines them as inventions is irrelevant, since they will remain patentable due to the non-fulfilment of the inventive activity requirement provided by the same act. In addition, it is unlikely that if the remaining conditions of patentability are met, the courts will not find a 'transformation of matter or energy', or that if an industrial application exists, it will not also be considered a 'use by mankind'.

64. Novelty, as a condition of patentability, is defined in Article 4, sections (b) and (c), of the PA. Section (b) defines as novel 'every invention which is not comprised in existing technology'. Section (c) defines as existing technology 'the technical knowledge which has become publicly known before the date of filing of the patent application or, when relevant, of the applicable priority, by means of an oral or written description, exploitation or any other means of communication or information, domestically or abroad'.

Novelty shall not be affected, however, in the following cases:[424]

(a) If within one year prior to the date of filing of the patent application or, when relevant, of the applicable priority, the inventor or his or her heirs, legatees or assignees have made the invention known by means of any means of communication. In this case, for the patent application to be valid, the applicant must file a sworn affidavit including a copy of the means of communication through which the invention was disclosed, if such means were printed or electronic. If the means were audio-visual, it will be enough to mention such means, together with the indication of their geographical location, of the disclosure and of the date of such disclosure.[425]
(b) If within one year prior to the date of filing of the patent application or, when relevant, of the applicable priority, the inventor or his or her heirs, legatees or assignees have exhibited the invention in national or international exposition. In this case, for the patent application to be valid, the applicant must file a sworn affidavit including adequate evidence of the participation of the inventor or of the applicant in the national or international exposition in which the invention was disclosed, as well as the date and scope of the disclosure.[426]

65. Inventive activity is defined by Article 4(d) of the PA as 'the creative process or its results which are not deducted from the state of technology in an evident way by a person with normal learning in the technical field involved'.

As in the case of other definitions of inventive activity or of similar concepts, such as inventive step or non-obviousness, it is unlikely that the PA's definition of inventive activity will provide a decisive guideline for the courts dealing with this aspect of patentability. The experience under the previous patent legislation – Law 111 – is enlightening. Law 111 did not include an express requirement of inventive

424. *Ibid.*, Art. 5.
425. *See* Regs, Art. 5.
426. *Ibid.*, Art. 5(c).

activity or non-obviousness.[427] However, the courts repeatedly inferred such requirement from other provisions of Law 111, such as those making reference to inventions that would not exist, in the courts' view, without inventive activity. In those cases, the courts had applied different standards to determine the existence of 'inventive merit', 'inventive level' or 'inventive step'. Thus, in some cases emphasis was placed on the existence of a 'creative activity' or an 'inventive spark'.[428] In other cases, the emphasis was placed on the fact that the innovation with respect to the pre-existing technology consisted in the exercise of mere professional ability or in the application of available expertise and experience.[429] Article 4(d) of the PA appears to combine these different tests, which in turn are well known in comparative law. In fact, the main merit and function of Article 4(d) is to place Argentine patent legislation within the prevailing positions taken in comparative law with respect to the element of 'inventive activity', 'inventive step' or 'non-obviousness'.

66. Industrial applicability is defined by Article 4(e) of the PA as taking place when the subject matter of the invention permits the attainment of an industrial result or product. The term 'industry' in this context is understood as being comprehensive of 'agriculture, forestry, animal husbandry, fishing, mining, manufacturing industries proper, and services'. This vague and rather unfortunate formulation[430] is unlikely to alter the approach traditionally used under Argentine law with respect to similar requirements included in Law 111,[431] which in turn were interpreted along the lines of those prevailing in other civil law jurisdictions.[432] The industrial applicability requirement will exclude the purely scientific or theoretical formulations,[433] as well as those that do not imply concrete effects on matter, such as psychoanalytical therapies. Whereas, regardless of the gaps found in the definition in Article 4(e) of industrial applicability, the economic area in which the invention is applied is unlikely to ever be an obstacle to patentability.

§4. Formalities

67. The procedure for the grant of patents under the Argentine PA is based on the prior examination by an administrative agency and the possibility of opposition by third parties.

427. *See* Chaloupka, '¿In dubio contra patentem?', 45 et seq.
428. *See Carl Braun Camera Werke v. Mira, G.*, National Court of Appeals for Federal Civil and Commercial Matters I, 24 Apr. 1979, *Jurisprudencia Argentina*, vol. 1979-III, 306.
429. *See Portaenvases Metálicos S. A. v. La Nación Argentina*, National Court of Appeals for Federal Civil and Commercial Matters I, 24 Oct. 1980, *Revista de la Dirección Nacional de la Propiedad Industrial*, nn. 499, 1981, 56.
430. Thus, while relatively minor activities, such as fishing, are expressly mentioned, major areas such as trade, communications and transportation have to be inferred from the general reference to services. Items such as exploration and scientific tools would meet the industrial applicability condition only through an ad hoc interpretation of the concept of 'services'.
431. *See* Law 111, Arts 1, 3 and 4.
432. *See* R. Fernández, *Código de Comercio comentado*, vol. 3 (Buenos Aires: R. Fernández, 1961), 274 et seq.
433. *Ibid.*, 274.

68. The procedure begins by means of the filing of an application with the National Patents Administration.[434] This application must include the following:[435]

(a) A formal request for the grant of a patent of invention.
(b) The name and personal data of the applicant.
(c) The domicile of the applicant.
(d) An ad hoc domicile of the applicant for purposes of the patent procedure.
(e) The name and domicile of the inventor.
(f) The name or title of the invention.
(g) If the invention is an addition to a prior invention, the identification of this basic prior invention.
(h) If the application refers to an invention that is part of a prior application, the number of such prior application.
(i) If the application results from the conversion of a prior utility model application, the number of this application.
(j) If a priority is claimed under the Paris Convention, the information necessary to determine the existence of such priority.
(k) If the application refers to microorganisms, the identification of the institution where they are deposited and of the date and registration number of such deposit.
(l) The name of the person or agent authorized to act in the procedure, as well as the number of his or her identification documentation.
(m) The signature of the applicant.
(n) A technical description of the invention, which must include a description of the technical field to which the invention belongs, a description of the state of technology in that field, including an indication of the documents in which such technology is disclosed, a detailed and complete description of the invention indicating the advantages over the prior state of technology, and a brief description of the graphs and drawings included in the application. The description of inventions must be comprehensible for a person knowledgeable in the field to which the invention pertains.
(o) One or more claims.
(p) The technical drawings necessary for the understanding of the invention.
(q) A summary of the description of the invention.
(r) A reduced-scale reproduction of the drawings included with the application, for publication purposes.
(s) If the application refers to microorganisms, a certificate of the deposit of the microorganisms in a depositary institution.
(t) Evidence of the payment of the application fees.
(u) Certified copies of the elements on the basis of which priorities are claimed.

434. *See* PA, Art. 12. The National Patents Administration is part of the National Industrial Property Institute.
435. *See* Regs, Art. 12.

69. The patent claim may be filed by the inventor or by his or her assignees, heirs or legatees.[436] They may act personally or by means of agents.[437] An inventor who is the original owner of the invention, pursuant to the rules on employee inventions,[438] may also file a patent application.[439]

70. If a priority right is claimed, pursuant to the Paris Convention, such priority right must be invoked in the patent application.[440] In such a case, the documentation on which the priority is based must be included together with the patent application.[441]

For the priority to be admissible, it must meet two conditions.[442] First, the application filed in Argentina should not be broader than the claims filed abroad on the basis of which the priority is claimed; if the claims filed in Argentina are broader, the priority will be limited to the claims filed abroad. Second, the country in which the first application was filed must grant reciprocity to Argentine applicants. This requirement does not appear to conform to the basic principles of the Paris Convention.

71. Each application must include only one invention or a group of inventions related in such a way that they constitute 'a single inventive concept'.[443] If these requirements are not met, the National Patents Administration may request the division of the application, and such division must take place within thirty days from the moment in which notice of the division request is served; otherwise, the application is considered to be abandoned.[444]

72. For the purposes of determining the priority of an invention and other legal effects based on the time of filing of a patent application, such patent application is considered to have been filed if it includes the following elements:[445] an affidavit requesting the patent grant, the identification of the applicant, a description of the invention, and one or more claims. If these conditions are met, the application is considered to have been filed – for the purposes of determining the timing of the filing – even if other formal requirements have not been complied with.[446]

If more than thirty days elapse from the filing date without meeting all the formal conditions required for patent applications,[447] the application shall be immediately rejected.[448] These formal conditions include filing the name and description of the invention, the technical drawings and graphs required for the proper understanding of the invention's description, one or more claims, and the summary of the description for purposes of publication and technical information.[449]

---

436. *See* PA, Art. 13.
437. *Ibid.*
438. *Ibid.*, Art. 10.
439. *See* Regs, Art. 10.
440. *See* PA, Art. 14.
441. *See* para. 68, *supra* .
442. *See* PA, Art. 14.
443. *Ibid.*, Art. 17.
444. *See* Regs, Art. 17.
445. *See* PA, Art. 18.
446. *Ibid.*
447. *See* PA, Art. 19, as amended.
448. *Ibid.*
449. *Ibid.*

73. Within a term of ninety days from the filing date, the applicant may present elements that complement, modify or correct the application, provided they do not imply an extension of the subject matter of the patent application.[450] Thereafter, the only possible changes will be those resulting from the suppression of defective elements, requested by the acting examiner.[451] If new examples of implementation of the invention are included in the file, they must serve for the better understanding of the invention.[452] No rights may be claimed on the basis of complements, corrections or modifications that imply an extension of the original application.[453]

74. The description of the invention in the patent application must be sufficiently clear and complete for an expert with average knowledge in the relevant field to be able to implement such invention.[454] It must also include an adequate description of the best-known method for the implementation and practical use of the invention.[455] The drawings, graphs and diagrams included with the application must be sufficiently clear for the proper understanding of the invention's description.[456]

The methods and procedures described as part of the patent application must be directly applicable for production activities.[457]

75. If the patent application refers to microorganisms, the application must include a description of the process that constitutes the subject matter of the patent claim, as well as of the product to be obtained with such process.[458]

In these cases, the applicant must deposit a specimen of the microorganism stock in an institution authorized for such purpose by the National Industrial Property Institute.[459] These institutions must either be institutions approved by the WIPO or meet the following conditions: they shall have a permanent character; they shall not be subject to the depositors' control; they must have adequate personnel and premises for purposes of showing the pertinence of the deposit and of assuring its storage and conservation without contamination risk; and they must offer the necessary security features to reduce to a minimum the risk of loss of the deposited material.[460]

At any moment after publication of the patent application, the public may obtain samples of a deposited microorganism from the depositary institution.[461]

76. The patent claims shall define the subject matter for which protection is sought in a clear and concise way.[462] Several claims may be included in an application, and they must be supported by the description of the invention, without exceeding the limits set by such description.[463] The first claim refers to the principal subject matter

450. *See* Regs, Art. 19.
451. *Ibid.*
452. *Ibid.*
453. *Ibid.*
454. *See* PA, Art. 20.
455. *Ibid.*
456. *Ibid.*, Art. 21.
457. *See* PA, Art. 20.
458. *Ibid.*
459. *See* Regs, Art. 20.
460. *Ibid.*
461. *Ibid.*
462. *See* PA, Art. 22.
463. *Ibid.*

of the invention, and the remaining claims must be subordinated to the first one.[464] Each claim must include the following:[465]

(a) A preamble or preliminary recital, with the same title as that given to the invention, describing all the aspects of the invention that have been derived from the technical area to which the invention belongs.
(b) An indication of the elements from which the novelty of the invention is derived and which are necessary for the implementation of the invention. These elements define the subject matter protected by the patent.
(c) If clarity and the better understanding of the invention so require, the principal claim may be followed by dependent claims, in which case the latter shall indicate the principal claim from which they depend and the additional characteristic they intend to protect. The same approach shall be used when a principal claim is followed by one or more subordinated claims related to particular varieties or implementations of the invention. Each independent claim must be a principal claim.

The Directives accept the use of 'Markush' claims but impose certain special requirements on their drafting and contents. The unity of invention requirement must be satisfied by this type of claim and the description of the invention must be sufficient for the obtention of all the different compounds falling within the scope of the claims.

77. The applicant may desist from his or her application at any time. If several applicants have filed a given application, such application shall only be considered abandoned if all the applicants have desisted from such application. If only some of them have desisted, their rights shall accrue in favour of those applicants who have not desisted from the application.[466]

It is also possible to convert a patent application into a utility model application. This conversion may only take place within thirty days from the filing of the application or within thirty days from the moment in which the National Patents Administration requests such conversion.[467] In this second case, if the applicant does not proceed to make the conversion, the application shall be considered abandoned.[468]

78. Once the patent application has been filed, the National Patents Administration undertakes a preliminary examination of the documentation;[469] as a result, it may require clarifications and the curing of omissions.[470] If applicants do not comply with these requirements within thirty days, the application shall be considered abandoned.[471]

---

464. *Ibid.*
465. *See* Regs, Art. 22.
466. *See* PA, Art. 16.
467. *Ibid.*, Art. 23 as amended.
468. *Ibid.*
469. *Ibid.*, Art. 24 as amended.
470. *Ibid.*
471. *Ibid.*

This preliminary examination, which the Regs qualify as 'formal',[472] must take place within twenty days from the moment in which an application including all the necessary documentation[473] has been filed.[474]

If the defects found in the preliminary examination refer to a priority based on a foreign application, the procedure related to the Argentine application may continue, but in that case the priority based on a foreign application will be considered as not having been invoked.[475]

79. The patent application and its appendixes are kept confidential up to the moment of its publication.[476] This publication is ordered by the National Patents Administration within eighteen months from the date in which the application is filed.[477] The applicant may request that the publication takes place before the expiration of the eighteen-month period.[478]

The publication of the patent application includes the following elements:[479]

(a) Number of the application.
(b) Date of filing of the application.
(c) Number of the priorities.
(d) Date of the priorities.
(e) Countries where the priorities originate.
(f) Name and domicile of the applicants.
(g) Name and domicile of the inventors.
(h) Registration number of the industrial property agent acting with regard to the application.
(i) Title of the invention.
(j) Summary of the invention.
(k) The most representative drawing of the invention, if any.

80. Upon termination and approval of the preliminary examination,[480] the applicant may request a substantive examination of the application.[481] This substantive examination is intended to determine that the conditions of patentability have been met.[482] For the request of substantive examination to be viable, the applicant must have previously paid an examination fee.[483] Within fifteen days from the filing of the

472. *See* Regs, Art. 24.
473. *See* para. 68, *supra* .
474. *See* Regs, Art. 24.
475. *Ibid.*
476. *See* PA, Art. 25.
477. *Ibid.*, Art. 26.
478. *Ibid.*
479. *See* Regs, Art. 26.
480. *See* para. 78, *supra* .
481. *See* Regs, Art. 27.
482. *See* PA, Art. 27.
483. *Ibid.* If the fee is not paid within eighteen months of the date of filing of the patent application, the application shall be considered abandoned.

substantive examination request, an examiner must be assigned to proceed with such examination.[484]

The substantive examination must take place within 180 days from the payment of the examination fee.[485] The substantive examination includes a search of anticipatory materials.[486] To this effect, the examiner will identify the documentation he or she deems necessary to determine whether the invention is new and implies inventive activity. This search covers all the relevant technical sectors and refers to the possible types of documents, as follows:[487] Argentine patent documentation, including that referred to patents and utility model rights already granted included in applications foreign patents and foreign published patent applications; and technical literature.

The examiner must determine, on the basis of this search and the preliminary examination, whether the application complies with the requirements of the PA.[488] In addition, the examiner may request that the applicant present a copy of the substantive examination undertaken with regard to the same invention by foreign patent offices.[489] Also, the examiner may request a report on the invention by researchers acting in universities or in scientific or technological research institutions.[490]

At the applicant's request, part of the substantive examination may take place in the applicant's premises, in particular to verify laboratory or equipment data.[491]

81. During the course of the substantive examination, the examiner may raise objections to the patent application.[492] The applicant is notified of these objections and has sixty days within which to answer these objections and present the additional information or documentation requested by the examiner. If the applicant does not comply with these requirements, the application is considered abandoned.[493]

All the objections raised by the examiner must be notified simultaneously, with the exception of preliminary clarifications or explanations requested from the applicant.[494]

In addition, any person may file objections to the application, including the documentary evidence supporting such objections, within sixty days from the publication of the patent application.[495] These objections are to be based on lack of novelty, lack of industrial application, lack of inventive activity or illegality of the subject matter of the application.[496] The examiner may reject these objections immediately if they are clearly unfounded.[497]

If the different objections raised to a patent application are not adequately answered and refuted by the applicant, the examiner issues a report advising the

484. *See* Regs, Art. 27(II).
485. *Ibid.*
486. *Ibid.*
487. *Ibid.*
488. *See* PA, Art. 27.
489. *See* Regs, Art. 27(III).
490. *Ibid.*
491. *Ibid.*, Art. 27(IV).
492. *See* PA, Art. 28.
493. *Ibid.*
494. *Ibid.*
495. *Ibid.*
496. *See* Regs, Art. 28.
497. *Ibid.*

National Patents Administration in favour of rejection of the application.[498] Before a decision on rejection is made, the applicant is given the opportunity to state his or her position with regard to the examiner's report.

82. If the examiner concludes that all the conditions for patentability have been met, he or she issues a report to that effect;[499] within thirty days from that recommendation, the National Patents Administration must issue a decision granting or rejecting the patent.[500] The applicant must be notified of this decision. The applicant has thirty days from this notice to appeal the decision.[501]

Following the decision to grant a patent, the National Patents Administration issues a patent certificate.[502] The patent grant is given subject to the condition that it does not affect the possible rights of third parties with regard to the invention and that no guarantee is given by the State with regard to the usefulness of the patented invention.[503] The patent grant is published in a special web page of the National Patents Administration.[504] This publication includes the basic information about the patent and the patented invention.[505]

§5. Ownership and Transfer

83. The right to obtain patent protection belongs to the inventor, or to his or her assignees, heirs or legatees.[506]

The PA provides a rebuttable presumption that the persons mentioned as inventors in patent applications are the actual inventors of the relevant invention.[507] No restrictions are provided with regard to the evidence that may be produced to rebut this presumption.

84. Article 10 of the PA provides the rules applicable to employee inventions.

The inventions obtained by an employee during the course of an employment or services contract or in the course of labour or service relationships whose purpose – totally or partially – is to undertake inventive activities belong to the employer. In these cases, the employee inventor is entitled to a supplementary remuneration for obtaining the invention if the employee's personal contribution to the invention and its importance for the enterprise and for the employer clearly exceed the scope of the contract or relationship in the context of which the invention was obtained.

If the conditions described in the preceding paragraph are not met, the employer may still have an option to acquire ownership of the invention or an exclusive right to exploit the invention. That is the case if the employee has obtained the invention in the course of his or her professional activity within the employer's enterprise,

498. *See* PA, Art. 29.
499. *See* Regs, Art. 30.
500. *Ibid.*
501. *Ibid.*
502. *See* PA, Art. 30.
503. *Ibid.*, Art. 31.
504. *Ibid.*, Art. 32 as amended.
505. *Ibid.*
506. *Ibid.*, Art. 8.
507. *Ibid.*, Art. 9.

provided the knowledge acquired by the employee in that enterprise or the means supplied by that enterprise have had a prevalent influence on the creation of the invention. The employer has ninety days to exercise this option, from the moment the invention is obtained. In addition, the employer's option is only viable if the invention is related to the employer's activities or to the work performed by the inventor in the course of his or her services for the employer.[508]

If the employer acquires rights on the invention under the option described above, the employee is entitled to fair compensation, based on the 'industrial and commercial importance of the invention', taking into account the value of the means or knowledge supplied by the employer's enterprise and the contributions made by the employee. If the employer who has acquired these rights grants a license to a third party, the inventor is entitled to up to 50% of the royalties the employer receives.

If – in the cases in which the employer is entitled to the option described above – the option is not exercised within the statutory term, the employee inventor becomes full owner of the patent rights related to the invention.[509]

For an invention to belong to the employer – directly or through the exercise of the option described above – based on its development during the course of an employment or services relationship, the patent application must be filed within one year from the moment in which the inventor ceased to be employed by the person claiming rights on the invention.[510]

The inventions that do not belong to employers – directly or through the exercise of the option described above – belong exclusively to the employee inventor.[511]

It is not legally admissible for employees to waive in advance their rights to inventions;[512] these rights are determined by the PA and may only be extended contractually in favour of the employee. However, there are no restrictions on the possibility of assigning the patents obtained by employees.

In case of disagreement between employers and employees, with regard to the determination of ownership of an invention pursuant to the rules described above, the parties may submit their claims to the National Patent Administration. In this case, the National Industrial Property Institute decides who will be entitled to the patent issued with regard to that invention.[513] This decision may be appealed before the Federal Civil and Commercial Courts.[514] A similar procedure is applicable in case of disagreement between employers and employees with regard to the latter's compensation in cases in which an employee invention becomes the property or is exploited by an employer.[515]

85. An inventor who has assigned his or her rights to an invention before the corresponding patent is granted is entitled to have his or her name mentioned in the

508. *See* Regs, Art. 10.
509. *Ibid.*
510. *See* PA, Art. 10(d).
511. *Ibid.*, Art. 10(e).
512. *Ibid.*, Art. 10(f).
513. *See* Regs, Art. 10.
514. *Ibid.*
515. *Ibid.*

patent documentation as inventor of the relevant invention.[516] Assignments of these rights prior to the patent grant are expressly allowed by Article 8 of the PA.

86. The patentee may assign his or her patent or rights thereof.[517] Although the PA does not expressly allow the fragmentation of patent rights – for example, through transactions leading to joint ownership of the patent – this fragmentation is possible on the basis of general civil law principles.

Patent assignments are registered in a special registry organized by the National Industrial Property Institute.[518] Between the parties, the assignment is valid regardless of recording in this registry. However, as against third parties, the transaction only becomes effective once the assignment has been recorded, except when recording takes place within ten working days from the date of the assignment agreement, in which case the effects of the recording – against third parties – are retroactive to the date of the agreement.[519] These restrictions on the effects of unrecorded agreements are especially relevant in cases of garnishments or other creditor actions against the assignor.

87. It is also possible for the patentee to grant licenses with regard to the patent.[520] As in the case of assignments, the contractual aspects of licenses are not regulated by the PA or the Regs but rather by the general civil law rules on contracts.[521]

Patent licenses may be exclusive, simple or sole; however, in the absence of contractual provisions to the contrary, licenses are considered to be simple, and the licensor retains the right to grant additional licenses and to exploit the subject matter of the licensed invention by himself or herself.[522]

Restrictive clauses included in license agreements are prohibited.[523] These prohibited clauses include those 'which affect the production, marketing or the technological development of the licensee, restrict competition or incur in any other conduct such as exclusive grant-backs, restrictions on the licensee's rights to challenge the validity of the licensed patent, package licensing' which infringe Competition Law.[524] This definition of restrictive clauses is clearly inadequate because practically every clause of a license agreement will 'affect the production, marketing or the technological development of the licensee'. It will probably be construed together with the provisions of the Competition Law,[525] which in turn are largely based on Articles 85 and 86 of the Treaty of Rome.

516. *See* Regs, Art. 9.
517. *See* PA, Art. 37.
518. *Ibid.*
519. *See* Regs, Art. 37.
520. *See* PA, Art. 37.
521. *See* G. Cabanellas, Contratos de licencia y de transferencia de tecnología en el derecho privado 2nd edn (Buenos Aires: Heliasta, 1994).
522. *See* PA, Art. 39.
523. *Ibid.*, Art. 38.
524. *Ibid.*
525. Law 25,156, as amended. On this law, *see* G. Cabanellas, *Derecho antimonopólico y de defensa de la competencia* (Buenos Aires: Heliasta, 2004). On the enforcement of the Competition Law in patent matters, *see* G. Cabanellas, *Contratos de licencia y transferencia de tecnología en el Derecho Económico* (Buenos Aires: Heliasta, 2010).

Under the previous Argentine patent legislation, licensees did not have the right to exercise directly the enforcement rights derived from the patent; they could only act by means of powers of attorney granted by the licensor. Article 40 of the PA partially reverses that rule, providing that the licensee may enforce the rights derived from the patent 'if the licensor does not exercise these rights by himself'. This provision is likely to cause practical difficulties because it does not state a clear framework to determine the time after which the licensor's inaction will allow the licensee to act by himself.

88. Licenses involving foreign licensors are subject to a special registration regime.[526] Under this regime, these licenses are valid regardless of registration, but unregistered licenses are subject to a less favourable tax regime, including the non-deductibility of royalties from the licensee's taxable income[527] and the application of a higher withholding rate to the royalties paid to foreign licensors.[528] Registration under this special regime is automatic[529] and does not imply a screening procedure with regard to the legal validity of the contractual clauses included in the registered agreements.[530]

§6. Scope of Exclusive Rights

89. Article 8 of the PA, as amended by Law 25,859, provides the basic rights derived from a patent, as follows:

(a) In the case of a product patent, the right to prevent third parties from manufacturing, using, offering for sale, selling or importing the patented product, without the patentee's authorization.
(b) In the case of a process patent, the right to prevent third parties from using the patented process and from using, offering for sale, selling or importing with these purposes the product directly obtained by means of such patented process, without the patentee's authorization.

90. The rights derived from a patent are defined by the first claim.[531] The effects of the remaining claims are subordinated to the defining effects of the first claim.[532] The description of the invention, the drawings, graphs and diagrams attached to such description, and the biological material deposited as part of the application procedure may be used to interpret the patent claims.[533]

526. Law 22,426, as amended.
527. *See* Law 22,426, Art. 9.
528. *Ibid.*
529. *See* Law 22,426, Art. 3; Decree 1,853, of 1993, Art. 8.
530. The validity of the clauses included in license agreements is determined by the authorities in charge of applying the Competition Law and by the ordinary courts.
531. *See* PA, Art. 11.
532. *Ibid.*, Art. 22.
533. *Ibid.*, Art. 11.

91. Several types of conduct are expressly excluded from the effects of the patentee's exclusive rights, as follows:

(a) The manufacturing of patented products or the use of patented processes as part of purely experimental activities of scientific or technological research, or as part of testing or teaching activities, in a context of not-for-profit private or academic activities.[534]
(b) The preparation of medicines, performed as a permanent activity by qualified professionals, and on a unit basis as required by medical prescriptions; the exception also extends to conduct related to the medicines thus prepared.[535]
(c) The employment of patented inventions, within the Argentine territory, in foreign vehicles – whether land, sea or airborne – that accidentally or temporarily are in circulation within the Argentine territory, if such inventions are employed exclusively for the needs of such vehicles.[536]

92. The PA does not include specific provisions on the territorial limits of patent rights. Thus, in principle, these rights would extend to conduct regarding which the patentee has the *ius prohibendi* provided by Article 8 of the PA[537] taking place within the Argentine territory.

In addition, Article 10(c) of the PA provides that patent rights do not extend against any person who acquires, uses, imports or in any way markets a patented product or a product obtained by means of a patented process, provided such products have been legally marketed in any other country. To determine, for these purposes, whether a product has been legally marketed abroad, Article 10(c) refers to the provisions included in Part III, section IV, of the TRIPS agreement. However, these provisions of the TRIPS agreement provide limited guidance as to the meaning of a 'product which has been legally marketed abroad'. Note 13 provides that the obligation to apply the procedures required by Part III, section IV, of the TRIPS agreement, does not apply to imports of merchandize marketed in a different country by the owner of the right or with his or her consent, or to merchandize in transit. It appears that the PA is based on the exclusion of the Argentine patentee's rights with regard to these imports. Article 36 of the Regs confirms this interpretation; it states that a product shall be considered to be validly marketed if the marketing has been authorized by the owner of the patent in the country where the merchandize was acquired or by a third party authorized to do the marketing.

On the whole, the Argentine rules on the patentees' rights with respect to imports are highly inadequate. The reference to the TRIPS agreement is in conflict with the tendency of this agreement – as it transpires from its Article 6 – not to define the limits of the exhaustion of patent rights. In addition, Article 36 of the Regs does not take into account the possibility – less likely with regard to patents than in trademark matters – that the patentee in one country will differ from the patentee in Argentina.

534. *See* PA, Art. 36(a).
535. *Ibid.*, Art. 36(b).
536. *Ibid.*, Art. 36(d).
537. *See* para. 89, *supra* .

§7. Limitations and Exceptions to the Scope of Patent Protection: Compulsory Licenses

93. Article 41 of the PA provides a general rule establishing limitations on the rights derived from a patent. According to Article 41, the National Industrial Property Institute, upon request by any competent authority, may provide limited exceptions to the rights granted by a patent. These exceptions should not interfere in an unjustified way with the normal exploitation of the patent nor cause unjustified damages to the legitimate interests of the patent owner, taking into account the legitimate interests of third parties.

This provision practically leaves in limbo the effective rights of patentees.

The National Industrial Property Institute is given the power to balance the 'legitimate interests' of patent owners and third parties, even though the basic patent rights already are the result of a protracted legislative effort to balance the interests of inventors and third parties.

Article 41 of the Regs limits to some extent the scope of Article 41 of the PA, providing that the Ministry of the Economy, the Ministry of Health and Social Action, and the Ministry of Defence shall be the competent authorities for purposes of requesting exceptions to the rights granted by a patent.

The limitations of the patent rights under Article 41 should be distinguished from the expropriation of a patent and from the use of a patented invention for public purposes. These restrictions derived from the Expropriations Law[538] require prior compensation to the patentee[539] and are only applicable to the extent that the expropriation or use is necessary to satisfy public purposes.[540]

94. The PA has repealed the restriction on the patentability of inventions in certain branches of trade that existed under prior law.[541] However, this elimination of restrictions was not immediately applicable but rather was subject to a special phase-out period. In particular, pharmaceutical products only became patentable after five years had elapsed from the publication of the PA.[542] Nevertheless, it was possible to file patent applications for pharmaceutical products before the five-year phase-out period expired, although the patents only could be granted after such expiration.[543]

A special set of rules applies in cases in which a third party has been using the invention during the phase-out period, once the pharmaceutical product patent is granted at the expiration of such period.[544] In such case, the third party has the right to continue exploiting the patented product, provided such third party undertakes the compromise to keep the local market fully supplied at the same prices, in real terms, applicable before patenting. In these cases, the patentee will have the right to obtain a fair and reasonable compensation from the third party exploiting the invention, from the moment the patent is granted until its expiration. This compensation is set by the

538. Law 21,499.
539. *Ibid.*, Art. 10.
540. *Ibid.*, Art. 1.
541. *See* PA, Art. 1.
542. *Ibid.*, Art. 100.
543. *Ibid.*, Art. 101.
544. *Ibid.*

National Industrial Property Institute, if the parties do not reach an agreement in that regard. The drafters of the PA, apparently unconvinced of the validity of these provisions in the context of the TRIPS agreement, have included a rule to the effect that the provisions on third parties' rights after the patent grant shall only be applicable to the extent that they do not have to be modified to comply with decisions of the World Trade Organization (WTO) adopted pursuant to the TRIPS agreement.

Article 101(II) of the Regs includes an additional restriction on the rights of third parties using the invention during the phase-out period. These rights would only exist if the third party has started the exploitation or has made significant investments to that effect before 1 January 1995. In practical terms, this is a severe restriction on the terms of these third parties' rights under the PA, of doubtful constitutional validity.

A further complication is introduced by Article 101(III) of the Regs. It provides a procedure where under the National Industrial Property Institute may grant exclusive marketing rights during the phase-out period. These exclusive marketing rights last for five years, unless a decision granting or rejecting the patent application is issued before the expiration of the five-year term. These exclusive marketing rights are not equivalent to the third party rights described above and are not patent rights. They therefore lack any legal foundation and are therefore unconstitutional. They are, in fact, a badly implemented compromise between the conflicting interests of foreign and local pharmaceutical companies. The granting of these exclusive marketing rights requires producing evidence with regard to the following matters:

(a) That the product is the subject matter of a patent application filed in Argentina.
(b) That the product has been the subject matter of a patent application after 1 January 1995, in another country that is party to the TRIPS agreement.
(c) That a patent has been granted for the same product, after 1 January 1995, in another country that is party to the TRIPS agreement, which must be the same country indicated in (b).
(d) That the marketing of the product has been authorized after 1 January 1995, in that same country.

Several additional restrictions are included in the PA with regard to inventions subject to the phase-out period described above – that is, those that are patentable under the PA but were not under Law 111. According to Article 102 of the PA, if a patent application in these cases reproduces a foreign patent application filed abroad before the enactment of the PA, the following conditions must be met for the Argentine application to be valid: the first application should have been filed less than a year before the enactment of the PA; the applicant must produce evidence of the foreign application; and exploitation or importation on a commercial scale of the invention should not have started. Patents obtained pursuant to these provisions expire together with the patent granted by the country in which the first application was filed, provided the extension of the patent rights does not thus exceed a total term of twenty years.[545]

Article 100 of the Regs includes a special set of restrictions on the filing of patent applications for pharmaceutical products during the phase-out period, which again contradicts the PA, particularly the latter's Article 102, described above. According

545. *Ibid.*, Art. 102(d).

to Article 100 of the Regs, patent applications for pharmaceutical products shall not be accepted if the first application was filed in Argentina or abroad before 1 January 1995, except when the applicants base their new application on a Paris Convention priority and such priority has been claimed after 1 January 1995. If the Paris Convention priority benefit is thus used, the first claim may date back to 1 January 1994. The same rules shall be applicable when the patent application for pharmaceutical products is the result of the conversion of a prior application for process patents.

By constitutional mandate, the regulations may not contradict the laws they are enacted to implement; as a result, the inconsistencies between the PA and the Regs, described above, resulted in substantial legal disputes and litigation.[546]

95. Article 43 of the PA provides that if within three years from the granting of a patent or within four years from the filing of a patent application, the corresponding invention has not been exploited, any person may ask for the authorization to use such invention without the patentee's consent. The same right arises if exploitation of the invention has been interrupted for more than one year.

However, this right does not arise if the reason for the non-exploitation by the patentee has been force majeure or if the patentee has made effective and serious preparations for the exploitation of the patented invention.

For the purposes of these provisions, a patented product shall be considered as exploited 'if it is sufficiently distributed and marketed so as to satisfy the national market's demand, in reasonable commercial conditions'.[547] It is not clear, however, whether the importation of goods manufactured with patented processes constitutes exploitation of such processes for the PA's purpose.[548]

Article 43 of the PA provides that force majeure shall be considered to exist in the cases legally qualified as such,[549] as well as when 'objective difficulties of a technical-legal character', beyond the patentee's control, make the exploitation of the invention impossible. Article 43 mentions, as one such 'objective difficulty', the delay in obtaining the registration with public offices necessary for a marketing authorization. It excludes as a justification for lack of exploitation the lack of economic resources or the absence of economic viability of the exploitation.

96. If the conditions for the grant of a compulsory licensing – derived from Article 43 of the PA – are met, and if a license is requested from the patentee and is denied by such patentee, after 150 days from the license request the petitioner may request from the National Industrial Property Institute a compulsory license for the manufacture and sale of patented products or for the use of patented processes.[550] The petitioner must produce evidence to the effect that a license with reasonable commercial terms has been requested from the patentee and that such request has had no positive

546. *See* L.M. Genovesi, 'El plazo de duración de las patentes: Prórroga de la protección a veinte años', in *Patentes de invención. Diez años de jurisprudencia*, J. Kors (Coord.) (Buenos Aires: La Ley, 2004), 49.

547. *See* Regs, Art. 43.

548. *See* C.M. Correa & S.D. Bergel, *Patentes y competencia* (Santa Fe: Rubinzal-Culzoni, 1996), 61.

549. Force majeure is defined by the Civil Code (Art. 514) as an unforeseen or unavoidable situation.

550. *See* Regs, Art. 42.

effect during a 150-day period.[551] The petitioner must also show that it has the technical and commercial capabilities to supply the domestic market in reasonable commercial terms.[552]

The patentee is informed of the compulsory license petition and thereafter has ten working days in which to answer and offer the evidence he or she deems relevant.[553] After the relevant evidence is produced – for which a forty-day period is provided[554] – the National Industrial Property Institute decides whether to grant the compulsory license.[555] This decision may be appealed before the pertinent administrative or judicial bodies within ten days from the moment it is notified.[556]

If a compulsory license is granted, based on lack of proper exploitation, and if the patentee and the licensee do not reach an agreement as to the applicable royalty rate, such rate shall be determined by the National Industrial Property Institute based on the economic value of the license and on the average royalty rate applied in the same field in commercial licenses between independent parties.[557]

97. Compulsory licenses shall also be granted if the patentee incurs in anti-competitive practices.[558] For these purposes, the PA states that the following conducts shall be considered anti-competitive practices:[559]

(a) Fixing comparatively excessive or discriminatory prices for patented products, 'with respect to the market average'. In particular, these conditions shall be considered to exist if there are offers to supply the market at prices significantly lower than those offered by the patentee for the same product.[560]
(b) The refusal to supply the local market in reasonable commercial terms.
(c) 'Hampering commercial or productive activities.'
(d) Any other violation of the Competition Law.[561]

551. *Ibid.*
552. *Ibid.*
553. *Ibid.*
554. *Ibid.*
555. *Ibid.*
556. *Ibid.*
557. *Ibid.*, Art. 43.
558. *See* PA, Art. 44.
559. *Ibid.*
560. The Patent Act, which frequently verges on the incomprehensible, here falls directly into the absurd. The purpose of patents is to allow patentees to obtain profit margins in excess of market averages with the aim of enticing patentees to make investments in research and development. 'Comparatively excessive' prices are not properly related to competition law as it applies to patents. An equally absurd category, from the point of view of competition law, is that of 'hampering commercial or productive activities', mentioned in (c), *infra* . *See* F. Rozanski, 'Nueva legislación argentina de patentes de invención', *Derechos Intelectuales* 7 (1996): 144.
561. Law 25,156. This Law follows the principles and, to some extent, the wording of Arts 85 and 86 of the Treaty of Rome.

For a compulsory license to be granted pursuant to these provisions, it is necessary for the authority in charge of applying the Competition Law[562] to issue an opinion stating that a violation of the Competition Law exists, that a compulsory license is a pertinent remedy, and what the conditions of such compulsory license should be.[563] If such an opinion is produced, the National Industrial Property Institute shall make several publications requesting bids from third parties interested in obtaining compulsory licenses.[564] These bids must be presented within thirty days from the publications.[565] The National Industrial Property Institute shall then decide on whose benefit the compulsory licenses shall be granted, and in what terms.[566] This decision is subject to administrative and judicial appeals.[567]

98. Compulsory licenses may also be granted on grounds of sanitary emergency or national security.[568] In these cases, the license is granted by the National Executive Power, acting with the advice of the Ministry of the Economy and of the National Industrial Property Institute, and of the Ministry of Health and Social Action or the Ministry of Defence, depending on the grounds being invoked for the license.[569]

99. Article 46 of the PA provides that compulsory licenses shall be granted to allow the exploitation of a second patent that may not be exploited without infringing a first patent, provided the following conditions are met:

(a) That the invention claimed in the second patent be a significant technical advance, with considerable economic importance, with respect to the invention claimed in the first patent.
(b) That the owner of the first patent be granted a cross license, in reasonable conditions, for the exploitation of the invention claimed in the second patent.
(c) That the compulsory license granted with respect to the first patent shall not be assignable independently from the second patent.

It is not clear what the relation is between the compulsory licenses provided by Article 46 of the PA and improvement patents. These are governed by Articles 51 and 52 of the PA. They are defined as patents granted for improvements of patented inventions.[570] They remain in effect as long as the patent on the improved invention or discovery is in effect.[571] In theory, an improvement patent could exist without meeting the conditions of Article 46 of the PA for compulsory licenses, particularly the requirement of 'economic importance' for the second patent. However, the Regs appear to take the position that compulsory licenses may be granted, pursuant to the regime of Article

562. The Secretary of Commerce, acting with the advice of the National Commission for the Defence of Competition.
563. *See* Regs, Art. 44.
564. *Ibid.*
565. *Ibid.*
566. *Ibid.*
567. *Ibid.*
568. *See* PA, Art. 45.
569. *See* Regs, Art. 45.
570. *See* PA, Art. 51 as amended.
571. *Ibid.*, Art. 52.

46 of the PA, in all cases of improvement patents.[572] These compulsory licenses are granted by the National Industrial Property Institute, and the latter's decisions in that respect are subject to appeal before administrative and judicial bodies.[573]

Compulsory licenses in favour of the owners of improvement patents are only possible if the owners of the first patent have refused to grant voluntary licenses in normal commercial terms.[574]

100. Article 47 of the PA provides several general rules applicable to all types of compulsory licenses. The following may be mentioned:

(a) The licenses shall extend to the patents related to components and manufacturing processes necessary for the exploitation of the licensed invention.
(b) The licenses shall be non-exclusive.
(c) The licenses shall be non-assignable, except in conjunction with the enterprise or part thereof where the exploitation of the license takes place.
(d) Except in cases related to competition law violations or to sanitary emergency or security needs,[575] the licenses shall be principally directed to supplying the domestic market.
(e) The patentee shall be entitled to a reasonable compensation, based on the economic value of the license. The procedure provided for compulsory licenses based on lack of proper exploitation[576] shall be applicable to other types of compulsory licenses.[577] In cases in which compulsory licenses are granted to correct anti-competitive practices, the need to correct the situation that led to such practices shall be taken into account when determining the patentee's compensation. Also in these cases, situations that would normally lead to having the compulsory license revoked – for example, lack of payment of the royalties – may not cause that effect if the preservation of the license is necessary to prevent the repetition of the anti-competitive practices that created the grounds for the compulsory license.[578]
(f) In cases of compulsory licenses derived from sanitary emergencies or national security needs,[579] the license shall be limited to the purposes that originated it and shall be terminated if the circumstances that originated the license have ceased to exist and are unlikely to repeat themselves;[580] the National Industrial Property Institute is in charge of determining the existence of these changes in the relevant circumstances.[581] If compulsory licenses are to be terminated due to changes in

---

572. *See* Regs, Art. 51. *See also* C.M. Correa & S.D. Bergel, *Patentes y competencia* (Santa Fe: Rubinzal-Culzoni, 1996), 172.
573. *See* Regs, Art. 51.
574. *See* PA, Art. 47(b).
575. *See* paras 97 and 98, *supra* .
576. *See* para. 96, *supra* .
577. *See* PA, Art. 47(h).
578. *Ibid.*
579. *See* para. 98, *supra* .
580. *See* PA, Art. 47(i).
581. *Ibid.*

the underlying circumstances, such termination shall take place in a way intended to minimize the impact on the persons who were granted the compulsory licenses.[582]

(g) In the case of semiconductor technology, compulsory licenses shall be granted after a judicial or administrative procedure.[583]

All decisions related to compulsory licenses are subject to appeal,[584] but such appeal does not suspend the effects of the decision granting or rejecting a compulsory license, until the appeal is decided.[585]

In all cases, persons requesting a compulsory license must show that they have the economic capacity and the necessary premises for an efficient exploitation of the licensed patented invention.[586]

§8. Duration of Protection: Maintaining and Termination of Patent Protection

101. The duration of patents is set by Article 35 of the PA at twenty years, counted from the date in which the patent application was filed. Article 35 provides that this term may not be extended.

102. Patents shall be declared void when they have been obtained in violation of the PA.[587] If voidness affects only part of the claims included in a patent, only such claims shall be declared void.[588] However, a claim may not be declared partially void.[589] If a claim is declared void, the rest of the patent shall continue in effect if the non-invalidated claims can exist independently from the void claim.[590]

If a patent is declared void, this shall not cause related improvement patents to be declared void, provided the latter's patentee requests the conversion of the improvement patent into an independent patent within ninety days from the moment he or she is notified of the voidness of the basic patent.[591]

103. Patents may lapse for the following reasons:[592]

582. *Ibid.*
583. It is difficult to determine the meaning of this provision, included in Art. 47(i) of the PA. If the 'semiconductor technology' is protected by patents, the PA's rules on compulsory licenses would be applicable, and the 'special' rules on semiconductor technology would add nothing to the PA's provisions on compulsory licenses. If the 'semiconductor technology' is not protected by patents, it is difficult to understand the reason why rules on such technology would be included in the PA, which has no specific regime on 'semiconductor technology'. In addition, the provisions of Art. 47(i) on semiconductor technology are so vague that they are practically irrelevant, since no rules are established as to what the applicable procedure should be.
584. *See* PA, Art. 48.
585. *Ibid.*, Art. 49.
586. *Ibid.*, Art. 50.
587. *Ibid.*, Art. 59.
588. *Ibid.*, Art. 60.
589. *Ibid.*
590. *Ibid.*
591. *Ibid.*, Art. 61.
592. *Ibid.*, Art. 62.

(a) Termination of the original term of duration.[593]

(b) Abandonment by the owner. If there are several joint owners, abandonment shall be effective only if all of them consent to such abandonment.[594] Abandonment shall not have prejudicial effects against third parties,[595] such as exclusive licensees.

(c) Lack of payment of the applicable yearly fees.[596] If payment is not made within a 180-day grace period from the required payment date, the patent will lapse unless the patentee shows that lack of payment was due to force majeure.[597]

(d) When the patented invention is not exploited within two years after a compulsory license has been granted with regard to such invention.[598] Literally understood, this rule would extend to all cases of compulsory licenses, even those in which the license is not based on lack of exploitation. Such a broad interpretation would probably be in violation of the Paris Convention.[599] It is therefore likely that this cause of lapsing will only extend to cases in which the compulsory license is based on lack of exploitation.

104. Pursuant to Article 63 of the PA, the expiration of a patent due to voidness or lapsing is automatic, taking place by operation of the law. The actual meaning of this provision is that if there is a conflict with regard to the validity or expiration of the patent, a judicial decision will be necessary to determine whether the patent is still in force; however, the effects of this decision will be retroactive to the moment in which the cause for expiration or lapse took place. Coherent with this interpretation, the PA states certain rules regarding the legal actions leading to a judicial declaration of voidness or lapsing. These actions may be filed by any person having a legitimate interest in such declaration.[600] Voidness or lapsing may be used as a defence in an action filed by the patentee.[601]

Once the voidness or lapsing of patent has been declared by a court and the decision is no longer subject to appeals, such decision shall be notified to the National Industrial Property Institute.[602] The PA does not define to what extent these decisions are valid against third parties that have not participated in the litigation.

593. *See* para. 101, *supra* .
594. *See* PA, Art. 62(b).
595. *Ibid.*
596. *Ibid.*, Art. 62(c).
597. *Ibid.*
598. *Ibid.*, Art. 62(d).
599. The provisions of the PA literally allow the combination of provisions based on non-exploitation with provisions based on other grounds (e.g., competition restraints) without establishing any necessary relation between each other. Article 5A(3) of the Paris Convention requires that the lapse of patent rights be related with the frustration of compulsory licenses as a remedy to abuses of patent.
600. *See* PA, Art. 64.
601. *Ibid.*, Art. 65.
602. *Ibid.*, Art. 66.

§9. Infringements and Remedies

105. The PA provides both civil and criminal remedies in cases of infringement of patent rights.

106. In case of violation of a patent right, the patentee and his or her licensees are allowed to file civil actions to obtain the prohibition of further conduct in violation of such patent right and the indemnification of the damages caused by such violation.[603] No distinction is made, for these purposes, between exclusive and non-exclusive licensees or between voluntary and compulsory licensees. For purposes of these civil actions, the PA does not define the meaning of 'violation of a patent right'; this concept is directly derived from the scope of the patent rights.[604]

Pursuant to general civil law principles, the indemnification of damages includes both the compensation of damages or losses actually caused as well as the compensation for the profits and chances foregone due to the patent violation.[605]

Civil actions are subject to a three-year statute of limitations period.[606]

107. In case of violation of patent rights, the injured party may obtain preliminary measures from the acting court.[607] To this effect it is necessary to present the patent certificate to the court[608] and to show that irreparable damage, in excess of what would result if the preliminary measure were not granted, would result if such measure were delayed.[609] Before ordering the preliminary measures, the court may ask for guarantees from the petitioner for the case in which the preliminary measure causes unjustified damages, and the court must appoint an expert witness to establish the prima facie validity of the patent and the reasonable probability that a violation of such patent exists.[610]

Pursuant to the PA, the preliminary measures may include the sequestration of infringing products; the description of the infringing process; the sequestration of the machinery used in violation of the petitioner's patent rights; the prevention of patent violations, particularly by avoiding the entry of infringing merchandize in the course of trade; and the preservation of relevant evidence.[611] In addition, the petitioner may request preliminary measures derived from procedural law. Procedural laws generally allow the courts to provide any preliminary measures that may be necessary for the effectiveness of the rights claimed by a plaintiff, provided prima facie evidence of that right and adequate guarantees are supplied by such plaintiff.[612]

603. *Ibid.*, Art. 81.
604. *See* paras 89–92, *supra* .
605. *See* Civil and Commercial Code, Art. 1738.
606. *See* PA, Art. 82; Civil and Commercial Code, Art. 2561.
607. *See* PA, Art. 83, as amended by Law 25,859. These amendments were introduced following an agreement between the US and Argentina, meant to adjust Argentine legislation to the standards provided by the TRIPS agreement.
608. *Ibid.*
609. *Ibid.*
610. *Ibid.*
611. *Ibid.*
612. *See* Regs, Art. 83; Civil and Commercial Procedure Code of the Nation, Art. 232.

Preliminary measures are undertaken by a court officer, who may be assisted by one or more experts.[613]

If, in the course of implementing preliminary measures, infringing products are identified, the person holding such products must supply information regarding the person who sold or supplied such products, as well as their amount and value, and the date in which supply began, under penalty of being considered an accomplice of the main infringer.[614]

If the requested preliminary measure consists of suspension of the defendant's exploitation, this preliminary request shall be granted if other adequate preliminary measures were not granted, unless the defendant posts a bond deemed sufficient by the court.[615] If no such bond is posted, the court may order the suspension of the exploitation, provided the plaintiff posts the bond determined by the court.[616]

When the preliminary measure is requested before the formal complaint is filed, the plaintiff has a fifteen-day period from the moment such measure becomes effective to file such complaint; if this requirement is not complied with, the preliminary measure lapses.[617]

108. Courts have the power in civil procedures related to the violation of process patents to place on defendants the burden of proof with regard to products that may have been produced with the process patent on which the action is based.[618] For purposes of exercising this power, courts may put on the plaintiff the burden of proof as to the violation of the process patent, if the product obtained by means of the patentee's procedure is not new.[619] In addition, courts shall presume that such product is not new if the defendant or an expert witness appointed by the court at the defendant's request shows that an identical non-infringing product was on the market at the time of the alleged patent violation that did not originate in the defendant or the patent holder.[620]

109. Civil actions with regard to patent infringement shall be subject to ordinary, non-abbreviated procedures and will be subject to the jurisdiction of the federal civil and commercial courts.[621]

110. Article 75 of the PA provides that cases of fraud against the rights of the inventor shall be considered a crime of falsification and punished with imprisonment from six months to three years and with fines. The amount of these fines is to be determined from time to time by the Ministry of the Economy.[622]

This rather cumbersome definition of the criminal violation of patent rights follows the lines of pre-existing Argentine legislation.[623] It generally includes conduct

613. *See* PA, Art. 84.
614. *Ibid.*, Art. 85.
615. *Ibid.*, Art. 87, as amended by Law 25,859.
616. *Ibid.*, *See also* PA, Art. 83.
617. *Ibid.*, Art. 86.
618. *Ibid.*, Art. 88, as amended by Law 25,859.
619. *Ibid.*
620. *Ibid.*
621. *Ibid.*, Art. 89.
622. *See* Regs, Art. 96.
623. *See* Law 111, Art. 53.

violating the exclusive rights of a patentee.[624] An element of wilful misconduct has generally been considered necessary for this type of violation to exist.[625]

More specific violations – also subject to the penalties provided by Article 75 – are listed in Article 76 of the PA. They include the following:

(a) Producing or having produced by third parties one or more objects in violation of the rights of a patentee. The provision does not require that the objects themselves be patented.
(b) Importing, selling, offering for sale, marketing, exhibiting or importing into the territory of Argentina one or more objects in violation of the rights of a patentee.

These 'special' violations defined by Article 76 cover, in practice, most of the violations that would fall under the broad terms of Article 75.

111. Several aggravated violations of inventors' rights are listed in Article 77 of the PA. These violations are punished with sanctions one-third higher than those applicable to the 'general' violations of Article 75.[626] These aggravated violations are the following:

(a) Making an illegal appropriation or disclosure of an invention that is not yet patented, if such conduct is undertaken by a partner, attorney, advisor, employee or worker of the inventor or of his or her assignees, heirs or legatees.
(b) Obtaining the disclosure of an invention by means of corruption of a partner, attorney, advisor, employee or worker of the inventor or his or her assignees, heirs or legatees.
(c) Violating the confidentiality obligations imposed by the PA.

112. Article 78 of the PA provides for fine penalties against any person who, not owning a patent or not enjoying the rights derived from a patent, uses in his or her products or advertisement statements that are likely to induce the public into error as to the existence of patent rights.

113. Those who participate in the criminal violations described above involving patents and inventions are subject to the penalties provided by the PA with regard to the authors of such violations, adjusted as generally provided by the Penal Code with regard to criminal participation.[627] These rules apply to instigators, accomplices, conspirators, aiders and abetters, and any other type of criminal participation.

In case of repetition of criminal violations of the PA, the applicable penalties shall double.[628]

114. Criminal actions with regard to violations of the PA are subject to a simplified type of criminal procedure – the so-called correctional procedure – to be conducted under the jurisdiction of the federal criminal and correctional courts.[629]

---

624. *See* J.C. Ledesma, *Derecho penal industrial* (Buenos Aires: Depalma, 1987), 158 et seq.
625. *Ibid.*, 170, 171.
626. *See* para. 110, *supra* .
627. *See* PA, Art. 80.
628. *Ibid.*, Art. 79.
629. *Ibid.*, Art. 89.

§10. Overlapping and Relation to Other Intellectual Property Rights

115. There have been few cases in connection with the relation of the PA with other intellectual property rights. The PA does show a tendency to protect inventions even before they have been patented,[630] thus creating a degree of overlapping with trade secret protection. As is characteristic of trade secret law,[631] the remedies derived from the PA would be added to those that already exist under other types of trade secret protection. It should be noted that the PA is vague with regard to the standards applicable to the protection of inventions before they are patented. Since the PA refers in these cases to 'inventions',[632] it would appear that the criteria of novelty, inventive activity and industrial application would be applicable to determine the existence of inventions that are protected while still unpatented.

With regard to software, the PA, as has been traditional under Argentine law, provides its non-patentability.[633] Software protection is based, under Argentine law, on copyright rules. However, this does not prevent the patentability of complex inventions in which software plays a part but does not constitute by itself the subject matter of a claim.

Industrial designs are generally distinguished from patents on the basis of the protection granted to ornamental characteristics by the former and to functional characteristics by the latter. An invention with both ornamental and functional characteristics could in principle be protected under both the patent and industrial design regimes, provided the ornamental elements of the design are not determined or imposed by the functional characteristics of the product.[634] Such double protection is unusual. If an industrial design has already been patented – on the basis of its functional characteristics – by one person, it may not be registered as an industrial design by a different person.[635]

630. *See* PA, Arts 75 and 77.
631. *See* Ch. 9, *infra* .
632. *See* PA, Arts 75 and 77.
633. *Ibid.*, Art. 6(c).
634. *See* Decree-law 6673, of 1963, Art. 6(c).
635. *See Collo GmbH v. Sed Metal*, 'National Court of Appeals for Federal Civil and Commercial Matters I', 27 Mar. 1987, *Revista del Derecho Indusrial*, 1989, vol. 10, 297.

Chapter 3. Utility Models

§1. Sources: Legislation

116. Utility models were introduced into the Argentine legislation by the PA of 1995. It was common, before that enactment, for the developers of utility models to use the rules on industrial designs for the protection of utility models,[636] although the rules on industrial designs prevent the protection of the ornamental elements of a design that are determined or imposed by the functional characteristics of the product.[637]

The rules on utility models are presently included in the PA, pursuant to the consolidated text approved by Decree 260, of 20 March 1996.[638] Additional provisions are included in the Regulations, also approved by that Decree. These statutory rules have received little application.

§2. The Protection of Utility Models

117. Article 53 of the PA defines utility models as every new form or device obtained or introduced in tools, working instruments, utensils, devices or objects already known that lend themselves to practical work, to the extent that they imply a better utilization of the function for which they are destined. An exclusive right is granted by Article 53 to the creators of utility models; such exclusive right shall be evidenced by utility model certificates.

The exclusive right on utility models extends to the new form or device described above.[639] It may not extend to subject matter already protected by a patent that is in effect.[640]

118. Utility models require novelty and industrial applicability to be legally protected as such.[641]

Novelty is a typical element of patentable inventions,[642] and the parallelism between the provisions on patent and utility model protection would immediately lead to an analogous interpretation of novelty both under patent and utility model law. However, this parallelism was broken by Article 55 of the PA, which provided that the fact that the utility model had been known or disclosed abroad did not impede the legal protection of the utility model. This could be understood to imply that the mere copying of foreign utility models would be enough to obtain certificates of utility models under Argentine law. Such an interpretation, however, would conflict with

636. *See* I.F. Poli, *El modelo de utilidad* (Buenos Aires: Depalma, 1982), 7.
637. *See* Decree-law 6,673, of 1963, Art. 6(c).
638. *See* para. 59, *supra* .
639. *See* PA, Art. 53.
640. *Ibid.*
641. *Ibid.*, Art. 55.
642. *See* para. 64, *supra* .

Article 53 of the PA, to the extent that it reserves the protection granted to utility models to its 'creator'. The mere copying of foreign utility models would not imply a 'creation'. In addition, priorities under the Paris Convention regime would additionally limit the possibility of obtaining certificates of utility models on the basis of mere copying of foreign utility models. Decree 27 of 2018 has amended Article 55 of the PA so as to eliminate the provision to the effect that knowledge or disclosure abroad does not impede the legal protection of utility models.

119. As has been the case under other utility model regimes,[643] protection for these models does not extend to new processes.

Also following comparative law precedents,[644] the PA requires, for the protection of utility models, that they imply a better utilization of the function for which they are destined. There must be a causal relationship between the new form or device in which the utility model consists and such 'better utilization'.[645] The following types of 'functional improvement' have been described:[646]

(a) A new benefit or effect derived from the function to which the model applies.
(b) An economy of time, energy or labour.
(c) An improvement in working conditions.
(d) A better efficiency or comfort in the application or use of the function to which the model applies.
(e) An increase or improvement in the benefits derived from the function to which the model applies.
(f) An increase in the yield of such function.

In addition, the utility model must refer to specific movable objects,[647] whose functions are improved by such model.

120. Obtaining a utility model certificate requires the filing of a petition with the National Patents Administration.[648] This petition must include the following elements:[649]

(a) The title given to the utility model.
(b) A description referred to the principal object of the new configuration or disposition of a tangible object with practical use, to the functional improvement, and to causal relationship existing between the new configuration or disposition and the functional improvement. The description must be such that the utility model may be reproduced by an average skilled person. An explanation of the drawings included with the application must also be attached.
(c) The claims referred to the utility model.
(d) The necessary drawings.

643. *See* I.A. Poli, *El modelo de utilidad*, 48, 49.
644. *Ibid.*, 64 et seq.
645. *Ibid.*, 65.
646. *Ibid.*
647. *Ibid.*, 67 et seq.
648. *See* PA, Art. 56.
649. *Ibid.*

According to Article 55 of the Regs, the filing date determines the existence of novelty, to the extent that foreign disclosures are not considered to destroy such novelty if they have been made by the petitioner abroad within the six months prior to the filing date. This would confirm the narrow interpretation of the substantive conditions of utility models proposed above,[650] but implies placing in the Regs a restriction that should have been explicit in the PA's text.

121. The utility model certificate application is examined to determine whether the substantive conditions for protection have been met.[651] In general, the procedure for such examination and the rest of the procedure leading to the granting of a utility model certificate are governed by the same rules applicable to patent applications,[652] described in Chapter 2. The opposition procedure applicable to patents[653] applies to utility models.[654]

122. There is a rebuttable presumption that the person mentioned in a utility model certificate as creator of the utility model is the actual creator of such model.[655] The rules on employee inventions applicable to patents[656] would also apply to utility models.

Utility models may be the subject matter of assignments and licenses.

123. The definition by the PA of the scope of the exclusive rights on utility models is imperfect. Article 53 of the PA grants an exclusive right as to the exploitation of utility models, without specifying the contents of such exclusive rights. However, it is possible to infer from other provisions of the PA certain additional rules that define the scope of the exclusive rights on utility models. First, Article 53 provides that these exclusive rights refer only to the new form or disposition that characterizes the utility model. Second, pursuant to Article 58 of the PA, the rules on the scope of protection of product patents[657] would be applicable to utility models.

124. It is not evident from the text of the PA whether compulsory licenses are applicable to utility models. The text of the PA provisions on compulsory licensing refers only to patents. However, Article 58 provides that the PA's provisions on patents are applicable to utility models to the extent that they are not incompatible with the basic rules applicable to such models. The rules in the PA on compulsory licenses are not incompatible with the basic structure of utility model protection. Probably more decisively, the PA's provisions on compulsory licenses are clearly based on the Paris Convention's rules on that matter, which in turn also extend to utility models.[658] Finally, the examination of each type of compulsory licenses – to be made forthwith – shows that they generally meet the same necessities in the case of utility models as in the case of patents.

650. *See* para. 118, *supra* .
651. *See* PA, Art. 57.
652. *Ibid.*, Art. 58.
653. *See* para. 81, *supra* .
654. *See* PA, Art. 57 as amended.
655. *See* PA, Art. 9.
656. *See* para. 84, *supra* .
657. *See* paras 89–92, *supra* .
658. *See* Paris Convention, Art. 5A(5).

With regard to compulsory licenses based on lack of proper exploitation,[659] the same lack of exploitation may take place in the case of utility models. The rules applicable to compulsory patent licenses based on lack of proper exploitation[660] would thus be extendable – *mutatis mutandis* – to utility models.

Compulsory licenses based on competition law violations[661] are also viable in the case of utility models, since such models may also be used as instruments for anti-competitive practices. However, it should be noted that utility models are generally far less likely than patents to be used as instruments for anti-competitive practices. To the extent that they are so used, the rules applicable to compulsory patent licenses[662] would also be extendable to utility models.

In a similar vein, it would be possible to extend compulsory licenses required by health emergencies or national securities[663] to utility models, although it is practically unlikely that these models would be relevant for such emergencies.

A far more practically significant situation is that in which a utility model improves on a patented invention. However, the possibility of obtaining compulsory licenses in these cases – following the rules provided for improvement patents – is blocked by the provision of Article 53 of the PA prohibiting the granting of utility model certificates if they are within the scope of pre-existing patents.[664]

125. There are no technical fields excluded from utility model protection.[665] Whereas, the subject matter excluded from patentability by the PA[666] would also be excluded from utility model protection. In addition, the definition of the scope of utility models excludes from protection certain types of technology, particularly processes, which may be protected by patents.[667]

126. The protection derived from utility model certificates extends ten years, counted from the filing of the relevant application.[668] This term may not be extended. Utility model certificates may be totally or partially void if they have been obtained in violation of the relevant PA's provisions.[669] If a utility model certificate has been declared partially void, the remaining elements of the certificate may continue to be legally effective, provided they may exist independently as the subject matter of a utility model certificate.[670]

The protection derived from utility model certificates may also expire due to the following reasons:[671]

659. *See* PA, Art. 43.
660. *See* para. 95, *supra* .
661. *See* PA, Art. 44.
662. *See* para. 97, *supra* .
663. *See* para. 98, *supra* .
664. A contrary position was held by I.A. Poli, *El modelo de utilidad*, 140 and 141, prior to the PA.
665. *See* PA, Art. 1.
666. *See* para. 62, *supra* .
667. *See* para. 119, *supra* .
668. *See* PA, Art. 54.
669. *Ibid.*, Art. 59.
670. *Ibid.*, Art. 60.
671. *Ibid.*, Art. 62.

(a) Abandonment by the owner. If there are several joint owners, abandonment shall be effective only if all of them consent to such abandonment.[672] The abandonment shall not have prejudicial effects against third parties,[673] such as exclusive licensees.
(b) Lack of payment of the applicable fees.[674] If payment is not made within a 180-day grace period from the required payment date, the utility model certificate will lapse unless the owner shows that lack of payment was due to force majeure.[675]
(c) When the utility model is not exploited within two years after a compulsory license has been granted with regard to such utility model.[676] As in the case of patents,[677] this cause of lapsing would only extend to cases in which the compulsory license is based on lack of exploitation. On this basis, this cause of lapsing is supported on the assumption that compulsory licenses for lack of exploitation are also applicable to utility models.[678]

127. The voidness or lapsing of a utility model certificate has retroactive effects.[679] The procedural rules applicable to the voidness or lapsing of patents are extendable to utility models.[680]

128. The civil and criminal rules on patent infringements and remedies[681] are also applicable to utility models. With regard to these rules, the PA has expressly included the rights on utility models together with patent rights as the subject matter of the remedies provided by such Act.[682]

129. As yet, no court decisions define the limits between utility models and other types of related subject matter of industrial property rights. However, on the basis of the PA's provisions on utility models, it is possible to draw such limits, at least partially. Utility models are distinguished from patents along the following lines:

(a) Utility models do not require an inventive step.[683] However, they require the existence of an 'invention',[684] and this may lead to requirements similar to those included under the inventive step doctrine for patents.
(b) The subject matter of utility models is more limited than that of patents.[685]

It is possible to convert a utility model certificate petition into a patent petition, and vice versa. Such conversion must take place within the first thirty days after the initial filing, or within thirty days after the conversion is requested by the National Patents

---

672. *Ibid.*, Art. 62(b).
673. *Ibid.*
674. *Ibid.*, Art. 62(c).
675. *Ibid.*
676. *Ibid.*, Art. 62(d).
677. *See* para. 103, *supra* .
678. *See* para. 124, *supra* .
679. *See* PA, Art. 63; para. 104, *supra* .
680. *See* para. 104, *supra* .
681. *See* paras 105–114, *supra* .
682. *See* e.g., PA, Arts 76 and 81.
683. *See* PA, Art. 55 as amended.
684. *Ibid.*
685. *See* paras 117 and 119, *supra* .

Administration.[686] The conversion requires that the conditions for granting the newly requested rights be properly met.[687]

Utility models are distinguished from industrial designs on the basis of the protection granted to ornamental characteristics by the latter and to functional characteristics by the former.[688] A creation with both ornamental and functional characteristics could in principle be protected under both the utility model and the industrial design regimes,[689] provided the ornamental elements of the design are not determined or imposed by the functional characteristics of the product.[690] If an industrial design has already been protected as a utility model – on the basis of its functional characteristics – by one person, it may not be registered as an industrial design by a different person.[691]

686. *See* PA, Art. 23 as amended.

687. Thus, the conversion of a utility model certificate petition into a patent petition will require compliance with the additional provisions applicable to the latter.

688. *See* I.A. Poli, *El modelo de utilidad,* 39.

689. *Ibid.*, 40.

690. *See* Decree-law 6673, of 1963, Art. 6(c).

691. *See* *Collo GmbH v. Sed Metal*, National Court of Appeals for Federal Civil and Commercial Matters I, 27 Mar. 1987, *Revista del Derecho Industrial*, vol. 10, 297.

Chapter 4. Trademarks

§1. Sources: Legislation

130. Argentine trademark law is characterized by legislative stability and a wide basis of judicial decisions. The basic statute governing this area is Law 22,362 (hereinafter, the Trademark Act or TA), enacted in 1980. Law 22,362 replaced Law 3,975 of 1900. Although Law 22,362 formally enacted a total replacement of Law 3,975, the change in practical terms was far less drastic than total replacement would suggest. Law 22,362 is based on the text of Law 3,975, with modifications that had already been introduced largely by judicial decisions in Argentine trademark practice. Thus, for example, the possibility that unregistered trademark rights may prevail over rights derived from registered trademarks, presently established by Article 24(b) of the TA, had already been recognized by the courts in the famous *La vache qui rit* decision[692] even in the absence of statutory provisions to that effect in Law 3,975. Decree 27 of 2018 has introduced several amendments to Law 22,362.

131. In addition to the TA, the following statutory provisions applicable to trademarks may be mentioned:

(a) Decree 558, of 1981, including the regulations applicable to the implementation of the Trademark Act (hereinafter the TM Regs).
(b) Decree 42,366, of 1934, on the use of the word 'national'.
(c) Decree 7,243, of 1961, on the use of the word 'Interpol' and other related signs.
(d) Decree 2,976, of 1893, on signs belonging to the Red Cross.
(e) Decrees 4,066, of 1932; 5,296, of 1938; 24,797, of 1945; and 3,775, of 1946, on industrial property agents.
(f) Regulation 81, of the National Industrial Property Institute, on the registration of liens on trademarks.
(g) Law 24,664, on the protection of Olympic symbols.
(h) Decree 753, of 2000, on the protection of Mercosur symbols.
(i) Decree 97/2001 on the registration of trademarks including references to ecology.
(j) Law 26,355 on collective trademarks.

132. Several international treaties with effects in the trademark area have been ratified by Argentina. The following may be mentioned:

(a) The Montevideo Convention of 1889. It provides certain minimum levels of trademark protection, applicable in the different member countries.
(b) The Paris Convention, ratified by Laws 17,011 and 22,195.
(c) The TRIPS Agreement, ratified by Law 24,425.

692. *See Fromageries Bel, Société Anonyme v. Ivaldi, E.*, National Federal Court of Appeals for Federal and Administrative Matters, Civil and Commercial section, 28 Feb. 1961, *La Ley*, vol. 107 (1961), 67.

(d) The Treaty of Asunción, of 1991. It created the *Mercado Común del Sur*, or Mercosur, a common market comprising Argentina, Brazil, Paraguay, Uruguay. Although it includes few provisions expressly applicable to trademarks, its rules on the circulation of goods are likely to have significant consequences on the effects of trademarks, which presently are purely national in scope.

§2. Subject Matter of Protection

I. Signs that May Serve as Trademarks

133. Article 1 of the TA includes a list of signs that may be registered as trademarks. These include: one or more words, with or without conceptual content; drawings; commercial symbols; monograms; engravings; prints; seals; images; stripes; colour combinations applied in a specific place of a product or a package; combinations of letters and numbers; the special graphics of letters and numbers; advertisement phrases; reliefs with distinctive capacity; and any other sign with distinctive capacity.

The last element of this list is the defining one, since the fact that an element is not included in the list will not prevent trademark protection provided such element has distinctive potential.

Several rules have been developed with regard to the admission as trademarks of these different elements.

134. Nouns may be registered, provided that they are not descriptive of the product or service they are intended to identify[693] and that they do not induce the public into error as to the quality, nature or other aspects of such product or service.[694] The fact that a sign may have certain suggestive or 'educating' character does not prevent its protection as trademark.[695] If a trademark includes a descriptive noun as part of a more complex set of words, courts will examine the trademark as a whole to determine whether it has a distinctive quality. Thus, the Spanish equivalent of the words 'tobacco flower' was admitted as a valid registered trademark for tobacco products, on the basis that the trademark as a whole was distinctive, although it included the word 'tobacco'.[696]

Adjectives have been admitted as trademarks, provided they do not refer to the defining properties of the product or service they identify.[697] In this respect, verbs are subject to similar rules, although they are less likely – except in the case of services – to infringe the minimum requirements of trademark protection.

693. *See* TA, Art. 2(a).
694. *Ibid.*, Art. 3(b).
695. *See Empaques S.A. v. Empaca S.A.*, National Court of Appeals for Federal Civil and Commercial Matters III, 26 Apr. 1982, *Revista del Derecho Industrial*, vol. 6, 190.
696. *See Manufactura de Tabacos Imparciales S.A.*, National Federal Court of Appeals for Federal and Administrative Matters, Civil and Commercial section, 31 Jul. 1970, *La Ley*, vol. 142 (1970), 598.
697. *See Maprico S.A. v. Arlistan S.A.*, National Federal Court of Appeals for Federal and Administrative Matters, Civil and Commercial section I, 30 May 1972, *Jurisprudencia Argentina*, vol. 16 (1972), 122.

Words without conceptual content are less likely to violate the distinctive capacity requirements of the TA. However, such violation may result when the word is 'transparent' in the sense that it may be perceived as a creation based on words with a current meaning. If such transparency exists, and if the underlying words are descriptive of the product or service to be identified or induce the public into error, the trademark will not be accepted. Thus, the word *Blancarina* was rejected as a possible valid trademark;[698] such word was the result of putting together the Spanish words *blanca* (white) and *harina* (flour), 'white flour' being in fact the product that the trademark was intended to identify.

There are no specific prohibitions against foreign language words. However, such words may be 'transparent', either because the foreign language is well known by consumers – as is often the case with English – or because the foreign language is similar to Spanish – as is often the case with words from Latin languages. In those cases, the courts will tend to apply tests similar to those used with regard to Spanish words to determine whether the foreign words have distinctive capacity or may induce the public into error.[699]

135. Personal names are admitted as trademarks, provided the person whose name is used authorizes such use.[700] If that person has died, the authorization of the living heirs will be necessary.[701]

Similar rules apply when a trademark consists of the pseudonym or portrait of a person.[702]

136. Courts have generally rejected the validity of trademarks consisting of deformed versions of the usual name or description of the article to be identified, such as *Hasucar* instead of *azúcar* (sugar) and *Kezo* instead of *queso* (cheese).[703]

137. Drawings and other images have generally been admitted as trademarks, provided they have distinctive qualities.[704]

Reliefs such as those included in shoe soles or in tires have been admitted as trademarks,[705] provided they are not 'the necessary form of a product'.[706] This would exclude reliefs with functional characteristics from trademark protection.[707]

---

698. *See Blancarina S.R.L. v. Molinos Río de la Plata S.A.*, National Federal Court of Appeals for Federal and Administrative Matters, Civil and Commercial section, 12 Sept. 1967, *La Ley*, vol. 130 (1968), 712.
699. Prior to Law 22,362, there were restrictions on the protection of foreign language words as trademarks.
700. *See* TA, Art. 3(h).
701. *Ibid.*
702. *Ibid.*, Art. 3(h).
703. *See* L.E. Bertone & G. Cabanellas, *Derecho de marcas* (Buenos Aires: Heliasta, 1989), vol. 1, 328.
704. *See* J. Otamendi, *Derecho de marcas* (Buenos Aires: Abeledo-Perrot, 1989), 30 et seq.
705. *See* Official Comments to the TA, Art. 1.
706. *See* E.M. Botacchi, 'La forma del producto como marca', *Revista del Derecho Industrial* 7 (1985): 361. *See also* TA, Art. 2(c).
707. *See Saez Merino, J.*, National Court of Appeals for Federal Civil and Commercial Matters III, 19 Apr. 1985, *Revista del Derecho Industrial*, vol. 7, 1985, 356.

Bands and stripes are admissible as trademarks, provided they are placed in a way that identifies a product and does not have merely ornamental functions.[708]

138. Trademarks may consist of colour combinations.[709] The natural colour of a product may not be used as a trademark.[710] For colour combinations to be admissible as trademarks, they must be located in specific places of the products to be identified.[711]

139. Tri-dimensional trademarks are admissible under Argentine law.[712] Packaging may be registered as a trademark, provided it has distinctive qualities.[713] However, the necessary shape of a product may not be protected as a trademark.[714]

140. Trademarks consisting in combinations of the different elements described above are admissible, provided they have the distinctive qualities required for all types of trademarks.[715]

141. Advertisement phrases may be protected as trademarks, provided they are 'original'.[716] This implies a certain level of intellectual creation higher than is generally required for trademarks in general and going beyond the distinctiveness requirement applicable to all trademarks.[717] It is not necessary, however, that the advertisement phrase meet the creativity requirements applicable for copyright protection.[718] For a phrase to be protected under the trademark rules on advertisement phrases, it must be potentially applicable in advertisement or publicity.[719]

If a trademark consists in an advertisement phrase, this will be indicated in the trademark certificate once the trademark is registered.[720]

142. The TA lists several types of signs that are not considered to be trademarks:

(a) The names, words and signs that constitute the necessary or usual designation of the product or service to be distinguished or that are descriptive of its nature, function, qualities or other characteristics.[721] Although this provision applies literally only to the actual designation of goods or services or to signs that are descriptive of their characteristics, different court decisions have extended this prohibition to signs that merely suggest a good or service[722] or that include the

708. *See* Official Comments to the TA, Art. 1.
709. *Ibid.*
710. *See* TA, Art. 2(d).
711. *Ibid.*, Art. 1.
712. *See* Official Comments to the TA, Art. 1.
713. *Ibid.*
714. *See* Botacchi, 'La forma del producto'.
715. *See* Otamendi, *Derecho de marcas*, 42 et seq.
716. *See* TA, Art. 3(j).
717. *See* J. Otamendi, 'El uso y otras cuestiones de la nueva Ley de Marcas', *La Ley* (1981-D): 911.
718. *See* *Mazza S.A. v. Dirección Nacional de la Propiedad Industrial*, National Court of Appeals for Federal Civil and Commercial Matters III, 16 Aug. 1984, *Revista del Derecho Industrial*, vol. 8, 1986, 73.
719. Comp. Otamendi, *Derecho de marcas*, 50.
720. *See* TM Regs, Art. 25.
721. *See* TA, Art. 2(a).
722. *See* Otamendi, *Derecho de marcas*, 63.

name of the good or service together with other words or signs.[723] It has, therefore, become difficult to distinguish between necessary or usual designations – barred as trademarks – and purely evocative trademarks, which do not actually restrict the possibility for third parties to properly identify with other signs their goods or services.[724] If a trademark is characterized as evocative, it will still be valid and registrable, but it will be qualified as 'weak' for the purposes of determining the scope of the rights derived from such trademark.[725]

(b) The names, words, signs and advertisement phrases that have become part of the general usage before registration is requested.[726] If a registered trademark becomes generally used as the name of a good or service, this will not cause the immediate loss of the pre-existing rights on such trademark.[727]

(c) The shape of products.[728] It is debatable whether this restriction extends to all trademarks on the form of a product or only to those in which the form chosen as a trademark is the necessary form of the product to be identified. Several decisions[729] and authors[730] understand that the restriction only applies to the necessary form of a product. However, the text of the law makes no distinction between necessary and unnecessary forms of products.

(d) The natural or intrinsic colour of products or one colour applied on such products.[731]

143. The TA also lists several types of signs that may practically act as trademarks but that are inadmissible as legally protected trademarks, namely the following:

(a) A trademark that is identical to an already registered trademark or to a trademark regarding which an application has been previously filed, provided the pre-existing trademark applies to the same products or services.[732] This limitation applies only if the pre-existing trademarks are still in effect – that is, they have not lapsed or expired – and if the registration application is still viable – that is, it has not been abandoned or rejected.[733] In the context of these provisions, the concept of 'same

723. For example, the trademark 'Mi té' (My tea), for tea. *See La Tijuca S.A. v. La Industrial Paraguaya S.A.*, Federal Supreme Court, 12 Mar. 1969, *Fallos*, vol. 273, 168.
724. *See* Otamendi, *Derecho de marcas*, 62 et seq.
725. *Ibid.*, 65.
726. *See* TA, Art. 2(b).
727. *See* Otamendi, *Derecho de marcas*, 74, 75.
728. *See* TA, Art. 2(c).
729. *See* J. *Saez Merino*, National Court of Appeals for Federal Civil and Commercial Matters III, 19 Apr. 1985, *Revista del Derecho Industrial*, vol. 7, 1985, 356.
730. *See* Otamendi, *Derecho de marcas*, 76 et seq.
731. *See* TA, Art. 2(d).
732. *Ibid.*, Art. 3(a).
733. *See Dirección de Vigilancia y Disposición Final de la Propiedad Enemiga v. Roger & Gallet de Paris*, National Federal Court of Appeals for Federal and Administrative Matters, Civil and Commercial section, 7 Apr. 1960, *La Ley*, vol. 100 (1960), 767.

products or services' extends to products or services regarding which use of an identical trademark is likely to cause confusion to the relevant public.[734]

(b) A trademark that is similar to an already registered trademark or to a trademark regarding which an application has been previously filed, provided the pre-existing trademark applies to the same products or services.[735] The difference with the situation described in (a), above, is that in this case similarity is enough to prevent the protection of the trademark. This similarity is determined on the basis of the possibility of confusion between the pre-existing and new trademark,[736] taking into account elements such as the following: the visual, phonetic and conceptual similarity of both trademarks;[737] the perception by the relevant consumers;[738] the type of products involved; the consumption and purchasing habits with regard to such products;[739] and generally any other aspect that may bear on the perception by the public of the signs involved.[740]

(c) Denominations of origin. The prohibition is applicable regardless of whether they refer to foreign or domestic origins.[741] For purposes of this rule, a denomination of origin is defined as the name of a given country, region or geographical area that is used to designate a product originating in such territories and whose qualities and characteristics are exclusively determined by the geographical environment. The definition also includes geographical areas that are determined or defined for purposes of identifying certain products.[742]

The legal definition of 'denominations of origin' is open to criticism. The qualities and characteristics of products are not 'exclusively determined by the geographical environment' even in traditional cases such as Port wine. Case law has followed a rather independent construction of the concept of 'denominations of origin'. For example, it has rejected applications for the registration as trademarks of the names of different villages in the Cognac region in France on the grounds that

734. *See* *Sistemas Operativos Argentinos S.A. v. Saipe S.A.*, National Court of Appeals for Federal Civil and Commercial Matters II, 15 Mar. 1983, *Revista del Derecho Industrial*, vol. 7, 1985, 123.

735. *See* TA, Art. 3(b).

736. *See* Otamendi, *Derecho de marcas*, 80.

737. *See* L.E. Bertone & G. Cabanellas, *Derecho de marcas* (Buenos Aires: Heliasta, 1989), vol. 2, 41 et seq.

738. *Ibid.*, 32 et seq.

739. *Ibid.*

740. *See* *Sportlandia S.A. v. Vilas, G.*, National Court of Appeals for Federal Civil and Commercial Matters II, 5 May 1981, *Revista del Derecho Industrial*, vol. 4, 1982, 644.

741. *See* TA, Art. 3(c).

742. For example, the Cognac region, which is recognized as such for purposes of defining denominations of origin, regardless of its existence for other geographical or political purposes.

this was an indirect method to appropriate the denomination of origin function that such names could potentially play.[743]

(d) Trademarks that are likely to induce to error with regard to the nature, properties, merit, quality, manufacturing techniques, function, origin, price or other characteristics of the products or services to be distinguished by such trademarks.[744]
(e) Words, drawings and other signs contrary to morals.[745]
(f) The letters, words, names, logos or symbols that are used or that must be used by the Argentine government, provinces, municipalities and religious or health organizations.[746]
(g) The letters, words, names or symbols used by foreign nations and by international organizations that have been recognized by the Argentine government.[747] The exclusion does not extend in this case to foreign provinces, municipalities or religious or health organizations.
(h) The name, pseudonym or portrait of a person without such person's consent or without the consent of the relevant heirs.[748]
(i) The designation of activities, as well as corporate and partnership names, provided they describe an activity and are used to distinguish products.[749] The prohibition is meant to prevent the registration of this type of trademarks for defensive purposes,[750] a practice that was common before the enactment of Law 22,362. This prohibition has been criticized on the ground that its relevant scope may be adequately dealt with by means of more basic provisions against misleading and descriptive trademarks.[751] The prohibition does not extend to letters, words or other signs that are part of the designation of activities or of corporate and partnership names, provided they have sufficient distinctive capacity as required by the usual trademark principles.[752]
(j) Advertisement phrases lacking originality.[753]

---

743. *See Destilico S.R.L. v. Institute National des Apellations d'Origine des Vins et des Eaux de Vie*, National Federal Court of Appeals for Federal and Administrative Matters, Civil and Commercial section, 14 Sept. 1967, *La Ley*, vol. 131 (1968), 1138. Denominations of origin are specifically protected by Laws 25,380 and 25,966. *See* E.M. Schiavone, Indicaciones geográficas y denominaciones de origen, in R.A. Etcheverry (dir.): *Código de Comercio y normas complementarias* (Buenos Aires: Hammurabi, 2006), vol. 6, 55.
744. *See* TA, Art. 3(d).
745. *Ibid.*, Art. 3(e).
746. Article 3(f).
747. *Ibid.*, Art. 3(g).
748. *Ibid.*, Art. 3(h).
749. *Ibid.*, Art. 3(i).
750. *See* Official Comments to the TA, Art. 3.
751. *See* TA, Arts 2(a) and 3(d).
752. *Ibid.*, Art. 3(i).
753. *Ibid.*, Art. 3(j). *See* para. 141, *supra* .

II. Different Categories of Trademarks

144. Argentine statutes and court law have distinguished different categories of trademarks, with distinct legal effects.[754] The following may be mentioned:

(a) On the basis of the type of signs that constitute a trademark, the following categories have been distinguished[755] and are usually employed in legal practice: Words, with or without conceptual meaning; drawings; commercial symbols; monograms; engravings; prints; seals; images; stripes; colour combinations; wrapping; packaging; letters and numbers combinations; the special configuration of letters and numbers; advertisement phrases; reliefs; and other signs with distinctive capacity. Each of these categories is subject to specific rules, described in this chapter, with regard to matters such as the determination of their distinctive capacity or of the rights granted in terms of protection against confusion with other signs.

(b) Fantasy trademarks: This category includes the so-called fanciful trademarks and arbitrary trademarks. It covers words without meaning, as well as words whose usual meaning is unrelated to their trademark use. Fanciful trademarks may be evocative, and as such they may be disqualified if they exceed the evocative strength allowed by Argentine courts.[756]

(c) Evocative or suggestive trademarks: These trademarks are allowed provided they do not hinder the identification by other parties of the goods or services identified by the suggestive trademark.[757] A trademark qualifies as suggestive depending on its perception by the public, regardless of whether it is a new sign or implies the use of a pre-existing word or sign. If a sign may be confused with the name or sign used to identify a good or service, it will be deemed to exceed the acceptable level of suggestion. Suggestive trademarks may also be considered invalid if they are misleading about the nature or other characteristics of the goods or services to which such trademarks refer.

(d) Descriptive trademarks: They describe the nature, function, qualities or other characteristics of the goods or services to which they apply.[758] They are unacceptable as trademarks under Argentine law.[759]

(e) Meaningful trademarks: They consist of words with conceptual meaning. They are subject to the same rules as fantasy trademarks. They will be declared invalid if they are descriptive trademarks, as defined above, or if they are suggestive trademarks that exceed the acceptable level of evocative strength.

754. *See* Bertone & Cabanellas, *Derecho de marcas*, vol. 1, 236 et seq.
755. *See* TA, Art. 1.
756. *See* *Llorca Hnos. S.R.L. v. Nestle Argentina S.A.*, National Court of Appeals for Federal and Administrative Matters, Civil and Commercial section, 7 Mar. 1961, *La Ley*, vol. 107 (1961), 63.
757. *See* para. 142, *supra* .
758. *See* TA, Art. 2(a).
759. *Ibid.*

(f) Denominative trademarks: They consist of the generic denomination of a good or service. They are unacceptable as trademarks[760] and are more properly identified as mere generic terms.

(g) Strong and weak trademarks: This distinction is used in Argentine court decisions.[761] The distinction does not apply a radical difference between strong and weak trademarks; rather, there is a gradual loss of 'strength', depending on certain circumstances. This loss of 'strength' implies that the protection granted to a trademark with respect to potentially confusing signs becomes more limited. Weakness may result from reasons inherent to the trademark or from reasons external to that sign. The first group of reasons relates to the proximity of a trademark to a generic term as well as to the suggestive character of the trademark.[762] A reason external to the trademark itself is the fact that certain elements of the trademarks have been widely used for similar goods or services.[763]

(h) Compulsory trademarks: This concept existed under Law 3,975. It includes trademarks that must be used with regard to certain goods.[764] The TA has repealed the provisions requiring the use of compulsory trademarks.

(i) Product and service trademarks: The TA introduced this distinction into Argentine trademark law. Both types of trademarks are generally governed by the same rules, with certain exceptions. Trademarks implying the designation of activities may not be used as product trademarks.[765] Also, in the case of service trademarks, the physical relation between the trademark and the subject matter to be identified is less precise; this bears on matters such as the area of exclusive rights granted to trademark owners and the meaning of use for purposes of complying with compulsory use requirements.

(j) Registered and factual trademarks: In principle, full rights on a trademark only result after registration of such trademark.[766] However, by means of statutory provisions[767] and court decisions,[768] Argentine law has greatly expanded the rights derived from trademarks that are used but not registered. This use may be claimed to oppose the registration of the trademark by another party.[769] Prior use may also

760. *Ibid.*
761. *See Panificación Argentina v. Marcolla, L.*, National Court of Appeals for Federal and Administrative Matters, Civil and Commercial section, 5 Sept. 1967, *La Ley*, vol. 128 (1968), 670.
762. *See Organo Argentina S.A. v. Laboratorio Inca de Especialidades Medicinales S.A.* National Court of Appeals for Federal and Administrative Matters, Civil and Commercial section, 19 Sept. 1967, *La Ley*, vol. 128, 996.
763. *See Productos Stani S.A. v. Paulista S.A.*, National Court of Appeals for Federal Civil and Commercial Matters I, 22 Oct. 1981, *Revista del Derecho Industrial*, vol. 4, 1982, 679.
764. *See* Law 3,975, Art. 7.
765. *See* TA, Art. 3(i).
766. *Ibid.*, Art. 4.
767. *Ibid.*, Art. 24(b).
768. *See Fromageries Bel, Societe Anonyme v. Ivaldi, E.*, National Federal Court of Appeals for Federal and Administrative Matters, Civil and Commercial section, 28 Feb. 1961, *La Ley*, vol. 107, 67.
769. *See* TA, Art. 24(b).

serve as basis to prevent the use of the trademark by another person[770] and to recover damages against third parties that acted in bad faith using the trademark knowing its prior use by another person.[771] Nevertheless, the rights derived from factual trademarks are more limited than those derived from registered trademarks. In particular, registered trademarks are granted criminal law protection that is not available for unregistered trademarks.[772] Also, registration creates a presumption of knowledge by third parties of the registered ownership of the trademark.[773]

(k) Collective trademarks: They are governed by Law 26,355. They are defined as signs distinguishing products or services produced or rendered by associations formed with the purpose of developing a social economy.[774] Only associations duly registered as such and formed by producers or suppliers of services are allowed to register such trademarks. They are governed by the general trademark rules to the extent that they are compatible with Law 26,355. To be registered as such, the relevant application must include the regulations that will govern the use of the collective trademark.

(l) Well-known trademarks: A trademark is characterized as well known or 'notorious' if it is widely known by the relevant customers or potential customers in Argentina. It is then protected against use or registration by third parties.[775] The fact that a trademark is well known abroad would not be sufficient to obtain this level of protection. In general, the category of well-known trademarks has been used to protect unregistered foreign trademarks. However, the fact that a trademark is well known may also be used to extend its protection within Argentina, if it is already registered, or to strengthen its protection if it has been used within Argentina.[776]

(m) High reputation trademarks: This category has been recognized in court decisions.[777] These trademarks enjoy not only the protection granted to well-known trademarks, but also an additional protection in terms of the rights against dilution or against the coexistence of similar trademarks.[778]

(n) Defensive trademarks: They are registered with the purpose of preventing use or registration by third parties, and not with the intention of actual use by the owner. A trademark may be registered in several classes for defensive purposes, and

770. *Giuso, A. v. Société Anonyme des Usines Remy*, National Federal Court of Appeals of the City of Buenos Aires, 28 Jul. 1949, *La Ley*, vol. 57, 189.
771. *Ibid.*
772. *See* TA, Art. 31.
773. Protection of a non-registered trademark requires evidence of bad faith by the purported infringer or of the fact that the trademark was well known within Argentina.
774. *See* Law 26,355, Art. 1.
775. *See Mack Trucks, Inc. v. Aira, G.J.*, National Court of Appeals for Federal Civil and Commercial Matters I, 9 Oct. 1984, *Revista del Derecho Industrial*, vol. 8, 68.
776. *See Santa Ana Maderas S.A. v. Siam Di Tella Ltda.*, National Court of Appeals for Federal Civil and Commercial Matters II, 28 May 1982, *Revista del Derecho Industrial*, vol. 6, 1984, 212.
777. *See Hijos de Antonio Barcelo S.A. v. Sancor Cooperativas Unidas* National Court of Appeals for Federal Civil and Commercial Matters I, 16 Jun. 1981, *Revista del Derecho Industrial*, vol. 4, 1982, 678.
778. *Ibid.*

such registration may remain indefinitely in effect, provided the trademark is used in connection with at least one of such classes.[779]

(o) Reserve trademarks: Argentine law does not require an immediate use or intention to use with regard to registered trademarks. However, if use does not take place within five years in at least one class, the registration may lapse.[780]

(p) National and foreign trademarks: This distinction is purely theoretical. Argentine law does not distinguish between national and foreign trademarks.[781] If a trademark is registered in Argentina, the fact that it is also registered abroad does not alter the rights resulting from the local registration. However, trademarks that qualify for protection under the Paris Convention will enjoy the same rights under Argentine law.

§3. Conditions of Protection

145. The basic condition for full protection of a trademark is its registration.[782] Use is not a requisite for protection, although lack of use may result in the lapsing of the trademark rights after a period of five years.[783] In spite of the basic principle that registration is the basis of trademark rights, several rights result from the mere use of a trademark, regardless of its registration, namely the following:

(a) The prior user of a trademark may oppose the registration of the same trademark by another party.[784]

(b) The user of a trademark may have a registered trademark declared void if the person who obtained the registration knew or should have known that the user had prior rights on the trademark.[785]

(c) The user of a trademark may file civil actions to obtain the indemnification of the damages caused by an infringing use of such trademark.[786]

(d) The user of a trademark may request a court injunction ordering the termination of the use of the trademark in violation of the rights obtained by the prior user.[787]

(e) The user of a trademark is not allowed to obtain the special preliminary measures granted by the TA in favour of registered trademark owners.[788] However, the user of an unregistered trademark may obtain the general preliminary measures – injunction, attachments, etc. – provided by the general rules on civil procedure

779. *See* TA, Art. 5.

780. *Ibid.*

781. *See A. Natterman & Cie. GmbH v. Inca Laboratorios de Especialidades Medicinales S.A.* National Court of Appeals for Federal Civil and Commercial Matters III, 10 Aug. 1982, *Revista del Derecho Industrial*, vol. 6, 1984, 217.

782. *See* TA, Art. 4.

783. *Ibid.*, Art. 5.

784. *See* TA, Art. 24(b); Otamendi, *Derecho de marcas*, 14.

785. *Ibid.*

786. *See* para. 145(j), *supra* .

787. *Ibid.*

788. *See* Otamendi, *Derecho de marcas*, 13.

to assure the effectiveness of all types of private rights, including those of the owners of factual trademarks.

(f) The user of an unregistered trademark is not protected by the criminal law provisions included in the TA in favour of registered trademark owners.[789] However, the users of unregistered trademarks may be protected by the criminal law provisions against unfair competition,[790] though these are much broader than those enacted in favour of registered trademarks and do not specifically contemplate trademark violations as a type of unfair competition.

§4. Formalities: Procedure for Obtaining Protection, Establishing and Maintaining Trademarks

146. Full protection for trademarks is obtained under Argentine law by means of the registration of the trademark.[791] Registration takes place in connection with specific classes of goods and services, which are listed in the TM Regs[792] and which are based on the international classification provided by the Nice agreement.[793]

147. The registration procedure begins with a filing application to be presented at the National Industrial Property Institute.[794] One application must be filed for each class.[795] The application must include the name, real domicile and electronic domicile of the applicant, as well as a description of the trademark and the indication of the goods or services to which it will apply.[796] The registration application may also be filed in specially authorized post offices located in the provinces,[797] in which case the application will be recorded in a special book located at such offices[798] and then sent for purposes of the continuation of the registration procedure to the National Industrial Property Institute.[799]

If the applicant is a juridical person, the application must also include indication of the relevant registration data of such person.[800]

The application must also include the elements necessary for the printing of the publications required by the TA.[801] Also, if the trademark includes a drawing, image or engraving, eleven copies of such elements must be included together with the application.[802]

789. *See* TA, Art. 31.
790. *See* Otamendi, *Derecho de marcas*, 15.
791. *See* TA, Art. 4.
792. Article 1.
793. *See* Official Comments to the TA, Preliminary Message.
794. *See* TA, Art. 10 as amended.
795. *Ibid.*
796. *Ibid.*
797. *See* TM Regs, Art. 5.
798. *Ibid.*, Art. 6.
799. *Ibid.*, Art. 7.
800. *Ibid.*, Art. 8.
801. *Ibid.*, Art. 9.
802. *Ibid.*, Art. 10.

The special domicile to be included together with the application is valid for purposes of establishing local jurisdiction and for purposes of serving notice with regard to judicial complaints related to voidness, revindication or lapsing of the trademark, as well as with regard to notices related to the registration procedure.[803] However, in the case of the aforementioned judicial complaints, the special domicile will not prevent the applicability of the procedural rules that grant more extended terms to defendants located outside the court's jurisdiction for purposes of answering the complaint.[804] The defendant's real domicile will be used to determine the applicability of such extended terms.[805]

148. The registration application may be filed by any of the following:

(a) the individual requesting the registration;
(b) a duly authorized officer of a legal entity requesting the registration;
(c) an attorney-in-fact with a general management power of attorney;
(d) a certified industrial property agent.[806]

If the industrial property agent files an application acting as attorney-in-fact, it is not necessary for the agent to include a copy of the power of attorney together with the application, but such copy may be required by an interested party or by the registration authorities.[807] If such agents act for a third party without having the necessary powers of attorney, they must obtain such powers within sixty days from the filing.[808] Thereafter, the application will only be valid if it is ratified by the person in whose name it was made.[809]

149. A statutory fee must be paid before the registration application is filed.[810] This is a condition for the continuation of the registration procedure.[811]

150. Once the registration application is filed, the applicant is given a receipt that identifies the filing and indicates the time when it was presented.[812]

Within a term of ten days, the registration authorities determine whether the formal requirements of the application have been met and whether the classes for which the trademark application was filed agree with the goods or services for which the trademark will be used according to the application.[813] If there are mistakes or missing elements in the filing, the registration authorities inform the applicant about such obstacles.[814] Thereafter, the applicant has a ten-day term within which to cure such defects or refute the authorities' observations.[815] Ten days after the expiration of

803. *See* TA, Art. 11.
804. *Ibid.*
805. *Ibid.*
806. *See* TM Regs, Art. 30.
807. *Ibid.*, Art. 31.
808. *Ibid.*
809. *Ibid.*
810. *Ibid.*, Art. 3.
811. *Ibid.*, Art. 4.
812. *Ibid.*, Art. 11.
813. *Ibid.*, Art. 12.
814. *Ibid.*
815. *Ibid.*

this term, the registration authorities must decide whether to order the publication of the trademark application or to reject such application.[816]

151. Once the application is declared to have been properly filed, pursuant to the procedure described above, a summary of the application is published for one day in the Trademark Bulletin.[817] This summary includes the following: the name of the applicant; the date of filing of the application; the goods or services to be distinguished by the trademark; the class in which they are included; the number of the application; the priority being invoked, if any; and the number of the industrial property agent acting in the registration procedure, if any.[818]

Within thirty days from this publication, the registration authorities must issue a report on the acceptability and precedents of the application,[819] and any interested third parties may file opposition petitions against the registration application.[820] These opposition petitions, which must be filed electronically with the registration authorities, must indicate the name and the real and electronic domiciles of the opponent, and the basis of the opposition.[821]

Within fifteen days from the termination of the term for the filing of opposition petitions, the trademark registration applicant must be notified of the contents of the report issued by the registration authorities and of the opposition petitions filed against the application, together with a copy of such opposition petitions.[822]

If, at this stage, the only obstacle for registration is the report issued by the registration authorities, the applicant has a ninety-day term within which the objections raised in that report must be answered, or the defects indicated in that report corrected.[823] After such term has expired, the report has been answered or the defects cured, the registration authorities have a ninety-day period within which to issue a decision as to the registration application.[824]

If an opposition petition has been filed against the trademark registration application, the parties may reach an agreement as to such opposition.[825] If no such agreement is reached and the opposition has not been withdrawn by the opponent, three months after the opposition has been notified, the administrative registration authorities must issue a decision as to such opposition.[826] This decision is reached after a procedure which allows the opponent to further develop the grounds of his or her opposition, and the applicant to answer the opposition;[827] both parties are allowed to present the evidence backing their claims.[828] Once a decision is reached, it may be

816. *Ibid.*
817. *See* TA, Art. 12 as amended.
818. *See* TM Regs, Art. 13.
819. *See* TA, Art. 12 as amended.
820. *Ibid.*, Art. 13.
821. *Ibid.*, Art. 14 as amended.
822. *See* TM Regs, Art. 15.
823. *Ibid.*, Art. 16.
824. *Ibid.*
825. *See* TA, Art. 16 as amended.
826. *Ibid.*
827. *Ibid.*, Art. 17 as amended.
828. *Ibid.*

appealed within thirty working days following its notification, before the National Court of Appeals for Federal Civil and Commercial matters.[829]

152. Although the TA provides that a trademark may lapse after five years of non-use,[830] it is not necessary to comply with any formality with regard to such use, unless a party files a complaint requesting the judicial declaration of such lapsing, in which case it is necessary to produce evidence showing that the trademark has been duly used.[831]

153. Renewal of trademark registrations, upon their expiration, is basically governed by the same procedural rules applicable to registration applications.[832] In practice, however, the procedure is much simpler.[833] No opposition by third parties is permitted[834] and control by the registration authorities is limited to the formal aspects of the renewal petition, and not to the substantive elements of the trademark.[835] However, it is necessary to file, together with the renewal petition, a sworn affidavit stating that the trademark whose registration is to be renewed has been used during the preceding five years in connection with the marketing of a product or the rendering of a service or as part of the designation of an activity.[836]

154. Administrative decisions regarding the registration procedure, other than those related to opposition by third parties, are subject to appeal before the Federal Courts for Civil and Commercial Matters.[837] These judicial appeals must be filed within thirty days as from service of notice of the decision being appealed.[838]

§5. Ownership and Transfer

155. Argentine trademark law follows a policy of broad permissiveness with regard to the persons who may own a trademark or request a trademark registration. Only a 'legitimate interest' of the owner or applicant is required,[839] and even this requirement is interpreted liberally by the courts and administrative agencies. In fact, for purposes of obtaining a trademark registration, it is only necessary to show that the applicant is an individual or a legal entity.

No restrictions are imposed on foreign ownership of trademarks. Foreigners, as any other applicants, are only required to designate a special domicile within the city of Buenos Aires, for procedural purposes.[840]

156. Article 9 of the TA expressly allows the joint ownership of trademarks. Jointly owned trademarks are registered in the name of the different joint owners. Any

---

829. *Ibid.*
830. *Ibid.*, Art. 26.
831. *Ibid.*
832. *Ibid.*, Art. 20.
833. *See* Otamendi, *Derecho de marcas*, 212.
834. *Ibid.*
835. *See* Bertone & Cabanellas, *Derecho de marcas*, vol. 2, 209, 210.
836. *See* TA, Art. 5.
837. *Ibid.*, Art. 21 as amended. *See also* para. 151 *supra*.
838. *Ibid.*
839. *Ibid.*, Art. 4.
840. *Ibid.*, Art. 11.

individual joint owner may use the jointly owned trademark, without authorization from the other joint owners, unless a different agreement has been previously reached among the joint owners.[841] Licensing, assignment or renewal of the trademark requires the consent of all the joint owners;[842] again, it is possible to contractually elect a different mechanism for these transactions to become binding on all the joint owners. The opposition against the registration of infringing trademarks and other legal actions based on the jointly owned trademark may be filed by any of the individual joint owners, unless an agreement to the contrary has been previously made among the different joint owners.[843]

157. Since, under Argentine law, partnerships and business associations in general are legal entities,[844] they own directly their trademarks on the same basis as other legal entities, and not as a form of joint ownership by the partners or associates.

158. No restrictions exist under Argentine law with regard to the assignment of trademarks. Trademarks may be assigned together with the enterprise or going concern in the context of which they were used or exploited and separately or independently from the elements that originated the goodwill associated with such trademarks.[845]

The assignment or sale of a going concern implies the assignment, to the acquirer of the going concern, of the trademarks used in connection with such going concern, unless the parties agree otherwise.[846]

The assignment of a registered trademark only becomes effective against third parties once such assignment has been registered in the trademark registry.[847] This requirement becomes particularly important in the case of bankruptcy of the assignor or attachment of his assets. The same rule applies in the case of other trademark transfers such as those resulting from decedent estates.

159. It is possible to pledge trademarks. For the pledge to be effective, it must be registered in the trademark registry, as well as the chattel mortgage registry.[848] Once a pledge has been thus registered, every certificate to be issued with regard to the pledged trademark must indicate the existence of the registered pledge.[849]

160. There are no restrictions on trademark licenses under Argentine law. A license may be granted with total independence from any transfer of tangible assets or from control by the licensor of the licensee's activities. Quality of the licensee's production is considered to be a contractual matter, left for the parties to negotiate between themselves.

Trademark licenses may be simple or exclusive. The owner of the trademark retains the right to start legal actions against infringers, even if an exclusive license has been granted. However, in the case of criminal actions, the licensee may request

841. *Ibid.*, Art. 9.
842. *Ibid.*
843. *Ibid.*
844. *See* Law 19,550, Art. 2.
845. *Ibid.*, Art. 7.
846. *Ibid.*
847. *Ibid.*, Art. 6.
848. *See* Reg. 81, of the National Industrial Property Institute.
849. *Ibid.*

that the public prosecutor start the criminal action against infringers. Also, licensees may have civil actions against infringers on the basis of the damages suffered by their assets by reason of such an infringement; such actions are rare. The licensees' precautionary measures, such as preliminary injunctions, in case of trademark infringement are highly limited.[850] They do not exist under the TA and may only be obtained on the basis of general procedural rules and principles. They are seldom requested or granted.

If the license is granted by a foreign transferor, it is necessary for tax purposes to register it with the National Transfer of Technology Registry.[851] If the license agreement is not thus registered, it is still valid, but royalty remittances become subject to a higher withholding rate and may not be deducted from the licensee's taxable earnings.[852] Registration is automatic and does not imply a screening procedure or control over the provisions of the agreement.[853]

§6. Scope of Exclusive Rights

161. In principle, a registered trademark grants to its owner the exclusive right to use such trademark for the class of goods or services regarding which registration has taken place.[854] This basic principle is subject to multiple rules that determine the scope of the exclusive rights thus recognized in favour of the trademark owner.

162. The exclusive rights of the trademark owner extend not only to identical trademarks but also to those that are confusingly similar to the registered trademark. This implies that for the purpose of determining the scope of the trademark owner's exclusive rights, it is necessary to define what is meant by 'confusingly similar trademarks'. To this effect, several tests have been applied by the courts, as follows:

(a) Graphic or visual similarity: This is based on the visual perception of the trademark by the relevant persons. Visual similarity is in turn determined on the basis of several visual elements. In the case of trademarks that include words, the similar spelling of the relevant words will be taken into consideration.[855] In all trademarks, and particularly those that consist of colour combinations, the graphic similarity of the trademark as a whole will be taken into account.[856] In the case of tri-dimensional trademarks, the visual effect of the shape of the objects adopted as trademarks shall be taken into consideration.[857]
(b) Phonetic similarity: Courts will take into account the effect of the pronunciation of potentially similar trademarks on the public.[858] Differences in spelling may be

850. *See* Otamendi, *Derecho de marcas*, 280.
851. *See* Law 22,426, Art. 9.
852. *Ibid.*
853. *See* Decree 1,853, of 1993, Art. 8.
854. *See* TA, Art. 4.
855. *See* Otamendi, *Derecho de marcas*, 147.
856. *Ibid.*, 148, 149.
857. *Ibid.*, 149, 150.
858. *Ibid.*, 151, 152.

discarded if the actual pronunciation is confusing.[859] This applies even in cases of mispronunciation,[860] if such mispronunciation is likely to be common or is already common in practice. In the case of trademarks including foreign words, or words that suggest a foreign pronunciation, courts tend to weigh the way in which such words are actually pronounced by the public.[861] In the case of trademarks composed of letters or numbers that are likely to be pronounced separately, courts will take into account the effects of such pronunciation on the actual phonetic similarity of the signs being compared.[862]

(c) Ideological similarity: This is based on the ideas or concepts represented by the signs used as trademarks. The ideological similarity may result from the meaning of words, but also from the conceptual meaning of drawings.[863] Ideological similarity may also exist between a word and a drawing, if their conceptual meaning is similar.[864]

163. As a general rule, it is sufficient for one of the similarities described above to exist for a trademark to be considered confusingly similar to another trademark.[865] However, this and other rules developed by Argentine courts in connection with the definition of similarity are not inflexible or mechanically applied; rather, courts examine the circumstances of each case,[866] and they take into account multiple elements, so that a rather subjective evaluation of the overall similarity actually takes place.[867]

164. Argentine courts have taken into consideration the identity of the potential buyers of the goods or services identified with trademarks, to determine their similarity.[868] However, no clear test has evolved in connection to the weight to be given to such identity.[869] Some cases have taken into account the identity of the actual buyers of the goods and services involved.[870] Others, particularly in the case of pharmaceuticals, have taken into consideration the whole process of product selection and in particular

859. *Ibid.*
860. *Ibid.*
861. *Ibid.*, 152, 153.
862. *Ibid.*, 153.
863. *See Weil y Cía. v. Arrocera Argentina Frugone y Preve Ltda. S.A.*, National Federal Court of Appeals of the City of Buenos Aires, 15 Sept. 1939, *Jurisprudencia Argentina*, vol. 67 (1940), 951.
864. *See Caliquri, S. v. Salvado, A. et al.*, National Federal Court of Appeals of the City of Buenos Aires, 4 Dec. 1942, *Jurisprudencia Argentina*, vol. 1943-I (1940), 485.
865. *See Gente de Comunicación v. Editorial Atlántida S.A.*, National Court of Appeals for Federal Civil and Commercial Matters II, 27 Mar. 1981, *Revista del Derecho Industrial*, vol. 4, 1982, 648.
866. *See Molnlycke A.B. v. Johnson & Johnson*, National Court of Appeals for Federal Civil and Commercial Matters I, 10 Jul. 1981, *Revista del Derecho Industrial*, vol. 4, 659.
867. *See Astra S.A. v. Bel-Men S.R.L.*, National Court of Appeals for Federal and Administrative Matters, Civil and Commercial section, 31 Mar. 1965, *La Ley*, vol. 119, 49.
868. *See Riera, C. v. Sumotar S.R.L.*, National Court of Appeals for Federal Civil and Commercial Matters II, 20 Aug. 1982, *Revista del Derecho Industrial*, vol. 6, 1984, 182.
869. *See* Bertone & Cabanellas, *Derecho de marcas*, vol. 2, 32 et seq.
870. *See Compler S.A. v. Esbelta S.A.*, National Court of Appeals for Federal Civil and Commercial Matters II, 29 Sept. 1981, *Revista del Derecho Industrial*, vol. 4, 1982, 667.

the need to obtain a medical prescription for the products involved.[871] Other cases have taken into account the price of the goods involved, based on the assumption that consumers are more careful in the selection of highly priced items.[872]

165. Always within the framework of a flexible and non-mechanical application of the similarity criteria related to trademarks, Argentine courts have used a number of additional tests or rules that bear on the outcome of the comparison between different trademarks. The following are particularly relevant:

(a) Trademarks must be compared as a whole, before any analysis of their parts is made for purposes of applying the rules on similarity.[873] This takes into account the fact that consumers have an immediate non-analytical perception of trademarks. However, certain decisions[874] have followed the *mot vedette* theory, focusing the comparison in the main word or element of trademarks.
(b) Similarities are more relevant than differences.[875] A trademark will not be considered dissimilar simply on the basis that it includes elements that are not found in the trademark with which it is being compared.[876] In this context, it is not necessary that the elements that are considered *similar* be identical with each other; it is enough if the similar elements of the trademarks being compared create confusion in the relevant consumer group.[877]
(c) Certain syllables are considered more significant for comparison purposes than the rest of the words used as trademarks. In particular, the first syllable tends to receive more weight in trademark comparisons,[878] while the last syllable is generally given less weight than the remaining syllables of verbal trademarks.[879]

871. *See Cutter Laboratories v. Biobasal AG*, National Court of Appeals for Federal Civil and Commercial Matters III, 26 Nov. 1981, *Revista del Derecho Industrial*, vol. 4, 1982, 664.
872. *See Peugeot S.A. v. Calefones Heineken*, National Court of Appeals for Federal and Administrative Matters, Civil and Commercial section, 5 Apr. 1967, *La Ley*, vol. 128, 993.
873. *See Standard Oil Co. v. Ciba S.A.*, National Court of Appeals for Federal and Administrative Matters, Civil and Commercial section II, 13 May 1974, *Jurisprudencia Argentina*, vol. 23, 211.
874. *See Alpes S.R.L. v. Bonafide S.A.*, National Court of Appeals for Federal and Administrative Matters, Civil and Commercial section, 6 Aug. 1959, *La Ley*, vol. 100, 747.
875. *See Fabripez S.A. v. Molinos Río de la Plata S.A.*, Special National Court of Appeals, 4 Nov. 1957, *La Ley*, vol. 92, 29.
876. *See Laboratorios Wander S.A. v. Laplacette, E. (suc.)*, National Court of Appeals for Federal and Administrative Matters, Civil and Commercial section, 31 Dec. 1958, *Jurisprudencia Argentina*, vol. 1959-IV, 638.
877. *See Odol S.A. v. Instituto Sidus Industrial y Comercial S.A.*, National Court of Appeals for Federal and Administrative Matters, Civil and Commercial section II, 26 May 1970, *La Ley*, vol. 140, 189.
878. *See Hell, R. v. Cía. Standard Electric Argentina S.A.*, National Court of Appeals for Federal and Administrative Matters, Civil and Commercial section, 13 Nov. 1963, *La Ley*, vol. 114, 531.
879. *See Hulytego S.A. v. Congoleum Nairn Inc.*, National Court of Appeals for Federal and Administrative Matters, Civil and Commercial section, 12 May 1959, *Jurisprudencia Argentina*, vol. 1959-IV, 641.

(d) Courts will take into account the actual phonetic use of verbal trademarks, even if such trademarks are visually different.[880]
(e) In the cases of trademarks combining verbal and non-verbal elements, courts will give weight to the impact of the combination on consumers but will pay special attention to the similarities of the verbal elements.[881]
(f) Courts will consider the physical elements on which the trademark is reproduced to ascertain its actual impact on consumers.[882]

166. Argentine courts use the distinction between weak and strong trademarks.[883] To the extent that a trademark loses 'strength', the protection granted to such trademark with respect to potentially confusing signs becomes more limited. Weakness may result from the proximity of a trademark to a generic term or from the suggestive character of a trademark.[884] It may also result if certain elements of the trademark have been widely used for similar goods or services.[885]

167. The exclusive rights of a trademark owner only extend with regard to the use of the trademark in connection with goods and services that are similar to those for which the allegedly infringed trademark has been registered. The legal classification of goods and services is indicative of similarity; however, the exclusive rights of the trademark owners extend to goods and services which, while placed in a different class, may interfere with the perception of the protected trademark.[886]

Several tests have been used to ascertain whether certain goods and services are relevant to determine the rights of a trademark owner. A presumption has been used to the effect that goods and services included in the same class in which the trademark has been registered are included within the scope of legal protection of such trademark.[887] Also, the perception of the relevant public has been taken into account to determine whether such public may suffer confusion with regard to the trademarks, used for different goods or services, that are being compared.[888] Another relevant factor has been whether the goods or services to which the exclusive rights of the trademark owner wish to be extended are sold or marketed in the same shops or by means of the same channels.[889]

---

880. *See Fieltros Industriales S.A. v. De San Agustin, C.D.*, Special National Court of Appeals, 4 Oct. 1957, *La Ley*, vol. 90, 421.
881. *See Della Rosa, C. v. Ferrum S.A.*, National Court of Appeals for Federal and Administrative Matters, Civil and Commercial section, 28 Feb. 1964, *La Ley*, vol. 115, 264.
882. *See Sportlandia S.A. v. Vilas, G.*, National Court of Appeals for Federal Civil and Commercial Matters II, 5 May 1981, *Revista del Derecho Industrial*, vol. 4, 1982, 644.
883. *See* para. 144(g), *supra* .
884. *Ibid.*
885. *Ibid.*
886. *See* Bertone & Cabanellas, *Derecho de marcas*, vol. 2, 83 et seq.
887. *See Frigorífico La Pampa S.A. v. Primera Cooperativa Arrocera Argentina*, Federal Court of Appeals of Paraná, 16 May 1968, *La Ley*, vol. 133, 924.
888. *See Urbin S.A. v. Bodegas Arizu S.A.*, Federal Supreme Court, 18 Jul. 1973, *El Derecho*, vol. 50, 138.
889. *See Panamericana de Plásticos S.A. v. Pan American World Airways Inc.*, National Court of Appeals for Federal and Administrative Matters, Civil and Commercial section II, 12 Jun. 1973, *Jurisprudencia Argentina*, vol. 20, 143.

168. Well-known trademarks are generally granted a more extensive protection than other trademarks.[890] Their exclusive rights will extend to a broader range of goods and services. There is no mathematical rule to this effect. There is no binary distinction between 'well known' and 'not well known' trademarks; rather, trademarks are more or less notorious or well known, and the more they meet such condition, the broader the protection courts will tend to grant them.[891]

169. With certain limitations, Argentine law admits defensive trademarks.[892] These trademarks exist, under Argentine law, when they are registered in several or all classes, with the intent of using them for only one or a few classes; the trademark registration may then remain in effect indefinitely in all the classes, provided the registration is renewed periodically.[893] However, if a registration in a given class is considered to be defensive – in the sense described above – courts will tend to construe narrowly the scope of goods and services regarding which the trademark owner has exclusive rights.[894] This limitation is frequently circumvented by means of registration in all possible classes.

§7. Limitations of the Scope of Trademark Protection

170. Argentine law does not include in its methodology the category of limited trademark protection. Limitations of the scope of trademark protection actually exist, but they are indirectly implemented by means of other legal concepts. Once a trademark is registered, it will grant exclusive rights to its owner with regard to certain goods and services. However, as described above,[895] certain trademarks may not be registered and, therefore, lack legal protection, and the scope of the exclusive rights derived from registration will vary depending on aspects such as whether the trademark is well known or defensive.[896]

In the context of this methodology, the fact that a trademark has not been used will not prevent the effectiveness of the full extent of its legal protection, provided it remains registered. However, lack of use will indirectly limit protection, since the trademark will not be well known and may be characterized as defensive.

Argentine law will not limit the scope of trademark protection due to deterioration or changes in the quality of the goods or services identified by the trademark. It is considered that the consequences of this deterioration or changes will bear directly on the value of the trademark and, therefore, on its profitability for the owner. A similar

890. *See* E. Aracama Zorraquín, 'La protección de las marcas notorias en los tribunales argentinos', *Revista Mexicana de la Propiedad Industrial y Artística* 1966 (1966): 373; J. Otamendi, 'La marca notoria', *La Ley* (1975-A): 1260; Bertone & Cabanellas, *Derecho de marcas*, vol. 2, 93 et seq.
891. *See Dami S.A. v. Adidas Sportschuhfabriken K.G.*, National Court of Appeals for Federal Civil and Commercial Matters III, 27 Sept. 1983, *Revista del Derecho Industrial*, vol. 7, 1985, 125.
892. *See* Bertone & Cabanellas, *Derecho de marcas*, vol. 2, 96 et seq.
893. *See* TA, Art. 26.
894. *See Pepsico Inc. v. Coppa y Chego S.A.*, National Court of Appeals for Federal Civil and Commercial Matters I, 18 Dec. 1981, *Revista del Derecho Industrial*, vol. 4, 1982, 763.
895. *See* s. 2, *supra* .
896. *See* s. 6, *supra* .

reasoning is applied in not limiting trademark protection in cases wherein the trademark is licensed without exercising proper controls over the licensee.

Tolerance of trademark violations will not limit the scope of trademark protection, except to the extent that the statute of limitations limits the legal actions that may be directed against such violations. However, a pattern of tolerance of certain infringing, or potentially infringing, conduct may lead the courts to a narrower construction of the scope of the trademark owner's rights.[897]

§8. Use Requirements

171. Until 1980, Argentine trademark law included no use requirements. This resulted in the extensive registration of trademarks with no intention to use them, with the purpose of assigning them – for a price – to future users of such trademarks.

Albeit imperfectly, the TA of 1980 halted this brisk business. It includes two basic provisions to this effect. Article 5 of the TA provides that a trademark registration may be renewed provided the trademark owner supplies evidence of having used the trademark during the five years preceding the expiration of the prior registration, in connection with the marketing of a product, the rendering of a service or the designation of an activity. To this effect, a sworn affidavit must be filed by the applicant.[898] In addition, Article 26 of the TA, as amended by Decree 27 of 2018 provides that any party or the relevant administrative authority may request the lapse of a trademark registration, if such trademark has not been used within Argentina with regard to certain goods or services included in the relevant registration, in the five years preceding the filing of such request, unless such use has not been possible for force majeure reasons. Use with regard to a similar or related good or service, or as designation of a business activity, is enough for registration to remain in place.

Article 26 of the TA, as amended by Decree 27 of 2018, also requires trademark owners to file a sworn affidavit with the relevant administrative authority, five years after registration and before expiration of the sixth year, describing the use made of the registered trademarks up to the date of such filing.

The basic rule under these provisions of Argentine law is that a trademark registration is subject to lapse for lack of use if such non-use has lasted five years or more. However, if use takes place before any complaint is filed requesting the lapse of the trademark registration, the previous non-use is cured, and a new period of five years must run its course before lapse for non-use may again result.

The lapse of a trademark registration due to lack of use is only effective as from the date in which the lapse has been judicially declared,[899] except in cases where the effect of non-use is to prevent the renewal of the trademark registration. In such case, the registration and its effects lapse together with the expiration of the registration term. Thus, the violation of the trademark rights derived from a registration is fully actionable, if such violation has taken place before the judicial declaration of the

897. *See* Bertone & Cabanellas, *Derecho de marcas*, vol. 2, 125 et seq.
898. *See* TA, Art. 20.
899. *See* E. Aracama Zorraquín, 'Sobre el tema del uso obligatorio de la marca', *El Derecho* 97 (1982): 920.

lapsing of the trademark, even if the trademark had not been used for the statutory five-year term.[900]

The loss of rights due to lack of use only affects those rights derived from the trademark registration. The trademark owner whose registration has lapsed for lack of use still retains the right to continue using the trademark – provided no third party rights are infringed – and retains also the rights derived from the goodwill and prestige associated with the trademark.[901] Also, if such trademark owner had previously used the trademark, such use will be taken into account in deciding future trademark conflicts, even if the statutory term of non-use had elapsed.

Strictly speaking, Argentine law does not provide a use obligation, since no fines or other sanctions are imposed for non-use.[902] Rather, the TA conditions the rights derived from trademark registration to certain rather weak requirements of use, basically devised to prevent the blocking of the trademark registry by purely speculative registrations.

172. For use to be considered effective under the requirements of the TA, it must meet several conditions. It must be open and public; purely internal conduct of an enterprise does not qualify as effective use.[903] Also, use must be economically significant, and not merely formal or symbolic.[904] In addition, the use of the trademark must be as such – that is, as a sign that identifies goods, services or activities, and not a use with non-distinctive purposes.[905] However, it is not necessary for the trademark to be physically applied to products.[906]

Conduct that is the mere preparation for future use does not satisfy the statutory requirements.[907] In a similar vein, advertisement or publicity is not the use required by the statute.[908] The use of trademarks in invoices and other commercial documentation is not sufficient use, unless specific goods or services are thus identified by the trademarks.[909]

In general, any type of marketing constitutes proper use under the TA's provisions examined herein, provided the trademark identifies – in the course of such marketing – specific goods, services or activities.[910] Thus, it is not necessary for sales to be involved; leases, barters or any other type of commercial use of the trademarks is sufficient.[911]

900. *See* Bertone & Cabanellas, *Derecho de marcas*, vol. 2, 252.
901. *See* I.A. Poli, 'Caducidad por falta de uso en la nueva Ley de Marcas', *Revista del Derecho Industrial* 3 (1981): 62.
902. *Ibid.*, 69.
903. *See* J. Otamendi, 'El uso y otras cuestiones de la nueva Ley de Marcas', *La Ley* (1981-D): 903.
904. *Ibid.*
905. *Ibid.*, 902, 903.
906. *See* E. Aracama Zorraquín, 'Sobre el tema del uso obligatorio de la marca', *El Derecho* 97 (1982): 911.
907. *See* Bertone & Cabanellas, *Derecho de marcas*, vol. 2, 265; but *see* E. Aracama Zorraquín, 'Sobre el tema del uso obligatorio de la marca', *El Derecho* 97 (1982): 911.
908. *See* Bertone & Cabanellas, *Derecho de marcas*, vol. 2, 262, 263; but *see* Otamendi, 'El uso y otras cuestiones', 902.
909. *See* Otamendi, 'El uso y otras cuestiones', 902.
910. *See* Bertone & Cabanellas, *Derecho de marcas*, vol. 2, 267.
911. *Ibid.*

For use to be effective, it must imply the commercial exploitation of the trademark, with purposes of identifying goods, services or activities; the use of the trademark rights to act against infringers is not the commercial use required by the TA.[912]

The TA does not impose quantitative standards for the minimum relevant use. The significance of a given use is determined on the basis of the normal commercial activities of the user.[913] It is not necessary for the use to have lasted for a given period, provided its time span is long enough for such use to qualify as significant.[914]

For the use to be legally relevant, it must take place within the Argentine territory.[915] However, it is not necessary for the use to have a wide geographical extension, and it may be focused in a given location or outlet.[916]

173. Argentine law does not require that the relevant use be directly made by the trademark owner.[917] It is enough that the use be made by a person authorized by the trademark owner, such as an employee, a licensee, a sublicensee or a franchisee.[918] It is not necessary that the use authorization be granted in writing or expressly; however, evidence of an authorization, having taken place before proceedings directed to determining the use of the trademark have started, has to be produced in such proceedings for the use requirement to be considered satisfied.

The use of the trademark in violation of the trademark owner's rights is not a relevant use for purposes of satisfying the TA's use requirements.[919] If the use was not authorized by the trademark owner at the time it took place, the irrelevance of such use may not be cured by means of the waiver of the trademark owner's rights against the infringer.[920] Such waiver is only effective, for purposes of creating a relevant use, to the extent that it implies an authorization for future use, and only the use-taking place after such authorization shall be considered relevant for purposes of satisfying the TA's use requirements.[921]

174. In principle, the relevant use is that of the trademark as it has been registered.[922] However, if the trademark is used with minor changes with respect to the way it has been registered, this will not affect such use as qualifying to meet the TA's use requirements.[923] A proper test, for these purposes, is to determine whether a consumer would identify the trademark as used with the trademark as registered.[924] However, if several similar but not identical registrations have been made by the same trademark owner, the use of only one of such variations will only be attributed to the

912. *Ibid.*, 268.
913. *See* Otamendi, 'El uso y otras cuestiones', 904.
914. *Ibid.*, 903.
915. *See* TA, Art. 26.
916. *See* Otamendi, 'El uso y otras cuestiones', 903 and 904.
917. *See* Poli, 'Caducidad por falta de uso', 73.
918. *See* Bertone & Cabanellas, *Derecho de marcas*, 275.
919. *See* E. Aracama Zorraquin, 'Sobre el tema del uso obligatorio de la marca', *El Derecho* 97 (1982): 915.
920. *Ibid.*
921. *See* Bertone & Cabanellas, *Derecho de marcas*, vol. 2, 275.
922. *See* Zorraquin, 'Sobre el tema', 911.
923. *Ibid.*, 918.
924. *See* Bertone & Cabanellas, *Derecho de marcas*, vol. 2, 280.

registered trademark that is identical or closer to the trademark that has been actually used.[925]

175. Lack of use may be justified due to force majeure.[926] This exists not only when use of the trademark becomes impossible, but also – as is common – when it becomes unbearably expensive.[927]

The following have been considered possible force majeure circumstances:[928] government action or rules making the use of the trademark impossible, such as a prohibition on marketing the goods to be identified with the relevant trademark; impossibility of obtaining raw materials, labour or other elements necessary to produce the goods or services to be identified with the relevant trademark; and legal disputes on the ownership of the trademark, etc.

§9. Duration of Protection: Renewal and Termination

176. Trademark registration in Argentina lasts for a ten-year period.[929]

Registration may be cancelled for lack of use, as described in the preceding section. Upon expiration of the statutory ten-year term, the effects of the registration lapse immediately and automatically.

177. In principle, the expiration of a trademark registration implies that the trademark owner loses all rights derived from the prior extinguished registration. As a result, if such prior trademark owner wishes to register the same trademark again, it will be in the same legal position as any other applicant, and priority will be determined on the basis of the timing of the new applications.[930] However, this termination of the rights derived from a trademark registration has been weakened in several cases by the courts. Thus, if a trademark whose registration has expired and which was actively used by the trademark owner before such expiration becomes the subject matter of a new application by a third party shortly after the registration expiration, courts have allowed an opposition to such new registration by the prior owner of the trademark.[931] Also, if both the owner of the previously registered trademark and third parties apply for registration of such trademark shortly after the expiration of the previous registration, courts will tend to give priority to the previous owner of the trademark, even if the third party has made a prior filing.[932] However, certain effects of the registration expiration are irreversible. In particular, criminal prosecution for trademark violations will not be possible with regard to conduct taking place after the registration has

---

925. *See* Poli, 'Caducidad por falta de uso', 71.
926. *See* TA, Art. 26 as amended.
927. *See* Bertone & Cabanellas, *Derecho de marcas*, vol. 2, 282.
928. *Ibid.*, 283 et seq.
929. *See* TA, Arts 5, 20.
930. *See United States Playing Card Co. v. Julio Laje*, Federal Court of Appeals of Buenos Aires, 17 Jun. 1940, *La Ley*, vol. 19, 12.
931. *See Philip's Gloeilampenfabriken v. Philadelphia Storage Battery Co.* Federal Supreme Court, 9 May 1941, Jurisprudencia Argentina, vol. 74, 342.
932. *See Camauer v. La Toja S.A.* Federal Supreme Court, 11 May 1942, *Jurisprudencia Argentina*, vol. 1942-II, 1019.

expired.[933] Also, after a reasonable period has elapsed from the expiration of the registration, no rights may any longer be claimed based on the prior registration, on the assumption that the identity of the previously registered trademark and its relation to its owners becomes lost in the perception of the relevant consumers.[934]

178. Trademark registrations may be renewed indefinitely for ten-year periods.[935] Renewal requires an application to that effect, together with a sworn affidavit stating that the trademark has been used in connection with goods, services or activities within the five years prior to renewal.[936] Use in connection with relevant goods, services or activities is necessary for renewal of the registration of the trademark thus used in all classes.[937]

Renewal implies that the new registration is identical to the original one.[938] If any changes are introduced, the rules applicable to new registrations will govern the application.[939]

Once the formal requirements for registration renewal have been met, such renewal is automatic.[940] Third parties are not allowed to file oppositions against the registration renewal.[941] If they consider that such renewal is invalid, they may file an action in court to have the trademark registration annulled due to lack of use or because the registration is null and void.

179. Several causes of termination of trademark rights are admitted under Argentine law, as follows:

- Renunciation of rights by the trademark owner.
- Expiration of the term of registration.
- Judicial annulment.
- Judicial declaration of lapsing due to lack of use.

These causes, expressly provided by Article 23 of the TA, are subject to different rules. Renunciation and annulment will be examined below. Expiration of the term of registration and lapsing due to lack of use have been previously examined.[942]

180. Renunciation, to become effective, must be express and unconditional.[943] It becomes fully effective from the moment in which it is entered into the trademark registry.[944] A renunciation limited to specific classes or products is possible; however,

933. *See* TA, Art. 31.
934. *See Dirección de Vigilancia y Disposición Final de la Propiedad Enemiga v. Roger & Gallet de Paris*, National Court of Appeals for Federal and Administrative Matters, Civil and Commercial section, 7 Apr. 1960, *La Ley*, vol. 100, 767.
935. *See* TA, Art. 5.
936. *Ibid.*, Art. 20.
937. *Ibid.*, Arts 5 and 26 as amended.
938. *See Graffigna Ltda. v. M. Beresiart*, Federal Court of Appeals of Buenos Aires, 7 Dec. 1925, *Patentes y Marcas*, 1925, 469.
939. *Ibid.*
940. *See* Otamendi, *Derecho de marcas*, 212.
941. *Ibid.*
942. *See* paras 171–177, *supra* .
943. *See* Bertone & Cabanellas, *Derecho de marcas*, vol. 2, 213.
944. *Ibid.*

it is not possible to make a renunciation as to partial aspects of the signs registered as trademarks.[945]

Argentine law does not recognize the abandonment of trademark rights.[946] Lack of enforcement of such rights may result in certain actions becoming barred due to the effects of the applicable statute of limitations. Abandonment does apply to trademark applications for which the steps leading to registration are not duly made by the interested parties.[947]

181. The annulment of trademarks under Argentine law may result from judicial decisions, or – in the case if annulment based on violation of the trademark registration rules – from a decision of the administrative authority, subject to appeal before the National Court of Appeals for Federal Civil and Commercial matters.[948]

Argentine law applies certain basic distinctions as to possible typcs of annulment, derived from the Civil and Commercial Code. If any interested party or the State may request the annulment, a situation characterized as absolute voidness exists. If only certain specific parties may claim or request the annulment, the situation is characterized as of relative voidness. Whether absolute or relative voidness exists will depend on the identity of the parties in whose interest the voidness is legally provided, as well as on whether there is a public interest in the declaration of such voidness.

A second distinction is between void and voidable acts or transactions. An act or transaction is void if the cause of annulment is evident and does not require complex investigations or factual determinations; if the cause of annulment does not meet such conditions, the act or transaction is voidable. If a void act or transaction is judicially annulled, the effects of the annulment are retroactive to the date in which the cause of the annulment was originated. If a voidable act or transaction is judicially annulled, the effects of the judicial annulment extend as from the moment of the judicial annulment declaration.

These distinctions are applicable to the annulment of trademarks.[949]

182. Article 24 of the TA lists the following causes of annulment of trademarks: trademarks registered in violation of the TA; trademarks registered by a person who, at the time of registration, knew or should have known that the trademarks belonged to another person; and trademarks registered with the purpose of selling the trademark rights, by a person who repeatedly makes that type of registration. Some of these categories, particularly the first one, are extremely broad. It is therefore convenient to outline, in more detail, the causes of annulment which are more commonly applicable under Argentine law, as follows:

(a) Lack of distinctive capacity. Registered trademarks with this characteristic are considered to be absolutely void.[950]

945. *Ibid.*
946. *Ibid.*, 214.
947. *See* TA, Art. 16.
948. *Ibid.*, Arts 23, 24 and 45.
949. *See* Bertone & Cabanellas, *Derecho de marca*, vol. 2, 214 et seq.
950. *Ibid.*, 222.

(b) Signs whose registration is not permissible, such as unwritten sounds. They are also considered to be absolutely void.[951]
(c) Trademarks that are identical to other trademarks registered for the same goods or services.[952] They are absolutely void.[953]
(d) Trademarks that are confusingly similar to other trademarks registered for the same goods or services. They are generally considered to be absolutely void.[954]
(e) Denominations of origin, registered as trademarks. They are absolutely void.[955]
(f) Trademarks likely to induce errors as to the nature, identity or characteristics of goods and services. These trademarks are absolutely void.[956]
(g) Trademarks contrary to public morality. They are absolutely void.[957]
(h) Trademarks consisting of signs belonging to public entities or to religious or health organizations. They are absolutely void.[958]
(i) Trademarks consisting in the name, pseudonym or portrait of persons who have not authorized such use. These trademarks are relatively void, and such voidness may only be claimed or opposed by the persons whose name, pseudonym or portrait has been used without proper authorization or by their heirs or assignees.[959]
(j) Use of the designation of activities as a trademark identifying goods. In this case, the trademark is considered to be absolutely void, as causing possible confusions in the public.[960]
(k) Advertisement phrases without originality. They are absolutely void.[961]
(l) Trademarks that have been registered in violation of procedural rules applicable to such registration, as in, for example, when the publications of the relevant application required by the TA are not made as legally provided. These trademarks are void if the infringements of the procedural rules are of such importance as to affect the rights of third parties or the essential functions of the registration procedure. Thus, if the domicile of the applicant is omitted in one of the applicable procedures, this will not cause the voidness of the registration procedure. When voidness does apply, pursuant to the test described above, such voidness will be absolute.[962]
(m) Trademarks belonging to third parties. These trademarks, if registered with the knowledge that they belong to third parties, or in circumstances in which such

---

951. *Ibid.*
952. *See* I.A. Poli, 'Das neue argentinische Markengesetz', *Gewerblicher Rechtsschutz und Urheberrecht. Internationaler Teil* (1982): 237.
953. *See* Bertone & Cabanellas, *Derecho de marcas*, vol. 2, 222.
954. *See* Poli, 'Das neue argentinische Markengesetz', 237.
955. *See* Official Comments to the TA, Art. 3.
956. *Ibid.*
957. *See* P. Di Guglielmo, 'Marcas inmorales y marcas contrarias al orden público', *La Ley* 144 (1971): 881.
958. *See* Bertone & Cabanellas, *Derecho de marcas*, vol. 2, 225.
959. *Ibid.*
960. *See* Official Comments to the TA, Art. 3.
961. *See* Bertone & Cabanellas, *Derecho de marcas*, vol. 2, 226.
962. *See* P.C. Breuer Moreno, *Tratado de marcas de fábrica y de comercio* (Buenos Aires: Abeledo, 1946), 502, 503.

knowledge should have existed, are absolutely void.[963] Although, under Argentine law, the basic rule is that trademarks only become the property of a person upon registration, in the context of this cause of annulment, a trademark is considered to belong to a third party if it has been publicly used by such third party.[964] In the case of foreign trademarks, this condition is satisfied if the trademark is publicly used within Argentina or has acquired a significant reputation in this country.[965] Once evidence as to the public use or reputation of the trademark is produced, courts will apply a presumption that the party who registered the trademark knew or should have known about the rights of the user with regard to such trademark.[966]

(n) Trademarks registered with the purpose of selling the trademark rights, by a person who repeatedly makes that type of registration. This cause of annulment is expressly provided by Article 24(c) of the TA. These trademarks are absolutely void.[967] However, it has been decided that such voidness becomes inapplicable if the trademark has been acquired by a third party acting in good faith.[968]

§10. Infringement and Remedies

183. Argentine law provides both civil and criminal remedies applicable in cases of infringement of trademark rights. Only certain infringements result in both civil and criminal remedies. All infringements may result in civil remedies.

184. Only registered trademarks are entitled to criminal remedies.[969] These remedies are exercised by means of criminal proceedings, which may be initiated by public prosecutors.[970]

The following types of conduct may constitute criminal infringements of trademark rights:[971]

(a) Falsifying a trademark. This situation exists when a trademark is partially or totally reproduced without proper authorization.[972] Criminal infringement will also exist when the registered trademark is reproduced together with additional elements. Criminal infringement exists, in these cases, not only when the falsified

963. *See* TA, Art. 24(b).
964. *See Sportlandia S.A. v. Explomar S.R.L.* National Court of Appeals for Federal Civil and Commercial Matters III, 1 Dec. 1983, *Revista del Derecho Industrial*, vol. 6, 1984, 217.
965. *See A. Natterman & Cie. GmbH v. Inca Laboratorios de Especialidades Medicinales S.A.*, National Court of Appeals for Federal Civil and Commercial Matters III, 10 Aug. 1982, *Revista del Derecho Industrial*, vol. 6, 1984, 217.
966. *See Fratelli Fila S.p.A. v. Cueros Artesanales S.A.*, National Court of Appeals for Federal Civil and Commercial Matters I, 7 Apr. 1981, *Revista del Derecho Industrial*, vol. 4, 682.
967. *See Bonneterie Cevenole S.A. v. Roseda S.A. et al*, National Court of Appeals for Federal and Administrative Matters, Civil and Commercial section I, 10 Mar. 1980, *Revista del Derecho Industrial*, vol. 2, 1980, 393.
968. *Ibid.*
969. *See* TA, Art. 31.
970. *Ibid.*, Art. 32.
971. *Ibid.*, Art. 31.
972. *See* Otamendi, *Derecho de marcas*, 222.

trademark is manufactured, but also when it is affixed or merely held with illegal purposes.[973]

(b) Imitating a trademark. The essential element of this infringement is the possibility of creating a confusion with the registered trademark, as perceived by the relevant consumers.[974]

(c) Using a trademark without the authorization of the trademark owner. This violation exists when the use refers to a trademark identical to the registered one or confusingly similar to the latter.[975]

(d) Selling or offering to sell a falsified trademark or a trademark that has been illegally imitated. This refers to the sale of seals, stamps, packaging or other elements bearing an infringing trademark, even if such elements are not attached to a product nor actually used to identify goods or services, provided such elements may be used in the future to illegally identify goods or services.[976]

(e) Selling, offering to sell, or otherwise marketing goods or services identified with a falsified or illegally imitated trademark.

185. For a criminal infringement punishable under the TA to exist, it is necessary for the conduct attributed to the defendant to be a violation of a registered trademark owner's exclusive rights. Therefore, the extent of possible criminal infringements is a function of the extension of the exclusive rights of the trademark owner, which was previously examined.[977]

186. Criminal infringements of trademark rights are punishable with fines and imprisonment of up to two years.[978] In practice, criminal prosecutions based on the infringement of trademark rights are not common, and imprisonment is hardly ever imposed.

187. Any infringement of a trademark owner's exclusive rights results in certain possible civil remedies against the infringer. These civil remedies exist in favour of both registered and unregistered trademarks,[979] although the remedies are broader in the case of registered trademarks.

The trademark owner may obtain court orders requiring the termination of the use of the trademark.[980] Such owner may also obtain the attachment and sale of infringing merchandize and of the elements bearing illegally used trademarks.[981] The said owner may also obtain court orders requiring the destruction of the infringing trademarks and of any elements bearing such trademarks, from which it is practically impossible

973. *Ibid.*, 224, 225.
974. *Ibid.*, 226 et seq.
975. *See* Bertone & Cabanellas, *Derecho de marcas*, vol. 2, 163, 164.
976. *See* Otamendi, *Derecho de marcas*, 250, 251.
977. *See* paras 161–169, *supra* .
978. *See* TA, Art. 31.
979. *See Giuso, A. v. Société Anonyme des Usines Remy*, Federal Court of Appeals of Buenos Aires, 29 Jul. 1949, *La Ley*, vol. 57, 189.
980. *See* TA, Art. 35.
981. *Ibid.*, Art. 34(a).

to remove the illegal trademarks.[982] These remedies also exist in criminal cases,[983] although it is far more common to obtain them through civil actions.

188. In case of violation of a trademark owner's exclusive rights, such owner is entitled to recover damages from the infringer. This right is not regulated by the TA, but rather results from general principles of tort law, derived from the Civil and Commercial Code. Thus, matters such as the determination of the parties that are considered to have caused damages and are therefore liable for such damages, the quantification of the damages, and the effects of the joint liability of the infringers are governed by the Civil and Commercial Code rules on torts. Courts have not been consistent with regard to the calculation of damages derived from trademark infringements. In principle, these damages should comprise both the losses caused to the trademark owner as well as the profits and chances the latter has foregone due to the trademark infringement.[984] However, while some courts have decided that there is a presumption that trademark infringements cause damages that must be compensated by the infringer, other decisions require that such damages be clearly proven and have been denied recovery where the trademark owner had not previously used the trademark.[985] Other decisions have allowed the recovery of damages equivalent to the profits obtained by the infringer by means of the illegal use of the trademark.[986]

189. Civil actions are barred by a statute of limitations three years after the infringement took place or one year after the trademark owner learned about the infringement.[987]

190. If an infringement is determined pursuant to a criminal or a civil action, the trademark owner may request that the court decision be published at the defendant's expense.[988]

191. Trademark owners are entitled to different provisional remedies, resulting from the applicable rules of procedure or from the TA. The latter are available only in connection with registered trademarks.[989] The TA provides the following provisional remedies:

(a) Attachment of the infringing elements.[990]
(b) Inventory and description of the infringing elements.[991]
(c) Sequestration of samples of infringing elements.[992]
(d) Interruption of the use of the trademark, unless the defendant provides a bond to be determined by the relevant court.[993]

982. *Ibid.*, Art. 34(b).
983. *Ibid.*, Art. 34.
984. *See* Civil and Commercial Code, Art. 1738.
985. *See* Otamendi, *Derecho de marcas*, 292 et seq.
986. *Ibid.*, 299, 300.
987. *See* TA, Art. 36.
988. *Ibid.*, Art. 34.
989. *See* Otamendi, *Derecho de marcas*, 280.
990. *See* TA, Art. 38(a).
991. *Ibid.*, Art. 38(b).
992. *Ibid.*, Art. 38(c).
993. *Ibid.*, Art. 35.

(e) Court orders requiring a party to supply information with regard to the allegedly infringing elements, particularly with regard to the origin and purchase documentation of such elements, the amount and price of the sales of such elements, and the identity of the persons to which such elements were sold.[994] If this information is not duly supplied, the court may presume that the party that did not supply the required information participated in the infringement of the trademark rights involved.[995]

192. Courts may require the parties that have requested provisional remedies to post a bond to cover the damages that may result if the provisional remedy was improperly requested.[996]

§11. Overlapping and Relation to Other Intellectual Property Laws

193. Several cases have been decided under Argentine law with regard to the conflict between trademark rights and other intellectual property rights. The following are noteworthy:

(a) In the case of a trademark registration application with regard to a tri-dimensional object that had been previously patented, it was decided that the trademark registration was not legally possible, since it implied the intention to extend the term of patent protection.[997]
(b) In a case involving an element that had been registered as an industrial design, a trademark registration application was rejected on the basis that the trademark registration could affect the rights derived from the industrial design registration. The rejection also noted that the ornamental function of the design could not be conceptually divided from the alleged distinctive effect attributed for trademark registration purposes.[998]
(c) A work that has copyright protection may not be registered as a trademark without the authorization of the copyright owner.[999]
(d) Trademarks may be used as part of works protected by copyright, provided that the use does not extend to the identification or distinction of goods or services.[1000]

994. *Ibid.*, Art. 39.
995. *Ibid.*
996. *Ibid.*, Arts 35 and 38.
997. *See De Nicolo, V. v. Pandolfi, G.*, Federal Court of Appeals of Buenos Aires, 8 Sept. 1939, *La Ley*, vol. 16, 5.
998. *See Coquena S.A. v. Panamericana de Plásticos S.A.*, National Court of Appeals for Federal Civil and Commercial Matters II, 4 May 1982, *Revista del Derecho Industrial*, vol. 6, 1982, 184.
999. *See La Casa del Café S.A. v. DC Comics Inc.*, National Court of Appeals for Federal Civil and Commercial Matters I, 10 Nov. 1981, *Revista del Derecho Industrial*, vol. 4, 634.
1000. *See* Bertone & Cabanellas, *Derecho de marcas*, vol. 1, 233.

(e) With regard to subject matter that may be protected both under copyright law and under trademark law, it has been examined in connection with copyright.[1001]

1001. *See* para. 56, *supra*.

Chapter 5. Trade Names

§1. Sources: Legislation

194. Trade names are governed under Argentine law by the TA, particularly Articles 27–30. Several provisions of the TA, particularly those applicable to civil and criminal remedies, extend to trademarks as well as to trade names. In addition, trade name protection is governed by the multilateral industrial property agreements ratified by Argentina, in particular the Paris Convention and the TRIPS agreement.

The Business Associations Law – Law 19,550, as amended – includes several provisions on corporate names that have sometimes been applied to trade names. However, the prevailing view is that corporate names should be conceptually distinguished from trade names[1002] and that trade names are not governed by the rules on corporate names.

§2. The Protection of Trade Names

195. Trade names are described by Article 27 of the TA as names or signs that identify an activity; such activity may be with or without profit purposes.

Although the rules on trade name protection included in the TA follow the same approach provided by the pre-existing Argentine legislation and judicial precedents, the TA has changed the terminology used in this area. It refers to 'designations' (*designaciones*), instead of 'trade names' (*nombres comerciales*), as was the case before 1980. The purpose of this new terminology is to distinguish trade names from the names of individuals or legal entities.[1003]

196. Trade names are distinguished from other signs under Argentine law on the basis of the subject matter they serve to identify. Trademarks identify goods or services; corporate names identify legal entities; personal names identify individuals; and trade names identify the activities of individuals or legal entities.

This distinction may be illustrated by the following example. A corporation X sells hamburgers and fries under the brand Y and identifies the premises in which such activities take place under the name Z. X is a corporate name, Y is a trademark and Z is a trade name.

In practice, the same signs may be used as corporate or individual names, trademarks and trade names. In terms of concept, however, each type of use is governed by a different set of rules and protected by different rights.

1002. *See* Official Comments to the TA, Art. 27.
1003. *Ibid.*

197. Trade names are declared to be the subject matter of property rights, under Article 27 of the TA. This implies that the owner of a trade name has an exclusive right to use such trade name, within the scope of such rights derived from the TA.[1004]

198. The TA does not define which signs may be used as trade names. In principle, any name or sign used to identify an activity qualifies as a trade name.[1005] Words and signs that have been held to constitute trade names include individual names,[1006] corporate names,[1007] pseudonyms,[1008] and other names or signs with or without meaning. In general, any sign with distinctive capacity may serve as a trade name and be protected as such. All the signs that may be used as trademarks may normally be used as trade names, except in cases in which there are practical obstacles for the sign to identify an activity.[1009]

199. Certain signs may not be used as trade names because they cannot perform the essential function of identifying activities. This applies to signs that may not be identified by the public as distinguishing a given activity, such as – with some exceptions – the colour of products; generic names; signs that have become generally used in the pertinent trade; and the shape or colour of products.[1010]

Other signs, while potentially having a distinctive character, may not be legally protected as trade names. Signs falling in this category include signs that have become unavailable due to their prior ownership by third parties;[1011] signs likely to induce the public into error about the identity or characteristics of goods, services or activities; signs that are contrary to public morality; signs used by domestic or foreign governments; names, pseudonyms and portraits of persons who have not consented to such use; and phrases lacking originality. In general, these excluded signs are similar to those that are excluded from trademark protection.

200. Any activity may be distinguished by trade names.[1012] It is not necessary for such activity to have a profit motive or commercial value. In a similar vein, any person undertaking an activity may obtain rights on trade names.[1013] This includes individuals and legal entities, whether domestic or foreign.

201. The property of a trade name is acquired by means of its use in connection with the activity it identifies.[1014] No registration requirement is applicable.

1004. *See Diadema S.R.L. v. Diadema S.R.L.*, National Court of Appeals for Federal and Administrative Matters, Civil and Commercial section, 21 Apr. 1958, *La Ley*, vol. 95, 213.

1005. *See* TA, Art. 27.

1006. *See Pedro y Antonio Lanusse S.A. v. Horacio E. Lanusse S.A.*, National Court of Appeals for Federal Civil and Commercial Matters III, 5 Mar. 1986, *La Ley*, vol. 1986-C, 509.

1007. *See Diadema S.R.L. c/v. Diadema S.R.L.*, 213.

1008. *See* J. C. Rivera, *El nombre en los derechos civil y comercial* (Buenos Aires: Astrea, 1977), 138.

1009. *See* L.E. Bertone & G. Cabanellas, *Derecho de marcas* (Buenos Aires: Heliasta, 1989), vol. 2, 451 et seq.

1010. *Ibid.*, 456 et seq.

1011. *See* TA, Art. 28.

1012. *See* TA, Art. 27.

1013. *See* Official Comments to the TA, Art. 27.

1014. *See* TA, Art. 28.

For the use of a trade name to be legally relevant, it must be apparent to persons outside the organization that undertakes the activity identified by such trade name.[1015] The following examples have been considered as use of a trade name, for purposes of creating rights with respect to such trade name:[1016] placing the trade name in the premises where the activity to be identified takes place; using the trade name in stationary and documents; using the trade name in advertisement; and using the trade name in products or packaging related to the activity to be identified. Some types of use are unusual but nevertheless relevant; such is the case, for example, of the use of the colours of a soccer team in such team's shirts, which may lead to such colours being identified with the activities of the club for which such team plays.

There are no quantitative or time requirements with regard to the relevant use. The applicable criterion is that the use of the trade name should be such that the public identifies certain activity by means of such trade name. In this context, the required extent of the use will depend on the nature of the activity involved and of its clients.

202. The use of a trade name has a territorial dimension. Exclusive rights on a trade name are acquired only with regard to the territory in which the trade name is publicly known as identifying certain activities.[1017] This implies that within Argentina, the same trade name may be owned by different parties to identify the same type of activity in different parts of the Argentine territory.[1018] However, if the use of a trade name by a given person becomes public throughout the Argentine territory, such person will acquire exclusive rights with regard to such trade name for all the Argentine territory.[1019]

203. Use of a trade name outside the Argentine territory does not create rights on that trade name within Argentina. If the trade name used abroad has become well known within Argentina, such trade name may be protected pursuant to the rules on unfair competition,[1020] and not on the basis of trade name law.

204. The scope of trade name protection is subject to several limitations. Trade name rights only extend to the type of business in connection with which the trade name has been publicly used.[1021] In this context, the relevant line of business is defined on the basis of the relevant consumers' perception.[1022] An activity will be considered as being similar to that covered by the trade name protection if the activity that has originated such protection competes, in the relevant consumers' perception, with the activity whose status is being ascertained.

The scope of trade name protection also has a territorial aspect. This is determined by the territory in which the trade name has been publicly used.

1015. *See Wilsdorf, H. v. Rulex S.R.L.*, Federal Court of Appeals of Buenos Aires, 25 Aug. 1947, *La Ley*, vol. 48, 523.

1016. *See* Bertone & Cabanellas, *Derecho de marcas*, vol. 2, 472 et seq.

1017. *See Promosur S.A. v. Promosur S.A. Cía. Financiera*, National Court of Appeals for Federal Civil and Commercial Matters, 8 Jul. 1981, *Jurisprudencia Argentina*, vol. 1982-II, 260.

1018. *Ibid.*

1019. *See Confitería París v. Hahn y Cía.*, Federal Court of Appeals of Buenos Aires, 8 Apr. 1942, *La Ley*, vol. 26, 171.

1020. *See* Bertone & Cabanellas, *Derecho de marcas*, vol. 2, 485, 486.

1021. *See* TA, Art. 28.

1022. *See Confitería París v. Blanquet Gerard, J. et al*, Federal Court of Appeals of Buenos Aires, 17 Dec. 1941, *La Ley*, vol. 25, 734.

The scope of trade name protection must also be determined as to the signs included within that protection. Identical signs would obviously infringe the rights of the trade name owner. However, as in the case of trademarks, similar signs also fall within the scope of the exclusionary rights of the trade name owner.[1023] Whether a sign is similar to a legally protected trade name is determined on the basis of the likelihood of confusion that may be created in the relevant consumer group.[1024]

A method used to avoid the effects of trade name protection has been to add words or expression to a protected trade name. This has been the case with expressions such as 'former partner of (the firm whose trade name is involved)', 'former employee of ... ', 'former student of ... ', 'relative of ... ' and 'system ... '. These uses will not be considered legal, even if they do not imply any falsehood, if they are likely to create significant confusion in the relevant customers or if they are meant to profit from the goodwill of the pre-existing trade name.[1025]

205. The violation of trade name protection is generally subject to the same remedies applicable to trademark violations.[1026]

Criminal penalties are applicable in case of illegal use of a trade name belonging to another person or of an imitation or falsification of such trade name.[1027] Civil remedies consist of orders requiring the termination of the illegal use of trade name[1028] and in the reparation of the damage caused by the illegal use of a trade name.

In general, the preliminary measures applicable to protect trademark rights are not extendable to trade names. Only the general preliminary measures provided by the applicable procedural codes are applicable in case of violation of rights related to trade names. There is an exception with regard to preliminary measures consisting of orders to stop the illegal use of a trade name. In that case, the trade name owner may obtain a preliminary injunction ordering the interruption of the use of the trade name, by posting a bond established by the court as a condition for such injunction.[1029] The party to which the preliminary injunction is addressed may prevent the effects of such injunction by posting a bond, also determined by the court, to cover the possible damages that may result from the continuation of the trade name's use.[1030]

206. The use of a trade name in violation of the rights of third parties with regard to such trade name may become valid and not subject to legal actions if such use extends for more than a year from the moment in which the use became publicly known or in which it became known by the party wishing to attack such use.[1031] This has the double effect of extinguishing the civil and criminal actions based on the purported violation of trade name rights and of granting the originally illegal user a

1023. *See Turmo y Venecio v. Benes y Cía.*, Federal Court of Appeals of Buenos Aires, 28 Aug. 1946, *La Ley*, vol. 43, 871.

1024. *See Carauni, E. v. Carauni Hnos. S.R.L.*, Federal Court of Appeals of Resistencia, 23 Nov. 1961, *La Ley*, vol. 109, 669.

1025. *See J.A. Minotti y Cía. v. Torra, J.M.*, Federal Court of Appeals of Buenos Aires, 6 Nov. 1936, *La Ley*, vol. 4, 626.

1026. *See* TA, Arts 31–37.

1027. *Ibid.*, Art. 31.

1028. *Ibid.*, Art. 35.

1029. *Ibid.*

1030. *Ibid.*

1031. *Ibid.*, Art. 29.

separate right on the trade name – based on the trade name's use – which may be exercised against third parties.

207. The rights regarding a trade name may be assigned.[1032] If the trade name is used in connection with a going concern, the sale or transfer of such going concern will imply the transfer of the trade name rights, unless the parties have agreed otherwise.[1033] It is also possible to grant licenses with regard to trade names.[1034]

208. The rights with regard to a trade name may continue indefinitely, for as long as such trade name is used in connection with a given activity. However, if such activity ceases or if the trade name is no longer used, the rights with regard to such trade name will terminate.[1035] For this effect to take place, the interruption of the trade name's use or of the activity in connection with which it was used must be significant enough to presume an abandonment of such trade name.

209. A difficult, and as yet not clearly resolved, issue is that of the relation between trademark and trade name protection. A trademark is protected throughout the Argentine territory; therefore, a trade name's use infringing a registered trademark would be actionable pursuant to the trademark owner's exclusive rights. However, it is not clear whether the special one-year statute of limitations applicable in favour of trade name users[1036] is applicable against trademark owners. Some decisions have been favourable to such applicability,[1037] but this result appears to be in contradiction with the rules in the statute of limitations applicable to trademark rights, which provide significantly longer periods for legal actions to become barred.[1038]

If trade name rights have been acquired by means of the use of such trade name, the prevailing view is that the trade name owner may prevent the registration of such name as a trademark, even if use of such trade name was territorially limited.[1039] If a trademark is registered in violation of the trade name owner's rights, it is possible to obtain the annulment of the infringing trademark registration.[1040]

1032. *See* *Sorocabana S.R.L. v. Mangieri R.*, National Court of Appeals for Commercial Matters, s. A, 26 May 1960, *La Ley*, vol. 100, 367.

1033. *See* *Zanoni y Cuenca v. Toti Bisio, C. et al.*, Federal Court of Appeals of Buenos Aires, 22 Jul. 1938, *Jurisprudencia Argentina*, vol. 64, 69.

1034. *See* Bertone & Cabanellas, *Derecho de marcas*, vol. 2, 564 et seq.

1035. *See* TA, Art. 30.

1036. *See* para. 206, *supra* .

1037. *See* *Dr Madaus y Cía. v. Smolinksi, E.*, Federal Supreme Court, 21 Jun. 1977, *El Derecho*, vol. 75, 265.

1038. *See* TA, Arts 32, 36.

1039. *See* *Urriza, M. v. García, A.*, Federal Court of Appeals of Buenos Aires, 19 Apr. 1944, *La Ley*, vol. 34, 517.

1040. *See* Bertone & Cabanellas, *Derecho de marcas*, vol. 2, 525.

Chapter 6. Industrial Designs

§1. Sources: Legislation

210. Industrial designs – also known as industrial models under Argentine law[1041] – may be protected by copyright law or by rules specifically applicable to such designs.[1042] The first type of protection is governed by the rules examined in Chapter 1. The second type of protection, which will be examined in this chapter, is basically implemented by Decree-law 6,673, of 1963 (hereinafter, the Industrial Designs Law or IDL), as amended by Decree 27, of 2018. Decree 5,682, of 1965, includes regulations applicable to the enforcement of the IDL. In addition, industrial design protection is governed by rules included in multilateral intellectual property agreements, particularly the Paris Convention[1043] and the TRIPS agreement.

§2. Subject Matter of Protection

211. Article 3 of the IDL, as amended, sets out the basic elements of the subject matter protected under that law. It provides that an industrial design or industrial model consists of the forms or aspects embodied or applied to an industrial or craft product that confer ornamental character to such product. Several rules may be inferred from this basic provision. First, industrial design protection is limited to the ornamental aspects of certain products.[1044] These aspects must be exterior and visible.[1045]

Industrial design protection does not extend to the functional aspects of products.[1046] Furthermore, if the configuration of the elements of a given product is the necessary consequence of the function of such product, such configuration is not protected under the IDL.[1047]

1041. *See* Decree 6,673, of 1963. On industrial design protection, *see* generally I.A. Poli, *El modelo industrial* (Buenos Aires: Abeledo-Perrot, 2008).

1042. *See* J.C. Ledesma, *Derecho Penal Industrial* (Buenos Aires: Depalma, 1987), 202.

1043. *See* P. Di Guglielmo, 'La Convención de París. Modelos y dibujos industriales', *Revista del Derecho Comercial y de las Obligaciones* 6 (1973): 17.

1044. *See* *Valot, E.A. et al. v. Sainz y Cía.*, National Court of Appeals for Federal Civil and Commercial Matters, s II, 27 Dec. 1994, *La Ley*, 14 Aug. 1996, 6.

1045. *See* IDL, Art. 6(b).

1046. *Ibid.*, Art. 6(c).

1047. *Ibid.*

§3. Conditions of Protection

212. Several conditions have been identified as necessary for the protection of industrial models or designs under the IDL, as amended, namely the following:[1048]

(a) Originality: This condition is required by Article 6(b) of the IDL. Industrial designs are required to have 'a distinct configuration' and a 'novel and individual physiognomy' when compared with pre-existing industrial designs. This implies that an industrial design, to be legally protected, must imply a minimum level of creativity.[1049] The creative effort is not comparable to that required for patent protection; it is limited to ornamental aspects, and in this context courts have taken into account the 'modest' level that normally characterizes ornamental creations.[1050]
Originality need not apply to the model as a whole. It is sufficient that certain aspects of the industrial model or design embody the level of creativity required by the IDL. As a result, the necessary originality has been found to exist in the following cases:[1051]

- New combination of known elements. Such new combination must imply a significant level of creativity with regard to prior combinations.
- New application of known elements. The originality requirement is satisfied if the new application implies a novel ornamental function, not immediately evident from the prior use given to the elements involved.
- Fashion articles. In these cases, the ornamental originality may result from secondary aspects of the design; this will be enough for legal protection if the overall ornamental effect is novel and original.
- New materials. This innovation may be protected provided it implies a new ornamental effect that is not evident from industrial designs already in use.
- Changes of dimension or proportion. In general, they do not meet the required level of originality. However, this requirement may be satisfied if the changes create a novel ornamental effect that was not obvious in the industrial designs already in use.
- Mere changes in colour in industrial models or designs already known are excluded from protection by Article 6(d) of the IDL.

(b) Novelty: Article 6(a) of the IDL excludes from protection under that law the industrial models or designs that were publicly exploited or published, in Argentina or abroad, before the registration date. This exclusion does not apply if the industrial model or design was disclosed abroad, provided the registration application or the priority claim is filed in Argentina within six months from the foreign disclosure, and that the following conditions are met: disclosure should

1048. *See* Ledesma, *Derecho Penal Industrial,* 203 et seq.
1049. *See* *Valot, E.A. et al. v. Sainz y Cia.*, National Court of Appeals for Federal Civil and Commercial Matters, s. II, 27 Dec. 1994, *La Ley*, 14 Aug. 1996, 6.
1050. *Ibid.*
1051. *See* Ledesma, *Derecho Penal Industrial,* 206 et seq.

be the direct or indirect result of conduct attributable to the author or his or her successors, or result from a bad faith or breach of confidence conduct attributable to a third party, or from breach of contract or a tort against the author or a legitimate successor, or result from an erroneous or undue publication by the Argentine administrative authority.[1052]

(c) Industrial product: An industrial model or design must be embodied in or applied to an industrial or craft product.[1053] In this context, 'industrial or craft product' is a word of art, which implies a tangible product with any type of practical use.[1054] It is irrelevant whether such product is the result of industrial activities – in the economic sense of the word 'industrial' – or is to be applied in such activities.

(d) Ornamental character: This condition is expressly required by Article 3 of the IDL. In practical terms, it implies that only the ornamental aspects of an object registered as an industrial design are legally protected under the IDL. The aesthetic value of the design, in this context, is irrelevant. Also, the fact that the object may have non-ornamental functions will not prevent its protection under the IDL, provided the ornamental elements are not required by the functional aspects of the object.[1055]

(e) Visibility: The ornamental aspects of the industrial design must be visible. The industrial design will not be protected under the IDL if it refers to aesthetic aspects that are not visually perceptible, such as sounds or tastes.[1056]

(f) Morality: For an industrial model or design to be legally protected, it must not be contrary to public morality.[1057]

§4. Formalities: Procedure for Obtaining Protection

213. Protection under the IDL is obtained by means of registration in a special registry, which depends from the National Industrial Property Institute.[1058] Registration is based on a written application that must include the following elements:[1059] name and domicile of the applicant; a sworn affidavit to the effect that the applicant is the author of the model or design, or the heir, legatee or assignee of the author; payment of the applicable fees; drawings, photographs or digital reproductions of the model or design; description of the model or design; blueprints of the model or design and facsimile copies thereof and a power of attorney or authorization, if necessary, to act on behalf of the applicant.

A registration application may be rejected if it does not meet the formal conditions established by the applicable statutes.[1060] There is no opposition procedure, nor do the

1052. *See* IDL, Art. 6(a), as amended.
1053. *Ibid.*, Art. 3, as amended.
1054. *See* Ledesma, *Derecho Penal Industrial*, 215.
1055. *See* IDL, Art. 6(c).
1056. *See* Ledesma, *Derecho Penal Industrial*, 216, 217.
1057. *See* IDL, Art. 6(e).
1058. *See* IDL, Art. 4.
1059. *See* IDL, Art. 10, as amended; Decree 5,682, of 1965, Arts 2 and 3.
1060. *Ibid. See also* IDL, Art. 12, as amended.

authorities in charge of registration control the substantive aspects of the application. If the application is rejected, this administrative decision may be appealed before a higher administrative authority or before the federal courts.[1061] If registration is improperly granted, due to lack of the substantive conditions required for industrial design protection, the registration and the rights resulting therefrom may be annulled, by means of a court decision.[1062]

§5. Ownership and Transfer: Assignment and Licenses

214. Ownership of the rights granted for industrial models and designs belongs to their author.[1063] There is a rebuttable presumption to the effect that the first applicant of an industrial model or design registration is the author of such industrial model or design.[1064]

If an industrial model or design is created by a person engaged in an employment relationship, rights on that model or design will still belong to the author, unless that person was hired with the purpose of creating such model or design, or such person is a mere executor of instructions received from the persons for whom he works.[1065] If the model or design is the result of the joint work of an employer and an employee, rights to such model or design will jointly belong to both, unless they have agreed otherwise.[1066]

If an industrial model or design has been jointly created by two or more persons, in a context other than an employment relationship, such persons shall have joint ownership of the rights on the model or design.[1067] This implies that all of them are allowed to exploit the model or design and to register – in the name of all the joint owners – such model or design.[1068]

215. If an industrial model or design is registered in favour of a person who is not the author, heir, legatee or assignee of such author, the rightful owners of the industrial model or design may file a special action to obtain registration and title with regard to such industrial model or design.[1069] If the action succeeds, the rights derived from the originally improper registration shall be transferred to the plaintiffs.

216. Article 2 of the IDL provides that the rights granted by that law in favour of the authors of industrial models or designs and to their assignees, heirs and legatees also apply to models or designs created abroad, provided the countries where such creation took place grant reciprocal rights to creators with Argentine nationality or residence. This provision is still effective with regard to persons who are not nationals

1061. *Ibid.*, Art. 12, as amended.
1062. *Ibid.*, Art. 17.
1063. *Ibid.*, Art. 1.
1064. *Ibid.*, Art. 5.
1065. *Ibid.*, Art. 1.
1066. *Ibid.*
1067. *Ibid.*
1068. *Ibid.*
1069. *Ibid.*

of member countries of the Paris Convention. Those who are nationals of such member countries are entitled to the national treatment granted by that Convention.

217. The rights granted with regard to industrial models or designs may be assigned.[1070] The assignment is effective against third parties – for example, infringers and creditors of the assignor – only after it has been recorded in the registry of industrial models and designs.[1071]

The assignment may be agreed in exchange for a valuable consideration or free of charge.[1072] It may encompass all rights resulting from the registration or only part of such rights.[1073]

218. Industrial models or designs may be the subject matter of license agreements. No registration is necessary for the validity of these agreements.

§6. Scope of Exclusive Rights

219. The owner of rights regarding a registered industrial model or design has a property right over such model or design, and the exclusive right to exploit such model or design.[1074] This exclusive right refers to both industrial and commercial uses of the model or design.[1075] Only the owner of the model or design, or a person authorized by such owner, is allowed to manufacture articles reproducing the model or design.[1076] Also, only the owner of the model or design, or a person authorized by such owner, is allowed to sell or otherwise market articles reproducing the model or design, except if such articles have been originally marketed with the authorization of the owner of the model or design.[1077] The exclusive rights of the owner of a model or design extend not only to identical reproductions of such model or design but also to non-identical imitations.[1078] Minor or secondary variations, from the registered model or design, will not be sufficient to prevent a violation of the owner's exclusive rights.[1079] In a similar vein, changes in colour, size or materials used in the manufacture of certain articles will not prevent such violation.[1080] The identity of the process used for the manufacture of the product is irrelevant for the purposes of determining an infringement of the model or design owner's rights.[1081]

1070. *Ibid.*, Art. 15 as amended.
1071. *Ibid.*
1072. *See* Civil and Commercial Code, Art. 1614.
1073. *See* IDL, Art. 15 as amended.
1074. *Ibid.*, Art. 1.
1075. *Ibid.*, Art. 19.
1076. *Ibid.*, Art. 21(1).
1077. *Ibid.*, Art. 21(2).
1078. *See* Ledesma, *Derecho Penal Industrial*, 240 et seq.
1079. *Ibid.*, 241.
1080. *Ibid.*
1081. *Ibid.*

§7. Limitations of the Scope of Protection

220. Once an industrial model or design has been registered, there are no specific limitations on the scope of the exclusive rights derived from such registration. In this area, Argentine law does not introduce any requirement or obligation as to working, producing or manufacturing the industrial model or design.

§8. Duration of Protection

221. The rights derived from the registration of an industrial model or design last for a five-year period, counted from the date of filing the relevant application.[1082] This registration may be renewed for two successive five-year periods if the owner requests such renewal.[1083] To this effect, a renewal application must be filed by the owner at least six months before the expiration of the period still in effect; however, the renewal application may also be filed up to six months after expiration of the previous period of protection, if a special fee is paid.[1084] The renewal application is generally subject to the same formal requirements applicable to an original application.[1085]

222. The protection derived from the registration of an industrial model or design expires not only together with the termination of the protection period described above, but also if the registration has been annulled by a court decision, due to lack of the substantive conditions required for industrial model or design protection, particularly if the registered owner is not the author of the model or design or an assignee, heir or legatee of such author.[1086]

§9. Infringement and Remedies

223. The infringement of the exclusive rights of the owner of an industrial model or design results in civil and criminal remedies. For these remedies to apply, the industrial model or design must be duly registered;[1087] otherwise, the applicable remedies are those that result from rules other than those specifically applicable to models and designs, particularly those on unfair competition.

224. Article 21 of the IDL, as amended, lists certain types of conduct that are subject to criminal penalties. For these penalties to apply, the conduct must be done in bad faith, that is, in circumstances in which the party engaged in the conduct knew or should have known that a violation of the model or design owner's exclusive rights was taking place.[1088] The types of conduct thus subject to criminal remedies are the following:

1082. *See* IDL, Art. 7.
1083. *Ibid.*
1084. *Ibid.*, Art. 11 as amended.
1085. *Ibid. See also* Decree 5,682, of 1965, Arts 14 and 15.
1086. *See* IDL, Art. 17.
1087. *Ibid.*, Art. 19.
1088. *See* Ledesma, *Derecho Penal Industrial*, 233, 234.

- Manufacturing or having other person manufacture industrial products including the characteristics that are protected by means of the registration of a model or design.
- Selling, offering to sell, exhibiting, importing, exporting or otherwise marketing infringing products.
- Holding infringing products.
- Concealing the identity of the manufacturer of infringing products.
- Falsely invoking the ownership of an industrial model or design.
- Selling the blueprints of designs belonging to another person.

225. Only the owner of a model or design, whose rights have been affected by a criminal infringement, may request the imposition of the applicable penalties from the relevant courts.[1089] These penalties consist of fines, which are increased in case of recidivism,[1090] and in the destruction or confiscation of infringing merchandize.[1091] Destruction and confiscation become inapplicable if the merchandize has been sold to third parties acting in good faith.[1092]

226. In case of infringement of the exclusive rights of the owner of industrial models or designs, such owner is entitled to obtain full reparation of the damages caused by such infringement, including foregone profits.[1093] In addition, if the infringer has acted in bad faith, the owner is entitled to recover any profits obtained by the infringer through the infringing use.[1094]

It is also possible to file civil actions with the purpose of obtaining injunctions against further use of the industrial model or design.[1095]

227. In the context of both civil and criminal actions, it is possible to obtain different types of special preliminary measures, in addition to those generally provided by the applicable law of procedure. First, by filing a bond and evidence of registration of the model or design, the owner may obtain a court order for the sequestration of one infringing item and for the drawing of an inventory of infringing items by a court officer.[1096] In these cases, if the holder of the infringing item is not the manufacturer of such item, the owner plaintiff may request from the holder of infringing items information as to the origin of such items; if such information is denied or is false, the holder may not thereafter claim to have acted in good faith.[1097]

Second, the owner may request the immediate suspension of the exploitation of a registered industrial model or design, once such owner has posted a bond required by the court to make effective such request; in these circumstances, the request will be enforced by means of a preliminary court order, unless the defendant in turn supplies

1089. *See* IDL, Art. 23.
1090. *Ibid.*, Art. 21 as amended.
1091. *Ibid.*, Art. 22.
1092. *Ibid.*
1093. *Ibid.*, Art. 20.
1094. *Ibid.*
1095. *Ibid.*, Art. 25.
1096. *Ibid.*, Art. 24.
1097. *Ibid.*

a bond of an amount sufficient to cover the possible damages that may result from the continuation of his exploitation of the model or design.[1098]

§10. Overlapping and Relation to Other Industrial Property Laws

228. The IDL includes several provisions to deal with the potential overlapping of the rights granted by that law and by other statutes.

According to Article 6(d) of the IDL, if the ornamental elements of a model or design are imposed by the practical function of such elements, the model or design is excluded from protection under the IDL. This implies that these functional elements may only be protected by means of patents.

If a model or design has ornamental characteristics, but does not include functional elements constituting a patentable invention, an applicant filing a patent or utility model application may request that such application – invalid from the perspective of patent law – be converted into an application for an industrial model or design registration.[1099]

Also, since models or designs may be protected under copyright law and be registered under such law, the owner of rights with regard to such models or designs under copyright law and under the IDL may choose to exercise the rights and legal actions derived from one or the other intellectual property, in a given case. The owner may not simultaneously claim protection under both regimes.[1100]

Other specific cases of overlapping with copyright, patent and trademark rights have been examined above in the context of the analysis of such rights.

1098. *Ibid.*, Art. 25.
1099. *Ibid.*, Art. 28, as amended.
1100. *Ibid.*

Chapter 7. Plant Variety Protection

§1. Sources: Legislation

229. Law 20,247, of 1973, on seeds and phytogenetic creations (hereinafter the Law of Seeds or LS) includes the basic provisions applicable in Argentina to plant variety protection. Different regulations have been issued pursuant to this law, included in Decrees 1,995, of 1978, 50, of 1989 and 2,183, of 1991.

Plant variety protection also results from the ratification by Argentina of the International Union for the Protection of New Varieties of Plants (UPOV), by means of Law 24,376, of 1994, and of the TRIPS agreement. Law 24,376 expressly provides that the provisions of the UPOV prevail over those of the LS, in case of conflict, with respect to nationals of the Member States of the UPOV. The regulations included in Decree 2,183, of 1991, are directed to the implementation of the UPOV in Argentina.[1101]

Patent protection of plant varieties is generally excluded under Argentine law.[1102]

§2. Subject Matter of Protection

230. The LS and the rules derived therefrom grant protection to plant varieties.[1103] A variety is defined by Article 1(c) of Decree 2,183, of 1991, as a set of plants belonging to only one botanical taxonomic category of the lowest known rank, which may be defined by the expression of the characteristics resulting from a certain genotype or from a combination of genotypes, provided that set may be distinguished from any other set of plants by the expression of at least one of such characteristics. Article 1(c) adds that a specific variety may be represented by several plants, only one plant or one or several parts of a plant, provided such part or parts may be used for the production of complete plants belonging to that variety.

Article 20 of the LS defines the basic scope of protection under that law. Protection is granted to phytogenetic creations and to cultivated varieties; these are considered as 'goods', meaning that a property right exists with respect to these creations or varieties, once the necessary legal conditions have been met.[1104]

A phytogenetic creation is defined as any cultivated variety, whatsoever its genetic nature, obtained by means of discovery or of the incorporation or application of scientific knowledge.

1101. *See* S.D. Bergel, 'La protección de las innovaciones biotecnológicas en la Ley 24,481', *La Ley* (30 Aug. 1996): 2.

1102. *Ibid.*, 1 et seq.

1103. *See* T. Zamudio, 'Protección jurídica de la propiedad industrial en el sector agrícola', *Jurisprudencia Argentina* (22 May 1996): 18.

1104. *See* LS, Art. 24.

Although plant variety protection does not require an inventive activity or an inventive level,[1105] it does require a minimum level of creation, discovery or development attributable to the originator of a protected variety.[1106]

§3. Conditions of Protection

231. Article 26 of Decree 2,183, of 1991, requires the following conditions for the protection of plant varieties:

(a) *Novelty*: This condition is satisfied if the variety has not been offered for sale or marketed, by the originator or with his or her consent, within the Argentine territory prior to the date of filing of the registration application in the National Registry of Variety Property. In addition, the variety should not have been offered for sale or marketed in countries to which Argentina is linked by bilateral or multilateral agreements on plant variety protection, more than four years before the date of filing of the registration application in the National Registry of Variety Property; in the case of trees and vines, this period is extended to six years.
(b) *Distinctiveness*: This condition implies that the protected variety should have one or more characteristics that permit its clear distinction from any other variety that is generally known at the time of filing the registration application. To this effect, once a variety has been the subject matter of a registration application in any country, it will be considered to be generally known, provided that application has resulted in the grant of a property right or in the recording of the variety in the National Registry of Varieties.[1107]
(c) *Homogeneity*: This means that the variety must maintain its most relevant hereditary characteristics in a sufficiently uniform way, subject to the pre-visible variations originated in the particular propagation mechanism of such variety.
(d) *Stability*: This condition is defined as requiring that the most relevant hereditary characteristics should remain as defined after successive propagations or, in the case of a special propagation cycle, at the end of each of such cycles.

§4. Formalities: Procedure for Obtaining Protection

232. Although it may be argued that the rights on a plant variety begin with the creation or development of such variety,[1108] full legal protection is only acquired by means of registration of such variety in the National Registry of Variety Property.[1109]

Registration in the National Registry of Variety Property requires filing a sworn affidavit, including the following elements:[1110]

1105. *See* T. Zamudio, 'Protección jurídica', 19.
1106. *See* LS, Art. 24; Decree 2,183, Art. 1(d).
1107. This Registry should not be confused with the National Registry of Variety Property.
1108. *See* LS, Art. 24.
1109. *Ibid.*, Art. 20.
1110. *See* Decree 2,183, Art. 29.

- The name and address of the originator or discoverer, and of his or her agent in Argentina, if any.
- The name, address, and professional registration data of the agricultural engineer sponsoring the registration.
- Common and scientific name of the species.
- Proposed name of the variety.
- Location where the variety was obtained.
- Description of the variety, including morphological, physiological, sanitary, phenological, physical and chemical characteristics of such variety, as well as its industrial or technological qualities, so as to allow a proper identification of the variety. Drawings, photographs and other technical elements may be used for purposes of the description of the morphological aspects of the variety.
- Justification of the novelty condition, including indications of the difference of the variety with respect to pre-existent plants.
- Evidence on the stability condition, including the indication of the date in which the variety was first reproduced meeting the stability condition.
- Origin of the variety, including the indication of its domestic or foreign origin, and in the second case, of the specific country of origin.
- Description of the applicable reproduction or propagation mechanism.
- Any additional information required for certain species by the National Seed Service.

In addition, the authorities may require field or laboratory tests from which evidence as to the characteristics attributed to the new variety may result.

233. If a registration application has been filed abroad, in a country with which Argentina is linked by bilateral or multilateral agreements of plant variety protection, a twelve-month priority period is granted, as from the first relevant foreign filing, for purposes of determining the priority of filings within Argentina. After expiration of this priority period, the applicant has twenty-four additional months within which to supply the documentation and material normally required for registration in Argentina.[1111]

234. Registration requires the prior evaluation of the existence of the substantive conditions of protection.[1112] Additional information, tests or cultivation may be required for purposes of this evaluation.[1113]

Third parties may file their opposition against registration applications.[1114]

§5. Ownership and Transfer: Assignment and Licenses

235. Property of the rights to a plant variety belongs to the person who developed such variety.[1115] The persons who participated in the work leading to a new variety

1111. *Ibid.*, Art. 30.
1112. *Ibid.*, Art. 31.
1113. *Ibid.*
1114. *Ibid.*, Art. 32.
1115. *See* LS, Art. 23.

have no rights to such variety – particularly, no rights to use it.[1116] However, if such persons have participated as independent parties in the creation or discovery of the new variety, joint ownership of the exclusive rights to the new variety would result.[1117] In this context, the level of participation that originates a joint ownership situation would be difficult to define. However, difficulties are practically reduced due to the fact that much of the participation in the work leading to new varieties is done in the context of employment relationships, and in such context a different set of rules applies to the determination of the ownership of plant varieties. These rules are those included in the Employment Contracts Law.[1118] Pursuant to such rules, intellectual creations made by an employee hired with the purpose of making such creations belong to the employer.[1119] Intellectual creations derived from procedures, technologies and other elements made available by the employer in the course of the employment relationship also belong to the employer.[1120] Other intellectual creations, developed independently by the employee, belong to such employee.[1121]

236. The rights to plant varieties are assignable.[1122] The assignment becomes valid as against third parties – particularly the assignor's creditors – upon recording the assignment in the National Registry of Variety Property.[1123]

237. The owner of rights to plant varieties may grant licenses with regard to the exploitation of such varieties. The licenses may be limited as to territory or volume of production.[1124] Licenses may also be limited to specific uses.[1125] The parties are granted broad contractual freedom to determine the terms and conditions of these licenses.[1126]

Licenses may also result from public offerings to grant such licenses, issued by the owner of rights on a plant variety.[1127] In these cases, if a person engages in conduct covered by the owner's exclusive rights included in the public offering, the person engaged in such conduct shall be considered as having accepted the public offering.[1128]

§6. Scope of Exclusive Rights

238. Article 41 of Decree 2,183, of 1991, defines the exclusive rights of the owner of registered plant varieties. These exclusive rights are defined with respect to the seed of a protected variety. To this effect a seed is defined by Article 1(a) of the

1116. *Ibid.*, Art. 24.
1117. *See* Decree 2183, Art. 40.
1118. *Ibid.*
1119. *See* Law 20,744, as amended, Art. 82.
1120. *Ibid.*
1121. *Ibid.*
1122. *See* LS, Art. 23.
1123. *Ibid.*, *See also* Decree 2,183, Art. 39.
1124. *See* Decree 2,183, Art. 42.
1125. *See* *Dekalb Argentina S.A. v. Las Compuertas*, National Court of Appeals for Commercial Matters E, 5 Oct. 1995, *Jurisprudencia Argentina*, 22 May 1996, 16.
1126. *See* Decree 2,183, Art. 42.
1127. *Ibid.*
1128. *Ibid.*

same Decree as any vegetal organ, including not only seeds in the strict botanical sense but also fruits, bulbs, tubercles, buds, cuttings, flowers and any other structure, including plants grown in tree nurseries, devised or used for sowing, planting or propagation. The exclusive rights apply to the following types of conduct, referred to seeds of protected varieties:

- Production or reproduction.
- Conditioning for propagation purposes.
- Offers.
- Sale or any other type of marketing.
- Exportation.
- Importation.
- Advertisement and exhibition of samples.
- Barter or exchange.
- Storage for any of the purposes listed above.
- Any other delivery, regardless of the legal transaction involved.

§7. Limitations of the Scope of Protection

239. Argentine law provides several limitations on the exclusive rights granted with regard to plant varieties, namely the following:

(a) A protected variety may be used as a source of variations or of contribution of desirable characteristics, in the context of plant improvement or development work.[1129] To this effect, it is not necessary to obtain the consent of the owner of rights on the protected variety.[1130] However, this limitation does not apply if the protected variety is used repeatedly or systematically for the production of commercially viable seed.[1131]

(b) An agricultural user of a protected variety may reserve all or part of the seed resulting from the exploitation of a protected variety and use such seed for further planting or reproduction of such variety.[1132] In addition, an agricultural user may sell as raw material or foodstuff the result of the exploitation of a protected variety, provided that exploitation is in itself authorized.[1133]

(c) A protected variety may be declared by the National Executive Power as subject to a regime of restricted public use.[1134] This declaration may be made if it is deemed necessary to assure an adequate supply within Argentina of the product resulting from the cultivation of the protected variety.[1135] Once this declaration is made, it is published with the purpose of obtaining bids from persons interested

1129. *See* LS, Art. 25; Decree 2,183, Art. 43.
1130. *Ibid.*
1131. *Ibid.*
1132. *See* LS, Art. 27; Decree 2,183, Art. 44.
1133. *Ibid,* at Art. 27.
1134. *Ibid,* at Art. 28.
1135. *Ibid.*

in exploiting the plant variety involved.[1136] These persons shall receive an authorization to exploit that plant variety if they are technically qualified to that effect.[1137] These licensees shall pay a fair consideration to the owner of the rights over the plant variety.[1138] If no agreement is reached to that effect between the owner and the licensees, the consideration is determined by the National Seed Service.[1139] If a restricted public use is granted pursuant to these provisions, the seed remaining at the moment of termination of such use must be returned to the owner of the rights over the protected variety.[1140] While the public use rights are in effect, the holder of such rights is entitled to use the name of the plant variety involved, even if it has been previously registered as a trademark.[1141] A declaration of restricted public use has a maximum term of two years but may be renewed by the National Executive Power for an additional term.[1142]

§8. Duration of Protection

240. Exclusive rights on registered plant varieties are granted for a maximum period of twenty years. The Secretary of Agriculture may establish shorter periods of protection with regard to particular species.[1143] Article 22 of the LS provides that the protection period may not be shorter than ten years.

241. In addition to the expiration of the applicable protection term, the exclusive rights on registered plant varieties may expire for the following reasons:[1144]

(a) Annulment of the property title due to lack of one or more substantive conditions of protection at the time such title was granted.[1145]
(b) Surrender of the rights by their owner.
(c) Obtainment of the exclusive rights in violation of the rights of third parties. In such case, if such third parties were entitled to the exclusive rights on the plant variety involved, title to such plant variety shall be transferred to such third parties.
(d) Lack of filing of the elements required by the authorities for purposes of controlling the existence of the variety involved.
(e) Lack of payment of the yearly fees to the National Registry of Variety Property, if a period of six months has expired after payment of such fees has been requested by the Registry.

1136. *Ibid*, at *see also* Decree 2,183, Art. 46.
1137. *See* LS, Art. 28.
1138. *Ibid.*
1139. *Ibid.*
1140. *See* Decree 2,183, Art. 48.
1141. *Ibid.*, Art. 49.
1142. *See* LS, Art. 29.
1143. *See* Decree 2,183, Art. 37.
1144. *See* LS, Art. 30; Decree 2,183, Art. 36.
1145. *See* Decree 2,183, Art. 35.

§9. Infringement and Remedies

242. Infringement of the exclusive rights on varieties are subject to criminal and civil remedies. Criminal penalties consist of fines, to be imposed by administrative authorities and subject to judicial appeal.[1146] Civil remedies consist of the indemnification of any damages caused by the infringement,[1147] including foregone profits; orders against further illegal exploitation of protected varieties; and the destruction of the crops or other products resulting from the illegal use of such varieties.[1148]

The general preliminary measures allowed by the applicable rules of procedure may be used in connection with plant variety protection.

§10. Overlapping and Relation to Other Intellectual Property Laws

243. Plant varieties are excluded from patent protection under Argentine law.[1149]

In relation with trademark rights, if public use rights have been granted with regard to a plant variety, the holder of public use rights is entitled to use the name of the plant variety involved, even if it has been previously registered as a trademark.[1150] It may be inferred from this provision that the name of a registered plant variety may be protected as a trademark, a conclusion that would be debatable if it had to stand exclusively on the basis of trademark law considerations.

1146. *See* LS, Arts 37, 46.

1147. *See* *Dekalb Argentina S.A. v. Las Compuertas*, National Court of Appeals for Commercial Matters E, 5 Oct. 1995, *Jurisprudencia Argentina*, 22 May 1996, 16.

1148. *Ibid.*

1149. *See* Bergel, 'La protección', 1 et seq.

1150. *See* para. 239(c), *supra* .

Chapter 8. Chip Protection

§1. Sources: Legislation

244. Argentina has enacted no specific rules on chip protection. Although Argentina is part of the WTO and has approved the TRIPS agreement, it has not yet implemented any rules on chip protection. This approach is based on the grace period provided by Article 65 of the TRIPS agreement in favour of developing countries.

Under Argentine law, ratified treaties are immediately applicable within Argentina.[1151] However, when a ratified treaty includes provisions that are not immediately applicable, but rather require the implementation of certain laws or regulations by the countries that are parties to that treaty, it is necessary under Argentine law for those laws or regulations to be enacted by the Argentine legislature. Only then do the rules included in the ratified treaty to become effective.

The provisions on chip protection included in the TRIPS agreement have not been deemed immediately applicable under Argentine law. In addition, Argentina has not ratified or implemented other multilateral treaties on chip protection, in particular the Treaty of Washington of 1989.

245. No specific treatment has been developed under more traditional branches of Argentine intellectual property law with regard to chips or semiconductors. This reflects not only the general lack of development of the intellectual property laws, but also the limited production capacity for semiconductor products. This means that the actual possibility of such production within Argentina to the detriment of third parties is, for the most part, purely theoretical. However, the increasing spread of computer use and manufacturing and the tendency to move the production of hardware and the inputs used therein to developing countries lend practical interest to the consideration of the rules presently applicable to the protection of semiconductors. This interest is enhanced by the substantial importation of semiconductors into Argentina, particularly as part of more complex hardware.

246. Semiconductor technology, generally, and topographies, in particular, may be protected under the traditional intellectual property rules applicable to all types of technology. To determine the extent of this possibility under Argentine law, one may start by observing that while the specific protection granted to topographies in the US and in other countries was traditionally linked to copyright law – at least from the point of view of the statutes in which such protection is included – it is not part of that law. Thus, for example, the US Semiconductor Protection Act was formally enacted as a part of the Copyright Act; however, it is in fact a sui generis law,[1152] specifically drafted to avoid its classification as copyright law, since such character would create an infringement of the international copyright conventions that prohibit the application of reciprocity requirements.

1151. *See* Federal Constitution, Art. 75(22).

1152. *See* J. H. Reichman, 'Legal Hybrids between the Patent and Copyright Paradigms', *Columbia Law Review* 94 (1994): 2478 et seq.

Copyright law – and, more specifically, Argentine copyright law – is inadequate for the protection of semiconductor technology and topographies. If that were not the case, it would not have been necessary in other countries with similar legal systems to introduce a special set of rules to achieve such protection. The subject matter to be protected in connection with semiconductors is not the literary, musical, artistic or scientific expression of an idea but rather its application and embodiment in certain tangible objects. This application is beyond the subject matter that may be protected by copyright, as may be noticed in connection with other fields. Thus, copyright on the blueprints for a given machine grants an exclusive right to the reproduction of such blueprints but none regarding the construction of the machine.

In the case of semiconductors and, in particular, in case of their topographies, the inadequacy of copyright, as traditionally understood and applied in Argentina, is stronger than in connection with software. In the case of semiconductors, what becomes embodied in a tangible object is not a work that is perceptible to the human mind beyond the perception of the tangible object in which it is embodied. The 'work' is limited to the embodiment of the topography if this is the subject matter being considered. There is in such case no element that transmits a 'message' or that expresses an idea or has an intellectual meaning, except in the trivial sense that every tangible object, up to the more common pebble, may have a 'message' for sensitive spirits. But these poetic subtleties have traditionally not been admitted under Argentine law to determine the limits of copyright protection, and it does not appear reasonable to begin with such poetic experimentation by means of computer technology. The reason why copyright protection has been advocated for semiconductor technology by means of this interpretation of copyright is the lack of an adequate alternative source of protection suited to this new type of technology. But this reason will disappear once the chip protection required by the TRIPS agreement is implemented within Argentina.

247. Semiconductor technology may be protected by patents; no exclusion in that respect is included in Argentine patent law. However, in practice, patent law provides an insufficient legal protection for the creative and development work that takes place in connection with semiconductors. Although this may be partly due to the fact that patents are normally considered to be more relevant for protecting industrial processes, the real obstacle appears to lie in the fact that semiconductors and their topographies, while being potentially new industrial products, or new means, frequently lack the necessary inventive step or non-obviousness required for their patenting. Thus, the specific legislations that in different countries grant protection to the topography of semiconductors tend to require the originality of the protected subject matter. This requirement differs from mere novelty in that it implies a certain minimum level of intellectual creation but without reaching the level required for patenting.[1153]

Notwithstanding these limits found in patent protection, there are no reasons to exclude a priori all semiconductors and their topographies from patenting; this will depend on the inventive level of the technological creation involved.

248. In some countries it has been proposed to use utility models to protect the topography of semiconductor products. This proposal is of interest in Argentina, due to the absence of inventive level requirements for granting utility model protection.[1154]

1153. *Ibid.*
1154. *See* PA, Art. 55.

However, this type of protection is likely to be superseded by the rules to be enacted in the future on the basis of the TRIPS agreement.

249. With regard to industrial models and designs, even though they have been used in some countries to protect certain aspects of semiconductors, they may not have a similar function in Argentina, since under Argentine law industrial models and designs have a purely ornamental or aesthetic subject matter,[1155] a condition not satisfied by semiconductor products. Also, the functional aspects of industrial models or designs are excluded from protection under Article 6(c) of the IDL, further limiting the applicability of this law for chip protection purposes.

250. The different aspects of chip protection, to be examined in the rest of this chapter, are determined by the lack of specific protection for chip technology. Thus, these aspects are a function of the type of legal protection used for the chip technology involved in each particular case.

§2. Subject Matter of Protection

251. There being no specific protection under Argentine law for chip designs, the subject matter of protection is determined on the basis of the applicable intellectual property right for which protection is claimed for a given chip technology.

§3. Conditions of Protection

252. In the absence of specific chip protection under Argentine law, the conditions of protection depend on the intellectual property right on the basis of which protection is claimed for a given chip technology. The applicable conditions of protection are those corresponding to such intellectual property right.

§4. Formalities: Procedure for Obtaining Protection

253. There are no specific formalities applicable to chip protection under Argentine law. The applicable formalities are those related to the intellectual property right on the basis of which protection is claimed for a given chip technology.

§5. Ownership and Transfer

254. Ownership of chip designs is acquired pursuant to the rules applicable to the specific intellectual property right on the basis of which chip protection is claimed. The assignment and transfer of these rights are governed by the rules related to the specific intellectual property right to be assigned, transferred or licensed.

1155. *See* IDL, Art. 3.

§6. Scope of Exclusive Rights

255. There is no specific scope for the exclusive rights on chip technology. This scope is determined pursuant to the rules applicable to the intellectual property right on the basis of which chip protection is claimed.

§7. Limitations of the Scope of Protection

256. The scope of protection of chip technology is governed by the general rules applicable to the specific intellectual property right on the basis of which chip protection is claimed. The particular limitations applicable on the basis of these general rules to chip protection were described in section 1, above.

§8. Duration of Protection

257. The duration of chip protection is determined by the duration of the specific intellectual property right on the basis of which chip protection is claimed.

§9. Infringement and Remedies

258. There are no specific categories of infringements of the rights on chip technology. The relevant infringements are those against the specific intellectual property rights on the basis of which chip protection is claimed.

§10. Overlapping and Relation to Other Intellectual Property Laws

259. . Since there are no specific rights on chip technology, the situations of overlapping between different intellectual property rights in this area are the same that arise in connection with the intellectual property rights on the basis of which chip protection is claimed.

Chapter 9. Trade Secrets: Confidential Information

§1. Sources: Legislation

260. Until 1996, there was no specific statute enacted in Argentina for purposes of trade secret and confidential information protection. Rights as to such secrets and information resulted from various statutory rules included in different branches of statutory law. In 1996, Law 24,766 on confidential information (hereinafter referred to as CIL) was enacted. Although the CIL purports to implement a general legal regime on confidential information, it includes little in terms of substantive or procedural protection of trade secrets and other confidential information. Rather, it tends to codify certain rules and principles previously applied by other legal sources. The CIL does not limit the protection of trade secrets and confidential information resulting from other legal sources. Case law in this area is rather limited; this reflects, to a large extent, the noticeable lack of litigation in Argentina involving trade secrets and confidential information.

In addition to the CIL, the principal statutory sources of protection are the following:

(a) Articles 153–156 of the Criminal Code include provisions on criminal infringements and remedies related to different types of secrets, including trade secrets.
(b) Article 159 of the Criminal Code includes provisions on unfair competition.
(c) Articles 82–88 of the Employment Contracts Law include provisions on trade secrets and other technology used or developed in the context of employment relationships.
(d) Trade secret and confidential information protection are implemented through the general rules and principles of tort law, particularly those included in Book II, section II, of the Civil Code.
(e) Article 77 of the PA defines certain infringements and remedies related to inventions that have not yet been patented and therefore still qualify as trade secrets or confidential information.

§2. The Protection of Trade Secrets and Confidential Information

261. Argentine law does not include a general statutory definition of trade secrets or confidential information. However, certain aspects of the concepts of trade secrets and confidential information may be derived from certain statutory formulations for general or specific purposes.

Article 1 of the CIL provides in general terms that confidential information is legally protected against unfair trade practices, provided such information meets the following conditions: it is secret, in the sense that it is not generally known or easily available – as a whole or with regard to the precise configuration and assembly of its components – for persons experienced in the trades in which such type of information is normally used: it has commercial value, due to its secrecy; and it has been the subject matter of reasonable steps, in view of the circumstances, to protect its secrecy, taken by the person who legitimately controls such information. The CIL applies to information included in documents, electronic or magnetic means, discs, films or other similar elements. This would not exclude, however, the protection that information included in other elements may have under other legal provisions. This indirect definition may be used to interpret the concept of trade secret or of confidential information, as used by criminal law or civil statutory provisions but does not by itself alter such law or provisions. The relation between the CIL and other provisions on trade secrets and confidentiality information is that the breach of the confidential obligations provided by the CIL may result in criminal or civil infringements, but such infringements shall be determined and punished pursuant to the specific criminal or civil law provisions applicable to the case.

Article 1 of Decree 580, of 1981, applicable to transfer of technology transactions, defines technology to include 'patents, industrial models and designs, (and) any technical knowledge for the manufacturing of a product or the supply of a service'. This definition, however, is only applied to determine the subject matter of the transfer of technology regulations and does not distinguish between secret and non-secret technology.

Article 156 of the Criminal Code treats the illegal communication of trade secrets as a punishable offence. However, it does not provide a definition of such secrets.

In *American Express S.A. v. Resolución del Sr. Secretario de Industria y Comercio Exterior* N. 356,[1156] a federal Court of Appeals followed the definition of technology adopted by Decree 580. However, this was in the context of a dispute about whether a transaction involving software was subject to transfer of technology regulations and did not involve trade secrets issues.

262. Argentine law includes several criminal law provisions directly or indirectly protecting trade secrets.

263. Article 153 of the Criminal Code imposes prison sentences on someone who illegally opens a letter, a closed file or other communication not directed to such person and on a person who illegally appropriates such documentation or any other private document. The penalty is increased if the contents of the private documents are communicated to third parties or published.

This provision permits a certain degree of protection for trade secrets. Thus, in the *Trivelli, E. J.* decision,[1157] this provision was used against an employee who made unauthorized copies of documentation including the description of industrial processes used by the employer.

However, this provision has severe limitations as a legal instrument for the protection of trade secrets. It only applies to information included in the specific type of documentation listed in Article 153. Thus, for example, it would not apply to secrets embodied in machinery or transmitted verbally to an employee.

1156. National Court of Appeals for Federal and Administrative Matters, 25 Aug. 1987.

1157. National Court of Appeals for Criminal and Correctional Matters 5, 6 May 1988, *Jurisprudencia Argentina*, 17 Jan. 1990, vol. 1990-I, 46.

264. Article 156 of the Criminal Code provides a fine levied against a person who, having knowledge of a certain secret due to his or her status, trade, employment, profession or craft, discloses such secret without a valid reason, provided such disclosure may be harmful.

This provision applies to any type of secret and not only to trade secrets. For Article 156 protection to apply, it is not enough that the information be kept confidential. It is necessary that it objectively be a secret.[1158] This means that the information must not only be kept by its legitimate holder as if it were a secret, but it must also be generally unknown to the public. The legitimate holder must, therefore, take adequate precautions to prevent dissemination of the information, not only to make clear his or her intent to maintain its secrecy, but also to prevent the actual loss of the secret character of the information. Information in the public domain is not protected under Article 156.[1159] If the information is generally available among personnel working in the technical field in which such information is applied, the information is considered to not be a secret, even though it may be generally unknown to the population at large.

A violation of Article 156 requires the existence of several persons having access to certain secret information. One or more of these persons are the 'owners' of the secret information.

The definition of who such owners are is left to the non-criminal law rules applicable to secrets, such as labour law rules on the ownership of technology developed by employees. The second category of persons consists of those who, although not 'owners' of the information, have access to it due their 'status, trade, employment, profession, or craft'. A violation exists if a disclosure is made by a person meeting the conditions of the second category, causing damage to one or more of the 'owners' of the secret.

265. On the basis of the elements described above, several types of persons and conduct have been considered the possible subject matter of an Article 156 violation, as follows:

- Employees, with regard to secrets they have access to in the course of their employment.
- Partners, with regard to secrets belonging to the partnership. This possibility may extend to any type of business organization.
- Independent professionals, such as engineers or accountants, with regard to secrets held by enterprises to which they render their services.
- Independent service workers or builders, in connection with information supplied to them for purposes of rendering their services or completing their work.
- Employees of a licensee, in connection with secrets that have been transferred to such licensee.
- Employers, in connection with information belonging to their employees, which the employees apply in the course of their employment, thus disclosing it to their employers but without transferring any rights as to such information.

1158. *See* S. Soler, *Derecho Penal Argentino* (Buenos Aires: Editorial Tea, 1951), vol. 4, 133.

1159. *See* J.C. Ledesma, 'Secretos de fábrica', *Enciclopedia Jurídica Omeba* (Buenos Aires: Editorial Omeba, 1968), vol. 25, 232.

266. Article 156 is inapplicable if an employee or another party meeting the subjective conditions described in that Article uses the technology for its own benefit, instead of disclosing it. This requirement limits to a significant extent the effectiveness of Article 156 in protecting trade secrets.

Article 156 is also inapplicable if an employee or another party meeting the subjective conditions described therein has a legally valid reason to disclose the secret information, such as the owner's authorization or a judicial order.

If the information is disclosed as provided by Article 156, the position of the person or persons to whom the disclosure is made is generally irrelevant for purposes of determining whether a violation of the provision exists. Such position is relevant only for purposes of determining whether the person to whom the disclosure was made is also liable under Article 156, because said person has acted in bad faith, for example, or has solicited an employee to make the disclosure.

Although Article 156 is a criminal law provision, the criminal prosecution based on that Article may be initiated only by the victim.[1160]

267. Article 159 of the Argentine Criminal Code includes an extremely broad provision imposing sanctions on unfair competition. Those sanctions apply to persons who 'by means of fraudulent machinations, false accusations or any means of unfair advertising, intend to divert, to themselves, clients of a commercial or industrial establishment'.

The applicability of Article 159 to conduct related to trade secrets is limited by several general conditions required in all cases for that provision to be effective. Article 159 only applies if the damaged party engages in industrial or commercial activity. It does not protect service activities.[1161] Such industrial or commercial activity must already be in operation at the time the purported unfair competition takes place. It is not enough if the establishment of a new potential activity is hindered by unfairly attracting its possible clients.[1162]

For Article 159 to apply, it is not enough that harm be caused to an operating enterprise. It is also necessary that clients be diverted to the party supposedly guilty of unfair competition.[1163] Hence, the disclosure of a trade secret to the public does not constitute unfair competition, although it damages the rightful owner of such secret, since it is not targeted to diverting clients to the person engaged in such disclosure.

It has also been considered necessary, for Article 159 to apply, that both the victim and the party guilty of unfair competition actually operate competing businesses in the same markets.[1164] The fact that one party profits illegally from the diversion of another's clients is not enough for that Article to be applicable, if such parties do not

1160. *See* Criminal Code, Art. 73(3).

1161. *See* *In re Ryan*, Criminal Court of Appeals of Buenos Aires, 5 Dec. 1941, *Jurisprudencia Argentina*, vol. 1942-II (1942), 72.

1162. *See* *In re Borgo*, Criminal Court of Appeals of Buenos Aires, 16 Aug. 1935, *Jurisprudencia Argentina*, vol. 51 (1936), 699.

1163. *See* *In re Chaud*, Supreme Court of Córdoba, 13 Feb. 1947, *La Ley*, vol. 47 (1947), 427.

1164. *See* *Maple y Cía. v. Espejo*, Federal Court of Appeals of Buenos Aires, 19 Jul. 1938, *Jurisprudencia Argentina*, vol. 63 (1939), 69.

operate in the same market. This condition has also been expressed as requiring that the activities of both parties be 'substitutes' for each other.[1165]

Unfair competition, as defined by Article 159, may take place even where a third party causes the unauthorized disclosure of trade secrets to a competitor of the original owner. In that case, however, it is necessary that said competitor act in bad faith, not only with respect to the origin of the trade secrets but also in terms of his intent to attract clients from the original owner of such information.[1166]

268. The following are some of the acts that have been considered to fall within the prohibition defined by the unfair competition law. It should be pointed out, however, that the list of such acts has been drawn from the general decisions involving unfair competition under Argentine law, although for several of the types of conduct listed, there are no specific judicial precedents:

- Use of confidential technology disclosed by a competitor's employees.
- Illegal appropriation of documents containing secret information, followed by the use of such information.
- Appropriation of confidential information by means of duress or fraud, followed by the use of such information.
- Appropriation of confidential information as a consequence of *culpa in contrahendo*, followed by the use of such information.
- Use of confidential information, disclosed in the course of a contractual relationship, beyond the limits defined by said relationship.
- Use of technology appropriated in the context of partnership or corporate relationships, beyond the limits allowed by such relationship.

269. Criminal law provisions on theft, particularly Articles 162 and 164 of the Criminal Code, may have some limited application in protecting trade secrets, particularly in cases where the misappropriation of such secrets takes place through the unauthorized removal of tangible media incorporating or describing secret technology. However, the misappropriation of the intangible intellectual elements of trade secrets – for example, by copying confidential documents – is beyond the scope of these rules.

270. Articles 172 et seq. of the Argentine Criminal Code include broad provisions against fraud. The prohibitions of these provisions may be extended to cases in which trade secrets are misappropriated through fraudulent action. The intangible nature of the misappropriated assets does not affect the applicability of the provisions on fraud, although these provisions do require that the victim suffer some economic damage. In practice, fraud cases involving trade secrets are rare.

271. The PA includes several punitive provisions against the unlawful communication or misappropriation of unpatented inventions. The following conducts are thus penalized by the PA:

1165. *See In re Natin*, Criminal Court of Buenos Aires, 5 Jul. 1957, *Jurisprudencia Argentina*, vol. 1957-IV, 215.

1166. *See In re Chaud*, 427.

- Misappropriating or disclosing an invention that has not yet been patented, if such conduct is done by a partner, agent, advisor, employee or worker of the inventor or of the inventor's assignees, heirs or legatees.[1167]
- Bribing a partner, agent, advisor, employee or worker of the inventor or of the inventor's assignees, heirs or legatees, so as to obtain the disclosure of an invention.[1168]
- Violation of the secrecy obligations provided by the PA,[1169] such as those bearing on employees of the National Patents Administration.

272. No civil law provisions apply specifically to trade secrets. However, several general civil law principles and provisions have been interpreted and applied to trade secrets, namely the following:

(a) Contract law: A possessor of trade secrets may enter into contracts with other parties defining or limiting these parties' rights to use or disclose such trade secrets. These contracts are generally enforceable under Argentine civil law,[1170] but they have certain limitations regarding their legal and practical effectiveness. A contractual restriction on the use of trade secrets may be judged illegal if it attempts to actually prevent the use of that information once it has entered the public domain through no fault of the recipient or otherwise attempts to restrict the use of technology in the public domain, particularly by workers.[1171] Contractual restrictions on the use of trade secrets may also be illegal when they have anti-competitive effects that are not justified by the context in which such restrictions are imposed. Argentine law follows, in this respect, the basic lines of European competition law. However, there are no cases under Argentine law in which a contractual restriction on trade secret utilization has been formally attacked as being anti-competitive. Contractual protection of trade secrets is widely used in Argentine practice and finds support in several judicial decisions. However, as in other jurisdictions, its practical effectiveness is limited by the fact that such protection is only effective with respect to parties with whom the trade secret holder has direct contractual relationships. It is of no effect as against third parties that act in good faith.

(b) Rules on privacy: Article 52 of the Civil and Commercial Code includes a broad provision protecting personal privacy. Some authorities have mentioned the possibility of applying these provisions to conduct that violates the confidentiality of trade secrets. These provisions, however, are generally not addressed to the economic aspects of confidential information, but rather to the emotional interest in preserving the privacy of personal matters; thus, they have little practical application in the trade secrets area.

1167. *See* PA, Art. 77(a).

1168. *Ibid.*, Art. 77(b).

1169. *Ibid.*, Art. 77(c).

1170. *See Ducilo S.A. v. Barcia, H.J.*, National Civil Court of Appeals A, 25 Mar. 1971, *El Derecho*, vol. 38, 407.

1171. *Ibid.*

(c) Unjust enrichment rules: Article 1794 of the Civil and Commercial Code includes a general provision allowing civil actions for the recovery of the consequences of unjust enrichment. Substantial case law has been developed in this area, and the misappropriation of trade secrets, detrimental to the previous possessor of such technology, has been considered to be a source of liability under unjust enrichment rules. Nevertheless, the practical application of these rules in trade secret cases has been very limited.

(d) Property rules: There has been a lengthy debate under Argentine law regarding whether unpatented technology constitutes proper subject matter for property rights.[1172] The dispute is basically theoretical, or else intended to achieve changes in the applicable law, since cases are rarely decided on the basis of whether trade secrets constitute property or not.

(e) Tort rules: There are no specific tort rules applicable to trade secrets or confidential information under Argentine law. However, the Civil and Commercial Code includes broad provisions that apply in principle to all types of illegal conduct that causes damage to another person or to his or her property and that could, therefore, be considered applicable to the damages caused by an illegal use or disclosure of trade secrets. Nevertheless, in the absence of definite statutory provisions defining illegal conduct in relation to trade secrets and of sufficient case law applying the broad tort law provisions of the Civil and Commercial Code, it is not possible to derive clear conclusions about the precise applicability of such provisions in this area. The rights held by a trade secret possessor must be derived from other rules, such as labour law rules, and tort law becomes applicable only once such rights are violated. The CIL includes a general provision prohibiting unfair trade practices regarding secret information. This prohibition extends to any person who, due to his or her work, employment, office, position, profession or business dealings, has access to secret information and has been forewarned of the confidentiality of such information. In this context, unfair trade practices are defined as those that imply the breach of contracts, the abuse of trust, the instigation to legal violations and the acquisition of undisclosed information by third parties who knew that the acquisition implied an unfair trade practice or did not know of such circumstance due to gross negligence. These provisions do not create a new type of protection for trade secrets, but rather imply that unfair trade practices related to secret information shall imply a tort, which in turn allows the recovery of damages and the possibility of preliminary injunctions and other preliminary measures.

273. Argentine labour law includes different types of provisions applicable to trade secrets and confidential information.

With regard to the ownership of trade secrets obtained with the participation of the employees, Law 20,744, as amended, on employment contracts, includes the following rules:

1172. *See* M.A. Laquis, '¿Es el 'know how' un derecho de propiedad?', *Revista del Derecho Industrial* 4 (1982): 287.

- The inventions and discoveries that are derived from industrial procedures, methods or equipment used in the employer's factory or premises, or from experiments, research or improvements based on technology used in such an establishment, belong to the employer.[1173] This rule applies both to patentable and unpatentable technology.
- The inventions, discoveries and technologies in general developed by an employee who has been hired with that purpose belong to the employer.[1174]
- The 'personal' inventions and discoveries made by the employee belong to the employee, even if he or she has used equipment belonging to the employer.[1175] However, if the employee decides to assign his or her rights to these technologies, the employer has a right of first refusal as to such assignment.[1176] Law 20,744 does not define 'personal' inventions and discoveries, but these are understood to be those that do not fall under the other two categories.

It follows from these principles that Argentine law is based, as to employee's inventions and technological creations, on the technical origin of the employee's technologies. If these are based on technology already used by the employer, the employee's inventions will belong to the employer; if not, such inventions will belong to the employee unless he or she was hired to develop the technology being considered.

274. In addition, Law 20,744 includes several provisions on the implied duties related to trade secrets in the context of employer-employee relationships. Under Article 83 of this Law, both the employer and the employee are under the obligation to maintain the secrecy of the technology developed by the employee during the course of his employment. It is understood, however, that if this technology belongs to the employer, this secrecy obligation implies that the employer may transfer the technology, but in a way that will preserve its secret character, usually by including confidentiality obligations in the agreement of transfer.

Also, under Article 85 of Law 20,744, the employee must preserve the confidentiality and secrecy of the information to which he has access in the course of his employment and which requires such confidentiality or secrecy. While the employer-employee relationship is in progress, this confidentiality obligation extends to all information that the employer maintains on a confidential basis. After the relationship terminates, this obligation would only extend to information that qualifies as a trade secret. In addition, the employee must refrain from competing with the employer or from working in competition with the employer,[1177] and this may indirectly restrict the employee's ability to use the information acquired during the course of employment. This non-competition duty does not apply after expiration of the employer-employee relationship – unless a contractual obligation is concluded to that effect. However, the employee's activities after termination of the employment relationship are restricted, precluding those that may result in the disclosure of the employer's secrets.

1173. *See* Law 20,744, as amended, Art. 82.
1174. *Ibid.*
1175. *Ibid.*
1176. *Ibid.*, Art. 83.
1177. *Ibid.*, Art. 88.

275. Covenants not to compete have been held to be enforceable, within certain limits, in the context of litigation related to trade secrets. In the *Barcia I* decision,[1178] an injunction was ordered against a former employee on the basis of a covenant not to compete, ordering the said employee not to render services in any enterprise that operated as a competitor of the owner of the trade secrets involved. The limits of this obligation were examined in more detail in *Barcia II*.[1179] The court examined whether an obligation not to compete included in an employer-employee agreement was contrary to the constitutional provisions on the right to work. The court stated that such an obligation was valid, provided its extension is not excessive in view of both the employer's legitimate interest and the need to preserve the employee's working possibilities. More specifically, the court stated that a three-year non-competition term was adequate, taking into account the time within which the trade secret involved would be likely to be legitimately available to the employer's competitors. Covenants not to compete must also comply with the limits set by competition law. There are no relevant decisions in this respect. However, the Argentine competition law (Law 22,262, as amended) follows the European Union model, and it is likely that Argentine courts would base their decisions on European precedents as to these issues. In view of the position taken by Argentine courts in the *Barcia* decisions, it is more likely that more stringent limits will be imposed on non-competition clauses on the grounds of protection of the freedom to work than because of competition law rules.

276. Contractual obligations of non-disclosure bearing on employees were generally upheld in the *Barcia* decisions. On the basis of these decisions, contractual non-disclosure obligations would be invalid if they interfere with the employee's constitutional right to work, particularly when they extend beyond the termination of the secret status of the technology involved. This is based on the employee's right to apply the expertise he or she has acquired in the course of employment, provided this does not negatively affect a prior employer's trade secrets.

277. Although there has been a strong debate, in Argentina and elsewhere, as to the obligations of member countries of the WTO, under Article 39(3) of the TRIPS agreement, regarding the protection of test data of pharmaceutical and other products, the CIL has taken a clear position on that matter, which has not been ruled contrary to the TRIPS agreement by the Argentine courts.[1180] CIL Article 9 protects confidential test data, delivered to the authorities in charge of authorizing pharmaceutical products, under the same standards applicable to other confidential information. The aforementioned authorities may use such information for the approval of the manufacturing and marketing of similar products, by suppliers other than those who supplied the information, without compensation, priority or other benefits in favour of the persons who supplied the test data.

1178. *Ducilo S.A. v. Barcia, H.J.*, National Civil Court of Appeals A, 7 Oct. 1966, *La Ley*, vol. 125 (1967), 770.

1179. 'Ducilo S.A. c/ Barcia, H.J.'s CNCiv. A, ED, 38, 1971, 407.

1180. *See* J.R. Vanossi, 'Constitucionalidad de la normativa que regula el registro o autorización de comercialización de productos farmacéuticos', *La Ley*, v. (2005-F): 869.

Chapter 10. Geographical Indications and Appellations of Origin

§1. Sources: Legislation

278. Until recently, Argentina had relatively few statutory rules on geographical indications and appellations of origin. The international rules included in the Paris Convention and the TRIPS agreement were applicable, but their enforcement was weak and ineffective. Additional rules were found in domestic unfair competition law, but they were far from creating an effective system of geographical indications and appellations of origin.[1181]

This picture has changed significantly in the last decades. A far more detailed legislation has been enacted on these matters, and business interest in geographical indications and appellations of origin has increased.

However, the content and meaning of the Argentine rules on geographical indications and appellations of origin differ to a significant extent from those found in other comparative law systems, specially European. First, locally developed geographical indications and appellations of origin are relatively few and have relatively weak limits and recognition; therefore, there is a lack of strong local interest in their protection. Second, terms which are viewed in Europe as geographical indications and appellations of origin are used in Argentina as generic terms, in part as a consequence of past European immigration, and their protection as geographical indications and appellations of origin may be viewed as misleading or as part of an effort to corner markets on the part of foreign suppliers. Third, the protection of geographical indications and appellations of origin has been traditionally intertwined with rules against misleading advertisement and on consumer protection, and this relationship still remains in contemporary law.

279. International statutory rules, applied in Argentina, on geographical indications and appellations of origin, include the relevant provisions of the Paris Convention and of the TRIPS Agreement. Although, for constitutional reasons, these international rules may be applied directly by the courts and by administrative authorities, this type of direct enforcement is not common.

Argentina is not a party to other widely used international arrangements such as the Madrid Agreement of 1891 and the Lisbon Agreement of 1958.

280. The following domestic statutory sources dealing with geographical indications and appellations of origin may be mentioned:

1181. On the Argentine regime of geographical indications and appellations of origin *see* E. Schiavone, 'Indicaciones geográficas', *Derechos Intelectuales* 10 (2003): 19 et seq.; M. García Sellart, 'Algunas reflexiones sobre el régimen legal de las indicaciones geográficas en la Argentina', *Derechos Intelectuales* 10 (2003): 41 et seq.; G. Cabanellas, P. Palazzi, A. Sánchez Herrero & D.H. Serebrinsky, *Derecho de la competencia desleal* (Buenos Aires, Heliasta, 2014) 469 et seq.

(a) The Argentine Foodstuffs Code[1182] (*Código Alimentario Argentino)* includes several rules on these matters. Article 236 prohibits the use of the geographical name of a country, region or place as the name of products manufactured in other locations, if this practice may induce errors or mistakes. Article 237 includes a specific case following from the general rule included in Article 236; it prohibits the identification of Argentine products with geographical indications which are not those of the region or place where such products are manufactured. Articles 1107 and 1135 include several provisions on the labelling and identification of wines and spirits; the general rule is that the use of geographical names must reflect the actual origin of such products, but certain exceptions are allowed, including the use of the expression 'type' accompanied by the indication of the actual geographical origin of the goods. These provisions have been largely superseded by the special regime of Law 25,163, on wines and spirits.

(b) The TA includes a legal definition of 'denomination of origin', and restrictions on the registration of such words as trademarks.[1183]

(c) The Fair Trade Law[1184] includes miscellaneous rules on unfair competition, identification of goods and services and commercial practices. Article 2 provides that goods manufactured and products produced in Argentina should bear – when marketed in Argentina — the indication 'Argentine industry', or 'Argentine production'. For these purposes, goods produced in Argentina are those manufactured or produced in Argentina, even if foreign raw materials or elements are used. Article 3 provides that goods or products with a foreign origin shall not be considered Argentine if they are only subject to assembly or finishing processes in Argentina, without changing their 'nature'. Article 7 prohibits any use of words, phrases or symbols that may be misleading about the characteristics or nature or goods or products, including their origin. Article 7 prohibits the use of national or foreign appellations of origin to identify a good or product whose origin is not in the relevant zone, except when the appellation of origin was registered as a trademark before Law 22,802 came into effect. Article 8 provides that appellations of origin which have become the common name or type of a product[1185] may be used freely.

(d) Law 25,163 includes a comprehensive regime on Argentine geographical names used in connection with wines and spirits derived from wine.

(e) Law 25,380 governs geographical indications and appellations of origin used in connection with the marketing of agricultural products foodstuffs, with the exception of wines and spirits derived from wine. Law 25,380 has been substantially amended by Law 25,966 and is complemented by the regulations included in Decree 556 of 2009.

(f) Law 26,355 protects collective trademarks. The regulations governing a given collective trademark may provide that such trademark be connected with a geographical origin defined by such regulations.

1182. Law 18,284, as amended.
1183. *See* para. 143 (c), *supra*.
1184. Law 22,802, as amended.
1185. A common practice in Argentina.

§2. The Legal Status of Geographical Indications and Appellations of Origin

281. Argentine law combines elements from different legal mechanisms to establish the protection of and the rights to geographical indications and appellations of origin. The following mechanisms may be distinguished in this context:

- Rules which provide absolute protection, preventing the use of geographical indications and appellations of origin by unauthorized persons, even if it is not misleading for the public. This system applies, e.g., to appellations of origin related to wines and spirits, registered pursuant to Law 25,163.
- Rules which provide protection against the use of geographical indications and appellations of origin, if it is misleading for the public. This type of protection applies under the Fair Trade Law.[1186]
- Rules which provide protection against the use of geographical indications and appellations of origin, if such use constitutes unfair competition. This type of protection is granted by the general rules on unfair competition applied in Argentina, in particular Article 10*bis* of the Paris Convention.
- Rules which provide protection against the use of false geographical indications and appellations of origin, regardless of whether such use is actually misleading or harmful for the public. This type of protection may result from the provisions of Article 10 of the Paris Convention.
- Rules which provide protection to geographical indications and appellations of origin in connection with collective trademarks.[1187]

282. On the basis of this complex system of protection, resulting from the operation of these different rules, geographical indications and appellations of origin are deemed to constitute intangible goods, which are part of intellectual and industrial property. These goods are subject to special regimes as to their use or exploitation, acquisition and transfer. Their use or exploitation is protected to the extent that it fits with the information and meaning conveyed by the relevant indication or appellation. A person having the right to use a given geographical indication is not free to use it in connection with goods which do not have their origin in the relevant location. Regarding acquisition, some rights are acquired by the mere location of a person, while in other cases it is necessary to go through a registration or certification procedure. Transfer of these rights is limited since the transferee must comply with the conditions attached to the use of the relevant geographical indication or appellation of origin, particularly location in a given area.

The fact that geographical indications and appellations of origin are part of intellectual and industrial property has significant legal effects. The rules of the TRIPS agreement and the Paris Convention – e.g., those on national treatment – are applicable in this area, as a consequence of this legal status. This is especially significant under Argentine law, since rules included in international agreements are immediately applicable and have a higher constitutional status than purely domestic laws.

1186. Law 22,802, as amended; *see* para. 280(c), *supra* .
1187. *See* para. 280(f), *supra.*

§3. Geographical Indications and Appellations of Origin under Law 25,380 and Its Amendments

283. The effective implementation of the international rules – especially those of the TRIPS agreement – on geographical indications and appellations of origin requires additional domestic legislation. This was initially achieved in Argentina by means of Law 25,380, which has been subsequently modified in several occasions.

Law 25,380 does not include a fully comprehensive regime of geographical indications and appellations of origin; it only governs agricultural products and foodstuffs, with the exception of wines and spirits. It does not reach industrial or mineral products, nor services.

284. In the system created by Law 25,380, its amendments and regulations, geographical indications (*indicaciones geográficas)* constitute a broad, general category and appellations of origin (*denominaciones de origen)* a specific category within the latter.

Geographical indications identify a product as originating in the territory of a country, or in a region or locality of that territory, provided a given quality or other characteristics of such product are fundamentally attributable to its geographical origin.[1188] Geographical indications exist as such and are legally protected without a previous formal procedure or registration, provided the objective conditions described in the preceding definition are met. However, they may be subject to a registration procedure, and this may facilitate the exercise of rights and claims related to such indications.

Appellations of origin are defined as the duly registered name of a region, province, department, district, locality or area of the national territory, which is used to design a product originating in any of them, whose qualities and characteristics are exclusively or essentially due to the geographical environment, including natural and human factors.[1189] In this case, a formal registration procedure is necessary.

Several provisions complement the legal definition of appellation of origin. Article 4 of Law 25,380 provides that an agricultural product or foodstuff may be the subject matter of an appellation of origin provided it has its origin in a region, province, department, locality, area or zone, it is well known for its character and originality and is produced in a given geographical environment, such that it may develop particular qualities which grant it a distinct character, different from other products, even if these are produced under similar environmental and technological conditions, due to the influence of the natural environment and human labour.

This complementary provision is legally significant, in that it stresses the fact that products included in an appellation of origin must have objective characteristics – resulting from the natural environment or from human labour – which distinguish them from comparable products. A general perception or reputation, or the mere attitude of consumers, is not enough for an appellation of origin to exist.

In addition, Article 4 of Decree 556 of 2009 includes two 'primary conditions of eligibility', applicable to appellations of origin. First, the qualities or characteristics of the relevant products must be derived 'exclusively or essentially' from the peculiar

1188. *See* Law 25,380, as amended, Art. 2.
1189. *Ibid.*

geographical environment of their origin. This includes natural factors, such as climate, soil, water or other similar factors; and human factors, such as knowledge or local or traditional practices. Second, the production of raw materials and their manufacture 'from the beginning to the end of the chain of production', must take place within the geographical area whose name is borne by the relevant products.[1190]

285. Special procedures apply for the administrative recognition and registration of geographical indications and appellations of origin.

In the case of geographical indications, a petition must be filed by producers located in the relevant area. If registration is accepted, other producers of the same area may also request to be registered as such.[1191]

Registration of an appellation of origin is more complex. An ad hoc council of appellation of origin must be created and incorporated – as a not-for-profit legal association – by producers from the relevant area. This council must then file a petition with the relevant agency, showing that the council has been duly incorporated and that the elements necessary for the recognition and registration of an appellation of origin are satisfied.[1192] This petition is published and subject to oppositions filed by third parties. Based on these different elements, the acting agency decides whether to admit the proposed appellation of origin.

286. Foreign geographical indications and appellations of origin may be registered as such in Argentina, provided they meet the relevant conditions applicable to such registration, described above.[1193] However, there are certain differences regarding the applicable procedure. Foreign geographical indications and appellations of origin require evidence of their protection in the country of origin, and a statement from an authority of that country indicating their existence and use.[1194] The Argentine authority may refuse protection if the foreign geographical indications and appellations of origin are no longer used or protected in their country of origin.[1195]

Protection resulting from these registrations is in addition to that resulting directly from international rules, such as the Paris Convention and the TRIPS Agreement.

287. Law 25,380, as amended, includes several prohibitions and restrictions on the registration and protection of geographical indications and appellations of origin, in particular:

(a) Indications and appellations that have become the generic name of agricultural products or foodstuffs may not be registered. An indication or appellation is deemed to be generic, for these purposes, if it is the common name of a product used by the public in Argentina.

1190. This second condition is impossible to satisfy if interpreted literally, since there are no geographically isolated chains of production in the modern world. The condition is interpreted and applied in a more relative way, requiring that the productive steps which define the quality or characteristics of the relevant products take place within the geographical area corresponding to the appellation of origin.

1191. *See* Decree 556 of 2009, Art. 16.

1192. *See* Law 25,380, Art. 17.

1193. *See* Law 25,380, as amended, Art. 23.

1194. *See* Decree 556 of 2009, Art. 23.

1195. *See* Law 25,380, as amended, Art. 23.

(b) Registration is not acceptable if the indication or appellation has been previously been registered in good faith as a trademark, or if it has been used in good faith as a trademark prior to 1 January 2000, or before the indication or appellation has become protected in its country of origin.
(c) An indication or appellation may not be registered if it is similar to previously registered appellations of origin.
(d) An indication or appellation may not be registered if it is likely to lead to misperceptions as to the qualities or characteristics of the relevant products, or about the actual geographical origin of such products.

288. Several rights are recognized by Argentine law in connection with geographical indications and appellations of origin:

(a) Right to use a geographical indication. This right is legally granted to registered producers and users.[1196] However, if a non-registered producer or user shows that he or she meets the geographical and production requirements of the relevant geographical indication, such producer or user will also be considered as legally use the geographical indication.[1197]
(b) Right to use an appellation of origin. This right belongs to registered producers or users and to the council formed in connection with the relevant appellation of origin.[1198] Other producers or users are prevented from using an appellation of origin if such use may mislead the consumers or induce them to misperceptions.[1199]
(c) Right to quality controls. The holders of rights on appellations of origin may request from the administrative authorities quality controls on relevant goods to assure that they meet the standards and specifications of goods bearing an appellation of origin.[1200]
(d) Rights against unauthorized or misleading use of geographical indications and appellations of origin. Forbidden practices include the use of such indications or appellations for goods that do not meet the applicable requirements – particularly geographical origin –- and the use of confusing terms or statements or any other practice that may induce consumers to misperceptions as to the real origin of a good or product.[1201] These practices are subject to injunctions and sanctions under the special statutory rules on geographical indications and appellations of origin, and in addition are subject to the prohibitions and sanctions bearing on unfair competition.

1196. *See* Decree 556 of 2009, Art. 26. *See also* Law 25,380, as amended, Art. 26.
1197. *Ibid.*
1198. *See* Law 25,380, as amended, Art. 26(b).
1199. *See* Decree 556 of 2009, Art. 26.
1200. *Ibid.*
1201. *See* Law 25,380 as amended, Art. 27.

§4. Geographical Indications and Appellations of Origin for Wines and Spirits

289. Law 25,163 includes a special set of rules applicable to geographical indications and appellations of origin used in connection with wines and spirits derived from wines. These rules – which have been enacted so as to comply with the TRIPS Agreement – have significant practical importance due to the value of Argentine wine and spirits production and to the peculiar practices in this country in connection with the identification of wines and spirits.

290. Law 25,163 uses legal categories, for the definition of geographical areas, different from those generally applied under Argentine law for geographical indications and appellations of origin.

First, Law 25,163 uses a general category of 'geographical names' (*nombres geográficos)* which includes the different special categories, defined by such Law, to which specific legal consequences are applied.

Second, Law 25,163 and its regulations[1202] uses the category of 'indications of origin' (*indicaciones de procedencia*). These apply to areas, defined by the National Winery Institute, meeting production and manufacturing conditions established by that Institute, such that only producers located in that area and using as a minimum 80% of grapes produced and manufactured within that area may use the relevant indication applied to that area for their table or regional wines.[1203]

Third, Law 25,163[1204] uses the expression 'geographical indication' (*indicación geográfica*) to identify products with special qualities and characteristics fundamentally attributable to the geographical origin of the product. The grapes must be totally produced within the area corresponding to the geographical name, and manufactured within that area; if manufacturing or bottling takes place outside that area, the name of the area where the grapes are produced and the name of the area where they are manufactured or bottled must both be used jointly.

Fourth, Law 25,163[1205] uses the category of 'controlled appellation of origin' (*denominación de origen controlada).* This is defined as the name which identifies a product originating in a given region, locality or limited production area within the national territory, whose particular qualities or characteristics are exclusively or essentially determined by the geographical environment, including natural and human factors. The grapes must be produced, manufactured and bottled within the relevant area, as certified by an administrative authority.

291. Law 25,163 establishes the procedures applicable to the recognition, registration and protection of the different types of geographical categories used in connection with wines and spirits.

1202. *See* Law 25,163, Art. 3; Decree 57 of 2004, Art. 3.
1203. 'Table' and 'regional' wines are categories traditionally used by the Argentine winemaking rules.
1204. *See* Law 25,163, Art. 4.
1205. *Ibid.*, Art. 13.

These procedures are particularly detailed with regard to controlled appellations of origin.[1206] Parties interested in the formal recognition of a controlled appellation of origin must create a 'promotional council', formed as a not-for-profit association by wine or grape producers. A promotional council is governed by its own set of regulations, governing matters such as the geographical limits of the controlled appellation of origin, the conditions to be met during the production of grapes and wines, compliance mechanisms and the organization of registries of authorized producers.

292. Different rights are provided with regard to the geographical categories used in connection with wines and spirits. These rights are particularly strong in the case of controlled appellations of origin, which may only be used with regard to grapes, wines and spirits produced by registered producers.[1207] In the case of other geographical categories, their use is generally restricted to producers and products meeting the conditions defined as to each category.[1208]

293. Law 25,163 defines different conducts which constitute violations of such Law and which are subject to the penalties provided therein.

Article 33 provides, generally, that the necessary legal steps may be taken to protect registered names applied to geographical areas defined by Law 25,163, so as to prevent any illegal use that may induce the consumer to errors or mistakes.

Article 34 defines and prohibits certain specific conducts related to such registered names:

(a) Their use for the identification of wines and spirits that do not have their origin in the areas identified by such names or which do not meet the conditions applicable to their registration.
(b) Their use so as to profit from the well-known character of such names, weakening or damaging their identity.
(c) Conduct which constitutes misappropriation, imitation or evocation by means of expressions such as 'class', 'in the manner of', 'type', 'style', even if the real origin is also indicated.
(d) Any other indication which is false or misleading, as to origin, provenance, nature or characteristics of wine products.
(e) Any other practice which may induce consumers to mistakes about the authentic origin of the product or which implies unfair competition.

1206. *See* Law 25,163, Arts 16 et
See Law 25,163, Art seq.
1207. *See* Law 25,163, Art. 30.
1208. In addition, producers of grapes, wines and spirits must comply with the detailed regulations on wine and spirit production, included in Law 14,878, its amendments and regulations.

Selected Bibliography

§1. Books

Altmark, D.R. & Molina Quiroga E. *Tratado de derecho informático*. Buenos Aires, La Ley, 2012.

Bensadon, M. *Ley de patentes comentada y concordada con el ADPIC y el Convenio de París*. Buenos Aires: LexisNexis, 2007.

Bertone, L.E. & G. Cabanellas. *Derecho de marcas*. Buenos Aires: Heliasta, 1989.

Breuer Moreno, P.C. *El nombre comercial en la legislación argentina*. Buenos Aires: Jesús Menéndez, 1929.

Breuer Moreno, P.C. *Tratado de las patentes de invención*. Buenos Aires: Abeledo-Perrot, 1957.

Breuer Moreno, P.C. *Tratado de marcas de fabrica y de comercio*. Buenos Aires: Perrot, 1946.

Cabanellas, G. 'Argentina'. In *Worldwide Trade Secrets Law*, vol. 3, edited by T. F. MacLaren. Deerfield, IL: Clark, Boardman, Calaghan, 1995.

Cabanellas, G. *Contratos de licencia y de transferencia de tecnología en el derecho privado*. Buenos Aires: Heliasta, 1994.

Cabanellas, G. *Derecho de las patentes de invención*. Buenos Aires: Heliasta, 2001.

Cabanellas, G. *Propiedad intelectual sobre los programas de computación*. Buenos Aires: Heliasta, 2011.

Cabanellas, G. *Régimen jurídico de los conocimientos técnicos*. Buenos Aires: Heliasta, 1985.

Cabanellas, G.; Palazzi, P.: Sánchez Herrero, A. & Serebrinsky, D.H. *Derecho de la competencia desleal*. Buenos Aires: Heliasta, 2014.

Cornejo Costas, E. *Tratado del nombre social*. Buenos Aires: Abaco, 1989.

Correa, C. M., et al. *Derecho informático*. Buenos Aires: Depalma, 1987.

Correa, C.M., et al. *Régimen legal de las patentes de invención*. Buenos Aires, La Ley, 2013.

Di Guglielmo, P. *La invención patentable*. Buenos Aires: Zavalía, 1968.

Di Guglielmo, P. *Tratado de derecho industrial*. Buenos Aires: Tea, 1948.

Emery, M.A. *Propiedad intelectual*. Buenos Aires: Astrea, 1999.

Goldstein, M.R. *Derecho de autor*. Buenos Aires: La Rocca, 1995.

Gutierrez, M. *El debate y el impacto de los derechos de obtentor en los países en desarrollo. El caso argentino.* Buenos Aires: IICA, 1994.

Harvey, E.R. *Derecho cultural latinoamericano.* Buenos Aires: Depalma, 1992.

Ledesma, J.C. *Derecho penal industrial.* Buenos Aires: Depalma, 1987.

Lipszyc, D. *Derecho de autor y derechos conexos.* Buenos Aires: UNESCO-Cerlalc-Zavalía, 1993.

Lipszyc, D. *Nuevos temas de derecho de autor y derechos conexos.* Buenos Aires: UNESCO-Cerlalc-Zavalía, 2004.

Mitelman, C.O. & D.R. Zuccherino. *Protección jurídica de la información confidencial y de los datos científicos.* Buenos Aires: LexisNexis, 2007.

Mitelman, C.O. *Marcas y otros signos distintivos.* Buenos Aires: La Ley, 2015.

Mouchet, C. & S. Radaelli. *Derechos intelectuales sobre las obras literarias y artísticas.* Buenos Aires: Kraft, 1948.

Otamendi, J. *Derecho de marcas.* Buenos Aires: Abeledo-Perrot, 1989.

Piñeiro, M., et al. *Reflexiones para la política tecnológica agropecuaria.* Buenos Aires: CISEA, 1984.

Poli, I. *El modelo de utilidad.* Buenos Aires: Depalma, 1982.

Poli, I. *El modelo industrial.* Buenos Aires: Abeledo-Perrot, 2008.

Rapela, M.A. (dir.). *Innovación y propiedad intelectual en mejoramiento vegetal y biotecnología agrícola.* Buenos Aires: Heliasta, 2006.

Rapela, M.A. *Derechos de propiedad intelectual en vegetales superiores.* Buenos Aires: Ciudad Argentina, 2000.

Rivera, J.C. *El nombre en los derechos civil y comercial.* Buenos Aires: Astrea, 1977.

Sánchez Herrero, A. *Confusión de marcas*, Buenos Aires, La Ley, 2013.

Villalba C.A. & D. Lipszyc. *El derecho de autor en la Argentina.* Buenos Aires: La Ley, 2009.

Wittenzellner, U. *Derecho de marcas en la Argentina.* Buenos Aires: Abeledo-Perrot, 1989.

Zavala Rodriguez, C.J. *Régimen legal de los dibujos y modelos industriales.* Buenos Aires: Depalma, 1962.

§2. Articles

Aracama Zorraquin, E.D. 'La jurisprudencia de la Corte Suprema y las marcas engañosas'. *El Derecho* 101 (1983): 636 et seq.

Aracama Zorraquin, E.D. 'La nueva Ley de Marcas y Designaciones'. *Legislación Argentina* (1981): 1147 et seq.

Selected Bibliography

Aracama Zorraquin, E.D. 'La piraterie des marques en droit argentin'. *La Propriété Industrielle* 98 (1982): 339 et seq.

Aracama Zorraquin, E.D. 'Sobre el tema del uso obligatorio de la marca'. *El Derecho* 97 (1982): 918 et seq.

Bensadon, M. & Poli, I.A., '¿Crisis en el sistema de patentes argentino?, *Revista del Derecho Comercial y de las Obligaciones* 46-A (2013): 683 et seq.

Bergel, S.D. 'Análisis crítico de la legislación latinoamericana relativa a invenciones biotecnológicas'. *Revista del Derecho Industrial* 15 (1993): 387 et seq.

Bergel, S.D. 'Las licencias obligatorias de patentes y el "derecho de propiedad" del inventor amparado por la Constitución Nacional'. *Revista del Derecho Industrial* 13 (1991): 519 et seq.

Bertone, L.E. 'La nouvelle loi argentine des marques'. *Revue Internationale de la Propriété Industrielle et Artistique* (1981): 450 et seq.

Bottaro, R.H. 'Contrato de edición'. *La Ley* (1981-D): 1112 et seq.

Breuer Moreno, P.C. 'La protección jurídica de las artes figurativas aplicadas al comercio y a la industria'. *Patentes y Marcas* (1939): 514 et seq.

Cabanellas, G. 'Aspectos económicos de la legislación de patentes'. *Revista del Derecho Comercial y de las Obligaciones* 16 (1983): 613 et seq.

Cabanellas, G. 'Protección jurídica de los elementos informáticos'. *Derechos Intelectuales* 5 (1991): 99 et seq.

Cabanellas, G. 'The Legal Protection of Computer technology under Argentine Law'. *Copyright World* II (1990): 34 et seq.

Chaloupka, P. '¿In dubio contra patentem?'. *Derechos Intelectuales* 2 (1987): 34 et seq.

Correa, C.M. 'Las nuevas reglas sobre propiedad intelectual y sus consecuencias en el comercio de tecnología'. *Revista del Derecho Industrial* 13 (1991): 3 et seq.

Correa, C.M. 'Los acuerdos de la Ronda Uruguay y las patentes'. *La Ley* (10 Oct. 1995): 1 et seq.

Correa, C.M. 'Patentes y biotecnología. Opciones para América Latina'. *Revista del Derecho Industrial* 12 (1990): 5 et seq.

De Las Carreras, D. 'Las patentes de invención y la información tecnológica'. *Derechos Intelectuales* 4 (1989): 122 et seq.

Di Guglielmo, P. 'Los proyectos de leyes sobre propiedad industrial'. *La Ley* 103 (1961): 1061 et seq.

Fernandez Madero, J.F. 'El nombre y la enseña comercial en la transferencia de fondo de comercio'. *El Derecho* 4 (1963): 1012 et seq.

García Sellart, M. 'Algunas reflexiones sobre el régimen legal de las indicaciones geográficas en la Argentina'. *Derechos Intelectuales* 10 (2003): 41 et seq.

Gonzalez, A.J. 'La prueba instrumental como destructiva de la novedad en las patentes de invención'. *Derechos Intelectuales* 3 (1988): 172 et seq.

Laquis, M.A. '¿Es el know-how un derecho de propiedad?' *Revista del Derecho* Industrial 4 (1982): 287 et seq.

Ledesma, J.C. 'Secretos de fábrica'. *Enciclopedia Jurídica Omeba* 25 (1968): 212 et seq.

Mille, A. 'La información ante el derecho de la propiedad intelectual'. *Derechos Intelectuales* 5 (1991): 76 et seq.

Musich, A.T. 'La propiedad intelectual en el escenario económico'. *Derechos Intelectuales* 6 (1994): 26 et seq.

Otamendi, J. 'El primer fallo sobre TRIPs'. *La Ley* (5 Feb. 1996): 5 et seq.

Otamendi, J. 'Respecto de un comentario sobre el acuerdo TRIPS y las patentes de invención'. *La Ley* (28 Nov. 1995): 1 et seq.

Schiavone, E., 'Indicaciones geográficas'. *Derechos Intelectuales* 10 (2003): 17 et seq.

Wassermann, M. 'Amplitud territorial de la protección del nombre mercantil'. *Jurisprudencia Argentina* 71 (1940): 7 (Doct.) et seq.

Wassermann, M. 'Colisiones entre nombres y marcas'. *Jurisprudencia Argentina* 74 (1941): 83 (Doct.) et seq.

Wassermann, M. 'La protección de los dibujos y modelos industriales'. *La Ley* 25 (1942): 966 et seq.

Zamudio, T. 'Protección jurídica de la propiedad industrial en el sector agrícola'. *Jurisprudencia Argentina* (22 May 1996): 18 et seq.

Zavala Rodriguez, C.J. 'Prescripción en materia de enseña comercial'. *Jurisprudencia Argentina* 47 (1934): 808 et seq.

§3. Law Reviews

Two law reviews are specifically directed to intellectual property issues: *Temas de Derecho Industrial y de la Competencia*, Ciudad Argentina, Buenos Aires; and *Derechos Intelectuales*, Astrea, Buenos Aires.

Index

The numbers here refer to paragraph numbers.

Index

Index

Index

Made in the USA
Monee, IL
18 October 2026

66041403R10111